HISTORIC BUILDINGS

*As Seen and Described
by Famous Writers*

With Numerous Illustrations

Edited and translated
by

Esther Singleton

Author of
Turrets, Towers and Temples
Great Pictures
Wonders of Nature
Famous Paintings
Paris
London
A Guide to the Opera

NATAL PUBLISHING LLC
ARS LONGA, VITA BREVIS

Preface

Two principles of selection have guided me in the preparation of this book, the sixth of a series which has met with a cordial reception. One is the beauty or interest from an artistic standpoint; the other, the historical associations. If the reader should miss some famous edifices, he will kindly remember that a small volume cannot contain a complete collection of all the historic buildings still standing, and that many other historic buildings have already appeared in my former books of this series, *Turrets, Towers and Temples* and *Romantic Castles and Palaces*.

I have endeavoured to find descriptions that deal with both views, giving the history of the building itself, and a description of its architectural features; and as this book contains, in consequence, a great variety of buildings of all periods and many countries, the student of both art and history will doubtless find pleasure in comparing these various styles of architecture and in composing a mental picture of events that have occurred within their walls.

Some of the buildings will aid him in realizing more fully, perhaps, than before some of the various influences that have aided in developing certain races; for instance, a study of the text and pictures of the cathedrals of Monreale and Palermo will demonstrate the presence of Norman and Saracen in Sicily. In other instances, it is not a long vanished race, but the still-felt presence of some strong personality like that of Shah Jehan, whose mosques and palaces and Taj Mahal stand as monuments not only to the great conqueror, but to the magnificence of his taste.

In this book, I have included several towers and fortresses as well as castles and baronial halls, and the Certosa of Pavia and La Grande Chartreuse, from which later historic home the Carthusian monks of France have lately been driven. In addition to the cathedrals and temples which have been the scenes of memorable historical events, I have added the particularly sacred shrines of the Holy Sepulchre, the Holy House of Loretto and the Campo Santo, Pisa, which attract thousands of the faithful.

Many of the extracts I have translated expressly for this book, and I have taken no liberties with the text, except a little cutting for the sake of space limitations.

E. S.
New York, *September, 1903*

Contents

The Castle of Angers *by Henry Jouin*

The Pagoda of Tanjore *by G.W. Steevens*

The Vendramin-Calergi, Venice *by Théophile Gautier*

A Visit to the Old Seraglio, Constantinople *by Pierre Loti*

The Duomo, Leaning Tower, the Baptistery and the
   Campo-Santo, Pisa *by H.A. Taine*

Rochester Castle *by Arthur Shadwell Martin*

Santa Croce, Florence *by John Ruskin*

The Certosea of Pavia *by John Addington Symonds*

ILLUSTRATIONS

India: *The Jumma Musjid*
Italy: *San Donato*
France: *The Palace of the Popes*
Palestine: *The Church of the Holy Sepulchre*
Kamakoura: *The Daïboudhs*
England: *Cathedral of Wells*
Italy: *The Coliseum*
India: *Golden Temple of the Sikhs*
Spain: *The Giralda*
Italy: *The Cathedral of Monreale*
France: *The Luxembourg Palace*
England: *Haddon Hall*
Italy: *Cathedral of Palermo*
India: *Fortress and Palace of Gwalior*
Italy: *The Holy House of Loretto*
Spain: *The Alcazar of Seville*
Portugal: *The Tower of Belem*
Italy: *The Foscari Palace*
France: *Saint Ouen*

England: *Carisbroke Castle*
Italy: *The Pantheon*
Germany: *St. Laurence*
Spain: *The Torre del Oro*
Italy: *Cathedral of Orvieto*
India: *The Pearl Mosque*
England: *The Church of St. Bartholomew*
Delhi: *The Kutb Minar*
England: *Kenilworth Castle*
Italy: *Santa Maria Della Salute*
France: *The Ramparts of Carcassonne*
Italy: *The Cathedral of Modena*
France: *The Cathedral of Rheims*
Italy: *The Castle of St. Angelo*
England: *Salisbury Cathedral*
France: *The Castle of Angers*
India: *The Pagoda of Tanjore*
Italy: *The Vendramin-Calergi*
Turkey: *Fountain of the Old Seraglio*
Italy: *The Duomo, Leaning Tower, Baptistery and Campo-Santo*
England: *Rochester Castle*
Italy: *Santa Croce*
Italy: *The Certosa of Pavia*

THE JUMMA MUSJID, INDIA
G. W. Steevens

Delhi is the most historic city in all historic India.

It may not be the oldest—who shall say which is the oldest among rivals all coeval with time?—though it puts in a claim for a respectable middle-age, dating from 1000 B.C. or so. It has at least one authentic monument which is certainly fourteen or fifteen hundred years old. At that time Delhi's master called himself Emperor of the World, and emperors, at least of India, have ruled there almost ever since. Mohammed, an Afghan of Ghor, took it in 1193; Tamerlane, the Mogul, sacked it two hundred years later; Nadir Shah, the Persian, in 1739; Ahmed Shah Durani, another Afghan, in 1756; the Marathas took it three years later. Half a century on, in 1803, General Lake took the capital of India for Britain. And British it has been ever since—except for those few months in 1857, when Mutiny brought the ghost of the Mogul empire into the semblance of life again; till Nicholson stormed the breach in the Kashmir Bastion, and dyed Delhi British for ever with his blood.

Look from the Ridge, whence the columns marched out to that last capture: the battered trophy of so many conquerors remains wonderfully fresh and fair. It seems more like a wood than a city. The rolls of green are only spangled with white, as if it were a suburb of villas standing in orchards. Only the snowy domes and tall minarets, the cupolas and gilded pinnacles, betray the still great and populous city that nestles below you and takes breath after her thousand troubles.

Let us go back to the city. Here at least is the Jumma Musjid, the great mosque, saved complete out of the storms—a baby of little more than two hundred years, to be sure, but still something. It is said to be the largest mosque in the world—a vast stretch of red sandstone and white marble and gold upstanding from a platform reached on three sides by flights of steps so tall, so majestically wide, that they are like a stone mountain tamed into order and proportion at an emperor's will. Above the brass-mounted doors rise red portals so huge that they almost dwarf the whole—red galleries above them, white marble domes above them, white marble minarets rising higher yet, with pillars and cupolas and gilded pinnacles above all. Beside the gateways the walls of the quadrangle seem to creep along the ground; then, at the corners, rise towers with more open chambers, more cupolas and gilded pinnacles. Within, above the cloistered quadrangle, bulge three pure white domes—not hemispheres, like Western domes, but complete globes, only sliced away at the base and tapering to a spike at the top—and a slender minaret flanks each side.

The whole, to Western eyes, has a strange effect. Our own buildings are tighter together, gripped and focused more in one glance; over the Jumma Musjid your eye must wander, and then the mind must connect the views of the different parts. If you look at it near you cannot see it all; if far, it is low and seems to straggle. The West could hardly call it beautiful: it has proportion, but not compass. Therefore it does not abase you, as other great buildings do: somehow you have a feeling of patronage towards it. Yet it is most light and graceful with all its bulk: it seems to suit India, thus spread out to get its fill of the warm sun. It looks rich and lavish, as if space were of no account to it.

You have passed below the cloud-capped towers, out

of the gorgeous palaces—and here is Silver Street, Delhi's main thoroughfare. The pageant fades, and you plunge into the dense squalor which is also India. Along the houses run balconies and colonnades; here also you see vistas of pillars and lattice-work, but the stone is dirty, the stucco peels, the wood lacks paint. The houses totter and lean together. The street is a mass of squatting, variegated people; bulls, in necklaces of white and yellow flowers, sleep across the pavements, donkeys stroll into the shops, goats nibble at the vegetables piled for sale down the centre of the street, a squirrel is fighting with a caged parrot. Here is a jeweller's booth, gay with tawdry paint; next, a baker's, with the shopkeeper snoring on his low counter, and everything an inch thick with dust. At one step you smell incense; at the next, garbage.

Inimitable, incongruous India! And coming out of the walls, still crumbling from Nicholson's cannon, you see mill-chimneys blackening the sky. Delhi, with local cotton, they tell you, can spin as fine as Manchester. One more incongruity! The iron pillar, the ruined mosque, the jewelled halls, the shabby street, and now the clacking mill. That is the last of Delhi's myriad reincarnations.

SAN DONATO, ITALY
MURANO
John Ruskin

We push our way on between large barges laden with fresh water from Fusina, in round white tubs seven feet across, and complicated boats full of all manner of nets that look as if they could never be disentangled, hanging from their masts and over their sides; and presently pass under a bridge with the lion of St. Mark on its archivolt, and another on a pillar at the end of the parapet, a small red lion with much of the puppy in his face, looking vacantly up in the air (in passing we may note that, instead of feathers, his wings are covered with hair, and in several other points the manner of his sculpture is not uninteresting). Presently the canal turns a little to the left, and thereupon becomes more quiet, the main bustle of the water-street being usually confined to the first straight reach of it, some quarter of a mile long, the Cheapside of Murano. We pass a considerable church on the left, St. Pietro, and a little square opposite to it with a few acacia trees, and then find our boat suddenly seized by a strong green eddy, and whirled into the tide-way of one of the main channels of the lagoon, which divides the town of Murano into two parts by a deep stream some fifty yards over, crossed only by one wooden bridge. We let ourselves drift some way down the current, looking at the low line of cottages on the other side of it, hardly knowing if there be more cheerfulness or melancholy in the way the sunshine glows on their ruinous but whitewashed walls, and sparkles on the rushing of the green water by the grass-grown quay. It needs a strong stroke of the oar to bring us into the mouth of another quiet canal on the farther side of the tide-way, and we are still somewhat giddy when we run the head of the gondola into the sand on the left-hand side of this more sluggish stream, and land under the east end of the Church of San Donato, the "Matrice" or "Mother" Church of Murano.

It stands, it and the heavy campanile detached from it a few yards, in a small triangular field of somewhat fresher grass than is usual near Venice, traversed by a paved walk with green mosaic of short grass between the rude squares of its stones, bounded on one side by ruinous garden walls, on another by a line of low cottages, on the third, the base of the triangle, by the shallow canal from which we have just landed. Near the point of the triangular space is a simple well, bearing date 1502; in its widest part, between the canal and campanile, is a four-square hollow pillar, each side formed by a separate slab of stone, to which the iron hasps are still attached that once secured the Venetian standard.

The cathedral itself occupies the northern angle of the field, encumbered with modern buildings, small out-house-like chapels, and wastes of white wall with blank square windows, and itself utterly defaced in the whole body of it, nothing but the apse having been spared; the original plan is only discoverable by careful examination, and even then but partially. The whole impression and effect of the building are irretrievably lost, but the fragments of it are still most precious.

We must first briefly state what is known of its history.

The legends of the Romish Church, though generally

more insipid and less varied than those of Paganism, deserve audience from us on this ground, if on no other, that they have once been sincerely believed by good men, and have had no ineffective agency in the foundation of the existent European mind. The reader must not therefore accuse me of trifling, when I record for him the first piece of information I have been able to collect respecting the cathedral of Murano: namely, that the emperor Otho the Great, being overtaken by a storm on the Adriatic, vowed, if he were preserved, to build and dedicate a church to the Virgin, in whatever place might be most pleasing to her; that the storm thereupon abated; and the Virgin appearing to Otho in a dream showed him, covered with red lilies, that very triangular field on which we were but now standing amidst the ragged weeds and shattered pavement. The emperor obeyed the vision; and the church was consecrated on the 15th of August, 957.

Whatever degree of credence we may feel disposed to attach to this piece of history, there is no question that a church was built on this spot before the close of the Tenth Century: since in the year 999 we find the incumbent of the Basilica (note this word, it is of some importance) di Santa Maria Plebania di Murano taking an oath of obedience to the Bishop of the Altinat church, and engaging at the same time to give the said bishop his dinner on the Domenica in Albis, when the prelate held a confirmation in the mother church, as it was then commonly called, of Murano. From this period, for more than a century, I can find no records of any alterations made in the fabric of the church, but there exist very full details of the quarrels which arose between its incumbents and those of San Stefano, San Cipriano, San Salvatore, and the other churches of Murano, touching the due obedience which their less numerous or less ancient brotherhoods owed to St. Mary's.

These differences seem to have been renewed at the election of every new abbot by each of the fraternities, and must have been growing serious when the patriarch of Grado, Henry Dandolo, interfered in 1102, and, in order to seal a peace between the two principal opponents, ordered that the abbot of St. Stephen's should be present at the service in St. Mary's on the night of the Epiphany, and that the abbot of St. Mary's should visit him of St. Stephen's on St. Stephen's day; and that then the two abbots "should eat apples and drink good wine together, in peace and charity."[1]

But even this kindly effort seems to have been without result: the irritated pride of the antagonists remained unsoothed by the love-feast of St. Stephen's Day; and the breach continued to widen until the abbot of St. Mary's obtained a timely accession to his authority in the year 1125. The Doge Domenico Michele, having in the Second Crusade secured such substantial advantages for the Venetians as might well counterbalance the loss of part of their trade with the East, crowned his successes by obtaining possession in Cephalonia of the body of San Donato, bishop of Euroea; which treasure he having presented on his return to the Murano basilica, that church was thenceforward called the church of Sts. Mary and Donato. Nor was the body of the saint its only acquisition: St. Donato's principal achievement had been the destruction of a terrible dragon in Epirus; Michele brought home the bones of the dragon as well as of the saint; the latter were put in a marble sarcophagus, and the former hung up over the high altar.

But the clergy of St. Stefano were indomitable. At the very moment when their adversaries had received this formidable accession of strength, they had the audacity "ad onta de' replicati giuramenti, e dell' inveterata consuetudine," to refuse to continue in the obedience which they had vowed to their mother church. The matter was tried in a provincial council; the votaries of St. Stephen were condemned, and remained quiet for about twenty years, in wholesome dread of the authority conferred on the abbot of St. Donato, by the Pope's legate, to suspend any of the clergy of the island from their office if they refused submission. In 1172, however, they appealed to Pope

---

[1] Perhaps in the choice of the abbot's cheer, there was some occult reference to the verse of Solomon's Song: "Stay me with flagons, comfort me with apples."

Alexander III, and were condemned again: and we find the struggle renewed at every promising opportunity, during the course of the Twelfth and Thirteenth Centuries; until at last, finding St. Donato and the dragon together too strong for him, the abbot of St. Stefano "discovered" in his church the bodies of two hundred martyrs at once!—a discovery, it is to be remembered, in some sort equivalent in those days to that of California in ours. The inscription, however, on the façade of the church recorded it with quiet dignity:—"MCCCLXXIV. a dì XIV, di Aprile. Furono trovati nella presente chiesa del protomartire San Stefano, duecento e più corpi de' Santi Martin, dal Ven. Prete Matteo Fradello, piovano della chiesa."[2] Corner, who gives this inscription, which no longer exists, goes on to explain with infinite gravity, that the bodies in question, "being of infantile form and stature, are reported by tradition to have belonged to those fortunate innocents who suffered martyrdom under King Herod; but that when, or by whom, the church was enriched with so vast a treasure, is not manifested by any document."

The issue of the struggle is not to our present purpose. We have already arrived at the Fourteenth Century without finding record of any effort made by the clergy of St. Mary's to maintain their influence by restoring or beautifying their basilica; which is the only point at present of importance to us. That great alterations were made in it at the time of the acquisition of the body of St. Donato is however highly probable, the mosaic pavement of the interior, which bears its date inscribed 1140, being probably the last of the additions. I believe that no part of the ancient church can be shown to be of more recent date than this; and I shall not occupy the reader's time by any inquiry respecting the epochs or authors of the destructive modern restorations; the wreck of the old fabric, breaking out from beneath them here and there, is generally

---

[2] "On the 14th day of April, 1374, there were found, in this church of the first martyr St. Stefano, two hundred and more bodies of holy martyrs, by the venerable priest, Matthew Fradello, incumbent of the church."

distinguishable from them at a glance; and it is enough for the reader to know that none of these truly ancient fragments can be assigned to a more recent date than 1140, and that some of them may with probability be looked upon as remains of the shell of the first church erected in the course of the latter half of the Tenth Century.

It is roofed by a concha, or semi-dome; and the external arrangement of its walls provides for the security of this dome by what is, in fact, a system of buttresses as effective and definite as that of any of the northern churches, although the buttresses are obtained entirely by adaptations of the Roman shaft and arch, the lower story being formed by a thick mass of wall lightened by ordinary semicircular round-headed niches, like those used so extensively afterwards in Renaissance architecture, each niche flanked by a pair of shafts standing clear of the wall, and bearing deeply moulded arches thrown over the niche. The walls with its pillars thus forms a series of massy buttresses, on the top of which is an open gallery, backed by a thinner wall, and roofed by arches whose shafts are set above the pairs of shafts below. On the heads of these arches rests the roof. We have, therefore, externally a heptagonal apse, chiefly of rough and common brick, only with marble shafts and a few marble ornaments; but for that reason all the more interesting because it shows us what may be done, and what was done, with materials such as are now at our own command; and because in its proportions, and in the use of the few ornaments it possesses, it displays a delicacy of feeling rendered doubly notable by the roughness of the work in which laws so subtle are observed, and with which so thoughtful ornamentation is associated.

We must now see what is left of interest within the walls.

All hope is taken away by our first glance; for it falls on a range of shafts whose bases are concealed by wooden paneling, and which sustains arches decorated in the most approved style of Renaissance upholstery, with stucco roses in squares under the soffits, and egg and arrow mouldings on the architraves, gilded, on a ground of spotty black and green, with a small pink-faced and black-eyed cherub on every keystone; the rest of the church being for the most part concealed either by dirty hangings, or dirtier whitewash, or dim pictures on warped and wasting canvas; all vulgar, vain, and foul. Yet let us not turn back, for in the shadow of the apse our more careful glance shows us a Greek Madonna, pictured on a field of gold; and we feel giddy at the first step we make on the pavement, for it, also, is of Greek mosaic waved like the sea, and dyed like a dove's neck.

Nor are the original features of the rest of the edifice altogether indecipherable; the entire series of shafts marked in the ground plan on each side of the nave, from the western entrance to the apse, are nearly uninjured; and I believe the stilted arches they sustain are those of the original fabric, though the masonry is covered by the Renaissance stucco mouldings. Their capitals, for a wonder, are left bare, and appear to have sustained no farther injury than has resulted from the insertion of a large brass chandelier into each of their abaci, each chandelier carrying a sublime wax candle two inches thick, fastened with wire to the wall above. The due arrangement of these appendages, previous to festa days, can only be effected from a ladder set against the angle of the abacus; and ten minutes before I wrote this sentence, I had the privilege of watching the candle-lighter at his work, knocking his ladder about the heads of the capitals as if they had given him personal offence. He at last succeeded in breaking away one of the lamps altogether, with a bit of the marble of the abacus; the whole falling in ruin to the pavement, and causing much consultation and clamour among a tribe of beggars who were assisting the sacristan with their wisdom respecting the festal arrangements.

It is fortunate that the capitals themselves, being somewhat rudely cut, can bear this kind of treatment better than most of those in Venice. They are all founded on the Corinthian type, but the leaves are in every one different: those of the easternmost capital of the southern range are the best, and very beautiful, but presenting no feature of much interest, their workmanship being inferior to most of the imitations of Corinthian common at the period; much more to the rich fantasies which we have seen at Torcello. The apse itself to-day (12th September, 1851), is not to be described; for just in front of it, behind the altar, is a magnificent curtain of a new red velvet with a gilt edge and two golden tassels, held up in a dainty manner by two angels in the upholsterer's service; and above all, for concentration of effect a star or sun, some five feet broad, the spikes of which conceal the whole of the figure of the Madonna except the head and hands.

The pavement is however still left open, and it is of infinite interest, although grievously distorted and defaced. For whenever a new chapel has been built, or a new altar erected, the pavement has been broken up and readjusted so as to surround the newly inserted steps or stones with some appearance of symmetry; portions of it either covered or carried away, others mercilessly shattered or replaced by modern imitations, and those of very different periods, with pieces of the old floor left here and there in the midst of them, and worked round so as to deceive the eye into acceptance of the whole as ancient. The portion, however, which occupies the western extremity of the nave, and the parts immediately adjoining it in the aisles, are, I believe, in their original positions, and very little injured: they are composed chiefly of groups of peacocks, lions, stags, and griffins,—two of each in a group, drinking out of the same vase, or shaking claws together,—enclosed by interlacing bands, and alternating with chequer or star patterns, and here and there an attempt at representation of architecture, all worked in marble mosaic. The floors of Torcello and of St. Mark's are executed in the same manner; but what remains at Murano is finer than either, in the extraordinary play of colour obtained by the use of variegated marbles. At St. Mark's the patterns are more intricate, and the pieces far more skillfully set together; but each piece is there commonly of one colour: at Murano every fragment is itself variegated, and all are arranged with a skill and feeling not to be taught, and to be observed with deep reverence, for that pavement is not dateless, like the rest of the church; it bears its date on one of its central circles,

1140, and is, in my mind, one of the most precious monuments in Italy, showing thus early, and in those rude chequers which the bared knee of the Murano fisher wears in its daily bending, the beginning of that mighty spirit of Venetian colour, which was to be consummated in Titian.

But we must quit the church for the present, for its garnishings are completed; the candles are all upright in their sockets, and the curtains are drawn into festoons, and a pasteboard crescent, gay with artificial flowers, has been attached to the capital of every pillar, in order, together with the gilt angels, to make the place look as much like Paradise as possible. If we return to-morrow, we shall find it filled with woeful groups of aged men and women, wasted and fever-struck, fixed in paralytic supplication, half kneeling, half couched upon the pavement; bowed down, partly in feebleness, partly in a fearful devotion, with their grey clothes cast far over their faces, ghastly and settled into a gloomy animal misery, all but the glittering eyes and muttering lips.

Fit inhabitants, these, for what was once the Garden of Venice, "a terrestrial paradise,—a place of nymphs and demigods!"

We return, yet once again, on the following day. Worshippers and objects of worship, the sickly crowd and gilded angels, all are gone; and there far in the apse, is seen the sad Madonna standing in her folded robe, lifting her hands in vanity of blessing. There is little else to draw away our thoughts from the solitary image. An old wooden tablet, carved into a rude effigy of San Donato, which occupies the central niche in the lower part of the tribune, has an interest of its own, but is unconnected with the history of the older church. The faded frescoes of saints, which cover the upper tier of the wall of the apse, are also of comparatively recent date, much more the piece of Renaissance workmanship, shaft and entablature, above the altar, which has been thrust into the midst of all, and has cut away part of the feet of the Madonna. Nothing remains of the original structure but the semi-dome itself, the cornice whence it springs, which is the same as that used on the exterior of the church, and the border and face-arch which surround it. The ground of the dome is of gold, unbroken except by the upright Madonna, and usual inscription, M R [** symbol] V. The figure wears a robe of blue, deeply fringed with gold, which seems to be gathered on the head and thrown back on the shoulders, crossing the breast, and falling in many folds to the ground. The under robe, shown beneath it where it opens at the breast, is of the same colour; the whole, except the deep gold fringe, being simply the dress of the women of the time. Le donne, anco elle del 1100, vestivano *di turchino con manti in spalla*, che le coprivano dinanzi e di dietro.[3]

Round the dome there is a colored mosaic border; and on the edge of its arch, legible by the whole congregation, this inscription:

"Quos Eva contrivit, pia Virgo Maria redemit;

Hanc cuncti laudent, qui Christi munere gaudent."[4]

The whole edifice is, therefore, simply a temple to the Virgin: to her is ascribed the fact of Redemption, and to her its praise.

"And is this," it will be asked of me, "the time, is this the worship, to which you would have us look back with reverence and regret?" Inasmuch as redemption is ascribed to the Virgin, No. Inasmuch as redemption is a thing desired, believed in, rejoiced in, Yes,—and Yes a thousand times. As far as the Virgin is worshipped in place of God, No; but as far as there is the evidence of worship itself, and of the sense of a Divine presence, Yes. For there is a wider division of men than that into Christian and Pagan: we ask what a man worships, we have to ask whether he worships at all. Observe Christ's own words on this head: "God is a spirit; and they that worship Him must worship Him in spirit, *and* in truth." The worshipping in spirit comes first, and does not necessarily imply the worshipping in truth. Therefore, there is first the broad division of men into Spirit

---

[3] "The women, even as far back as 1100, wore dresses of blue, with mantles on the shoulder, which clothed them before and behind."—Sansovino. It would be difficult to imagine a dress more modest and beautiful.

[4] "Whom Eve destroyed, the pious Virgin Mary redeemed;
All praise her, who rejoice in the Grace of Christ."

worshippers and Flesh worshippers; and then, of the Spirit worshippers, the farther division into Christian and Pagan,—worshippers in Falsehood or in Truth. I therefore, for the moment, omit all inquiry how far the Mariolatry of the early church did indeed eclipse Christ, or what measure of deeper reverence for the Son of God was still felt through all the grosser forms of Madonna worship. Let that worship be taken at its worst; let the goddess of this dome of Murano be looked upon as just in the same sense an idol as the Athene of the Acropolis, or the Syrian Queen of Heaven; and then, on this darkest assumption, balance well the difference between those who worship and those who worship not;—that difference which there is in the sight of God, in all ages, between the calculating, smiling, self-sustained, self-governed man, and the believing, weeping, wondering, struggling, Heaven-governed man;—between the men who say in their hearts "there is no God," and those who acknowledge a God at every step, "if haply they might feel after Him and find Him." For that is indeed the difference which we shall find, in the end, between the builders of this day and the builders on that sand island long ago. They *did* honour something out of themselves; they did believe in spiritual presence judging, animating, redeeming them; they built to its honour and for its habitation; and were content to pass away in nameless multitudes, so only that the labour of their hands might fix in the sea-wilderness a throne for their guardian angel. In this was their strength, and there was indeed a Spirit walking with them on the waters, though they could not discern the form thereof, though the Master's voice came not to them, "It is I." What their error cost them, we shall see here-after; for it remained when the majesty and the sincerity of their worship had departed, and remains to this day. Mariolatry is no special characteristic of the Twelfth Century; on the outside of that very tribune of San Donato, in its central recess, is an image of the Virgin who receives the reverence once paid to the blue vision upon the inner dome. With rouged cheeks and painted brows, the frightful doll stands in wretchedness of rags, blackened with the smoke of the votive lamp at its feet; and if we would know what has been lost or gained by Italy in the six hundred years that have worn the marbles of Murano, let us consider how far the priests who set up this to worship, the populace who have this to adore, may be nobler than the men who conceived that lonely figure standing on the golden field, or than those to whom it seemed to receive their prayer at evening, far away, where they only saw the blue clouds rising out of the burning sea.

THE PALACE OF THE POPES, FRANCE
Charles Dickens

Hard by the cathedral stands the ancient Palace of the Popes, of which one portion is now a common jail, and another a noisy barrack: while gloomy suites of apartments, shut up and deserted, mock their own old state and glory, like the embalmed bodies of kings. But we neither went there to see state-rooms, nor soldiers' quarters, nor a common jail, though we dropped some money into a prisoners' box outside, whilst the prisoners themselves, looked through the iron bars, high up, and watched us eagerly. We went to see the ruins of the dreadful rooms in which the Inquisition used to sit.

A little, old, swarthy woman, with a pair of flashing black eyes—proof that the world hadn't conjured down the devil within her, though it had had between sixty and seventy years to do it in—came out of the Barrack Cabaret, of which she was the keeper, with some large keys in her hands, and marshalled us the way that we should go. How she told us, on the way, that she was a Government Officer (*concierge du palais apostolique*) and had been for I don't know how many years; and how she had shown these dungeons to princes; and how she was the best of dungeon demonstrators; and how she had resided in the palace from an infant—had been born there, if I recollect right—I needn't relate. But such a fierce, little, rapid, sparkling, energetic she-devil I never beheld. She was alight and flaming all the time. Her action was violent in the extreme. She never spoke without stopping expressly for the purpose. She stomped her feet, clutched us by the arms, flung herself into attitudes, hammered against the walls with her keys, for mere emphasis: now whispered as if the Inquisition were there still: now shrieked as if she were on the rack herself; and had a mysterious, hag-like way with her forefinger, when approaching the remains of some new horror—looking back and walking stealthily, and making horrible grimaces—that might alone have qualified her to walk up and down a sick man's counterpane, to the exclusion of all other figures, through a whole fever.

Passing through the courtyard, among groups of idle soldiers, we turned off by a gate, which this She-Goblin unlocked for our admission, and locked again behind us: and entered a narrow court, rendered narrower by fallen stones and heaps of rubbish; part of it choking up the mouth of a ruined subterranean passage, that once communicated (or is said to have done so) with another castle on the opposite bank of the river. Close to this courtyard is a dungeon—we stood within it, in another minute—in the dismal tower *des oubliettes*, where Rienzi was imprisoned, fastened by an iron chain to the very wall that stands there now, but shut out from the sky which now looks down into it. A few steps brought us to the Cachots, in which the prisoners of the Inquisition were confined for forty-eight hours after their capture, without food or drink, that their constancy might be shaken, even before they were confronted with their gloomy judges. The day has not got in there yet, they are still small cells, shut in by four unyielding, close, hard walls; still profoundly dark; still massively doored and fastened as of old.

Goblin, looking back as I have described, went softly on, into a vaulted chamber, now used as a store-room: once the chapel of the Holy Office. The place where the tribunal sat was plain. The platform might have been removed but yesterday. Conceive the parable of the Good Samaritan having been painted on the wall of one of these Inquisition chambers! But it was, and may be traced there yet.

High up in the jealous wall are niches where the faltering replies of the accused were heard and noted down. Many of them had been brought out of the very cell we had just looked into, so awfully: along the same stone passage. We had trodden in their very footsteps.

I am gazing round me, with the horror that the place inspires, when Goblin clutches me by the wrist, and lays, not her skinny finger, but the handle of the key, upon her lips. She invites me, with a jerk, to follow her. I do so. She leads me out into a room adjoining—a rugged room, with a funnel-shaped, contracting roof, open at the top to the bright day. I ask her what it is. She folds her arms, leers hideously, and stares. I ask again. She glances round, to see that all the little company are there; sits down upon a mound of stones; throws up her arms, and yells out, like a fiend, "La Salle de la Question!"

The Chamber of Torture! And the roof was made of that shape to stifle the victim's cries! Oh, Goblin, Goblin, let us think of this awhile in silence. Peace, Goblin! Sit with your short arms crossed on your short legs, upon that heap of stones, for only five minutes, and then flame out again.

Minutes! Seconds are not marked upon the Palace Clock, when, with her eyes flashing fire, Goblin is up in the middle of the chamber, describing, with her sunburnt arms, a wheel of heavy blows. Thus it ran round! cries Goblin. Mash, mash, mash! An endless routine of heavy hammers. Mash, mash, mash! upon the sufferer's limbs. See the stone trough! says Goblin. For the water torture! Gurgle, swill, bloat, burst, for the Redeemer's honour! Suck the bloody rag, deep down into your unbelieving body, Heretic, at every breath you draw. And when the executioner plucks it out, reeking with the smaller mysteries of God's own Image, know us for His chosen servants, true believers in the Sermon on the Mount, elect disciples of Him who never did a miracle but to heal: who never struck a man with palsy, blindness, deafness, dumbness, madness, any one affliction of mankind; and never stretched His blessed hand out, but to give relief and ease!

See! cries Goblin. There the furnace was. There they made the irons red-hot. Those holes supported the sharp stake, on which the tortured persons hung poised: dangling with their whole weight from the roof. "But"—and Goblin whispers this—"Monsieur has heard of this tower? Yes? Let Monsieur look down then!"

A cold air, laden with an earthy smell, falls upon the face of Monsieur; for she has opened, while speaking, a trap-door in the wall. Monsieur looks in. Downward to the bottom, upward to the top, of a steep, dark, lofty tower: very dismal, very dark, very cold. The Executioner of the Inquisition, says Goblin, edging in her head to look down also, flung those who were past all further torturing down here. "But look! does Monsieur see the black stains on the wall?" A glance, over his shoulder, at Goblin's keen eye, shows Monsieur—and would without the aid of the directing key—where they are. "What are they?" "Blood!"

In October, 1791, when the Revolution was at its height here, sixty persons: men and women ("and priests," says Goblin, "priests"): were murdered, and hurled the dying and the dead, into this dreadful pit, where a quantity of quicklime was tumbled down upon their bodies. Those ghastly tokens of the massacre were soon no more; but while one stone of the strong building in which the deed was done remains upon another, there they will lie in the memories of men, as plain to see as the splashing of their blood upon the wall is now.

Was it a portion of the great schemes of Retribution that the cruel deed should be committed in this place? That a part of the atrocities and monstrous institutions, which had been, for scores of years, at work, to change men's nature, should in its last service tempt them with the ready means of gratifying their furious and beastly rage! Should enable them to show themselves, in the height of their frenzy, no worse than a great, solemn, legal establishment in the height of its power? No worse! Much better. They used the Tower of the Forgotten in the name of Liberty— their liberty; an earth-born creature, nursed in the black mud of the Bastille moats and dungeons, and necessarily betraying many evidences of its unwholesome bringing-up—but the Inquisition used it in the name of Heaven.

Goblin's finger is lifted; and she steals out again into the Chapel of the Holy Office. She stops at a certain part of the flooring. Her great effect is at hand. She waits for the rest. She darts at the Brave Courier, who is explaining something; hits him a sounding rap on the hat with the largest key: and bids him be silent. She assembles us all round a little trap-door in the floor as round a grave. "Voilà!" she darts down at the ring, and flings the door open with a crash, in her goblin energy, though it is no light weight. "Voilà les oubliettes! Voilà les oubliettes! Subterranean! Frightful! Black! Terrible! Deadly! Les oubliettes de l'Inquisition!"

My blood ran cold as I looked from Goblin, down into the vaults, where these forgotten creatures, with recollections of the world outside: of wives, friends, children, brothers: starved to death, and made the stones ring with their unavailing groans. But, the thrill I felt on seeing the accursed wall below, decayed and broken through, and the sun shining in through its gaping wounds, was like a sense of victory and triumph. I felt exalted with the proud delight of living, in these degenerate times, to see it. As if I were the hero of some high achievement! The light in the doleful vaults was typical of the light that has streamed in on all persecution in God's name, but which is not yet at its noon! It cannot look more lovely to a blind man newly restored to sight, than to a traveller who sees it, calmly and majestically, treading down the darkness of that Infernal Well.

Goblin, having shown *les oubliettes* felt that her great *coup* was struck. She let the door fall with a crash, and stood upon it with her arms akimbo, sniffing prodigiously.

When we left the place, I accompanied her into her

house, under the outer gateway of the fortress, to buy a little history of the building. Her cabaret, a dark low room, lighted by small windows, sunk in the thick wall—in the softened light, and with its forge-like chimney; its little counter by the door, with bottles, jars, and glasses on it; its household implements and scraps of dress against the wall; and a sober-looking woman (she must have a congenial life of it with Goblin) knitting at the door—looked exactly like a picture by Ostade.

I walked round the building on the outside, in a sort of dream, and yet with the delightful sense of having awakened from it, of which the light, down in the vaults, had given me the assurance. The immense thickness and giddy height of the walls, the enormous strength of the massive towers, the great extent of the building, its gigantic proportions, frowning aspect, and barbarous irregularity, awaken awe and wonder. The recollection of its opposite old uses; an impregnable fortress, a luxurious palace, a horrible prison, a place of torture, the court of the Inquisition: at one and the same time, a house of feasting, fighting, religion, and blood: gives to every stone in its huge form a fearful interest, and imparts new meaning to its incongruities. I could think of little, however, then, or long afterwards, but the sun in the dungeons. The palace coming down to be the lounging-place of noisy soldiers, and being forced to echo their rough talk and common oaths, and to have their garments fluttering from its dirty windows, was some reduction of its state, and something to rejoice at; but the day in its cells, and the sky for the roof of its chambers of cruelty—that was its desolation and defeat! If I had seen it in a blaze from ditch to rampart, I should have felt that not that light, nor all the light in all the fire that burns, could waste it, like the sunbeams in its secret council-chamber, and its prisons.

Before I quit this Palace of the Popes, let me translate from the little history I mentioned just now a short anecdote, quite appropriate to itself, connected with its adventures.

"An ancient tradition relates, that in 1441, a nephew of Pierre de Lude, the Pope's legate, seriously insulted some distinguished ladies of Avignon, whose relations, in revenge, seized the young man and horribly mutilated him. For several years the legate kept *his* revenge within his own breast, but he was not the less resolved upon its gratification at last. He even made, in the fullness of time, advances towards a complete reconciliation; and when their apparent sincerity had prevailed, he invited to a splendid banquet, in this palace, certain families, whom he sought to exterminate. The utmost gayety animated the repast; but the measures of the legate were well taken. When the dessert was on the board, a Swiss presented himself, with the announcement that a strange embassador solicited an extraordinary audience. The legate, excusing himself for the moment to his guests, retired, followed by his officers. Within a few moments afterwards, five hundred persons were reduced to ashes; the whole of that wing of the building having been blown into the air with a terrible explosion!"

After seeing the churches (I will not trouble you with churches just now), we left Avignon that afternoon. The heat being very great, the roads outside the walls were strewn with people fast asleep in every little slip of shade, and with lazy groups, half asleep and half awake, who were waiting until the sun should be low enough to admit of their playing bowls among the burnt-up trees, and on the dusty road. The harvest here was already gathered in, and mules and horses were treading out the corn in the fields. We came, at dusk, upon a wild and hilly country, once famous for brigands; and travelled slowly up a steep ascent. So we went on until eleven at night, when we halted at the town of Aix (within two stages of Marseilles) to sleep.

THE CHURCH OF THE HOLY SEPULCHRE, PALESTINE
Pierre Loti

The rain is nearly over. The sky is drying sadly and shows the first blue spaces. It is damp and cold, and water runs all along the base of the old walls.

On foot, with an Arab for a guide, I escape alone from the hôtel to hurry at last to the Holy Sepulchre. It is in the opposite direction to that of the Dominicans, almost in the heart of Jerusalem through narrow winding streets between walls as old as the Crusades, without windows and without roofs. On the wet pavements and beneath a still dark sky, circulate Oriental costumes,—Turks, Bedouins, or Jews, and women draped like phantoms, Musulmans beneath dark veils and Christians beneath white veils.

The city has remained Saracen. Vaguely I notice that we pass an Oriental bazaar, where the stalls are occupied by merchants in turbans; in the shadow of the roofed streets there slowly passes a string of enormous camels, that obliges us to enter one of the doors. Now, we must get out of the way for a peculiar and long defile of Russian women, all sexagenarians at least, who walk rapidly leaning on walking-sticks; old faded dresses, old parasols, old *touloupes* of fur, with faces of fatigue and suffering framed in black handkerchiefs; a black and sorrowful *ensemble* in the midst of this Orient of colour. They walk rapidly with a movement at once excited and exhausted, all hustling along without seeing anything, like somnambulists, with anæstheticized eyes wide open in a celestial dream. And hundreds of moujiks, having the same look of ecstasy follow them; all of them old, sordid, with long grey beards and long grey hair escaping from their felt hats; on their breasts many medals, indicating that they are old soldiers. Having entered the holy city yesterday, they are returning from their first visit to that sacred spot where I am going in my turn; poor pilgrims who come here by the thousand, on foot, sleeping out of doors in the rain or the snow, suffering with hunger and dying on the way.

In proportion as you approach, the Oriental objects in the stalls give place to objects of an obscure Christian piety: thousands of chaplets, crosses, religious lamps, and images or icons. And the crowd is denser, and other pilgrims, old moujiks and old matouchkas plant themselves to buy cheap little wooden rosaries and cheap little crucifixes for two sous, which they will carry from here as relics to be considered as sacred forever.

Finally, in an old and defaced wall resembling a rock, there opens a rude door, very low and narrow, and, by a series of descending steps, you arrive before a place jutting out from the high sombre walls, in front of the basilica of the Holy Sepulchre.

At this spot, it is customary to take off your hat, the very moment the Holy Sepulchre appears; every one passes bareheaded even if he is only going by on his way about Jerusalem. It is thronged with poor people who beg by singing; pilgrims who pray; sellers of crosses and chaplets who have their little booths on the ground upon the old and venerable flag-stones. Upon the pavement and among the steps there rise the still uprooted socles of columns that formally supported the basilicas, and that were razed, like those of St. Stephen, from far back and doubtful periods; everything is a collection of rubbish in this city which has been subjected to twenty sieges and which every kind of fanaticism has sacked.

The high walls, of reddish brown stone, forming the sides of this place, are convents or chapels—and it is said fortresses also. In the background, higher and more sombre than anything else rises that worn out and broken mass, which is the façade of the Holy Sepulchre and which has assumed the appearance and irregularities of a large rock; it has two enormous doors of the Twelfth Century framed with singularly archaic ornaments; one of them is walled up; the other is wide open permitting you to see thousands of little flames in the shadowy interior. Songs, cries and discordant lamentations, lugubrious to hear, escape through it with the perfume of incense.

Passing through the door, you find yourself in the venerable shadow of a kind of vestibule that reveals magnificent depths beyond, where innumerable lamps are burning. Some Turkish guards, armed as if for a massacre, occupy this entrance in a military fashion; seated like sovereigns on a large divan, they watch the devotees passing this place, which is always, from their point of view, the opprobrium of Musulman Jerusalem and which the most savage of them have never ceased to call El Komamah (ordure).

Oh! the unexpected and imperishable impression when you enter here for the first time. A maze of sombre sanctuaries, of all periods and of all aspects connected by openings, doors and superb columns,—and also by little gloomy doors, air-holes and cavernous hollowings. Some of these are elevated like high tribunals, where you perceive, in the remote distance, groups of women in long veils; others are subterranean, where you are jostled by shadows, between walls of rock that have remained intact, dripping and black.—All this, in a twilight where a few rays of light fall and accentuate the surrounding darkness; all this, starry with an infinite number of little flames in lamps of silver and gold, hanging from the vaults by the thousand.—And everywhere a crowd moving about confusedly as if at Babel, or quite stationary, seeming to be grouped by nationalities around the golden tabernacles where somebody is officiating.

Psalmody, lamentations and joyful songs fill the high vaults, or echo in the sepulchral depths below; the nasal melopœia of the Greeks cut through by the howlings of the Copts. And, in all these voices, an exaltation of tears and prayers which produce dissonance and which unite them; the whole effect becoming I know not what strange thing that makes this place like a great wail from mankind and the supreme cry of distress before death.

The rotunda with a very high cupola, which you enter first and which allows you to divine between its columns the obscure chaos of the other sanctuaries, is occupied in the centre by the great marble kiosk, of a luxury that is half barbaric and overcharged with silver lamps, that encloses the stone of the sepulchre. All around this very sacred kiosk, the crowd surges or stands still: on the one side hundreds of moujiks and matouchkas are kneeling on the flag-stones; on the other, the women of Jerusalem, standing up, in long white veils—groups of ancient virgins, one would, say, in the dreamlike shadow; elsewhere Abyssinians and turbaned Arabs prostrated with foreheads to the earth; Turks with sabre in hand; people of all communions and all languages.

You do not stay long in this habitation of the Holy Sepulchre, which is really the very heart of this mass of basilicas and chapels, people pass by one by one; lowering your head you enter it by a very little door of marble carved and festooned; the sepulchre is within, encased in marble and surrounded by gold icons and gold lamps. There entered at the same time as I did a Russian soldier, a poor old woman in rags, an Oriental woman in rich brocade; all kissed the cover of the tomb and wept. And others followed, and others eternally follow, to touch, embrace and wet with tears these same stones.

There is no plan of unity in this collection of churches and chapels which crowd close around this very holy kiosk; there are some large ones that are marvelously sumptuous and some little ones that are humble and primitive, crumbling away with age in these sinister nooks dug out of the natural rock and dark as night. And, here and there, the rock of Calvary, left bare, appears in the midst of richness and archaic gold work. The contrast is strange between so many collected treasures,—icons of gold, crosses of gold and lamps of gold,—and the rags of the pilgrims and the decay of the walls and the pillars, worn, corroded, shapeless and greasy from the rubbing of so many human bodies.

All the altars and all the different confessionals are so mingled here that it results in a continual displacing of priests and processions; they cleave through the crowds, carrying remonstrances and preceded by armed Janizaries who knock upon the resonant flag-stones with the hilts of their halberds. Make room! here are some Latins who pass in golden chasubles. Make room again! here is the Syrian bishop with a long white beard under a black *cagoule*, who issues from his little subterranean chapel. Then here are some Greeks still Byzantine in adornment, and Abyssinians with black faces. Quickly, quickly they walk by in their sumptuous vestments whilst before them the silver censers swung by children knock against the crowd which is thrown into confusion and separates. In this human sea there is a continuous rumbling and an incessant noise of psalmody and sacred bells. Almost everywhere it is so dark that in order to walk about, it is necessary to have a candle in your hand, and, beneath the high columns and in the dark corridors thousands of little flames follow or cross each other. Men praying in a loud voice, weeping and sobbing, run from one chapel to another, here to kiss the rock where the Cross was planted, there to prostrate themselves where Mary and Magdalen wept; some priests, crouching in the shadows, beckon to you to lead you through the funereal little doors in the holes of the tombs; old women with wild eyes and tears running down their cheeks come up from the subterranean blackness to kiss the stones of the sepulchres.

In black darkness, you descend to the chapel of Saint-Helena, by a wide stairway of about thirty steps, worn, broken, dangerous as falling into ruin and bordered with squatting spectres. In passing, our candles illumined the vague motionless creatures, of the same colour as the side of the rock, who are afflicted beggars, lunatics covered with ulcers, sinister all of them, with their chins in their hands and long hair falling over their faces.—Among these ghastly creatures, there is a blind young man, with magnificent blonde curls enveloping him like a mantle, who is as beautiful as the Christ whom he resembles.

Down below, the chapel of Saint-Helena, after that night, with its two rows of phantoms that you have passed through, is illumined by daylight, whose rays arrive pale and bluish through the loop-holes of the vault. Assuredly this is one of the strangest places in all that medley that calls itself the Holy Sepulchre; it is there that one experiences in the most distressing manner, the sentiment of the terrible Past.

It is silent when I arrive and it is empty, beneath the half dead gaze of those phantoms that guard the stairway at the entrance; you hear with difficulty the indistinct noise of bells and chants from above. Behind the altar, still another stairway, bordered with the same long-haired individuals, descends lower into a still darker night.

You would think this a heathen temple. Four enormous, dumpy pillars, of a primitive Byzantine type and exceedingly heavy, sustain the surbased cupola, from which hang ostrich eggs and a thousand uncouth pendants. Remains of painting on the walls indicating saints with nimbuses of gold in naïve and stiff attitudes are being effaced by the dampness and ancient dust. Everything is decaying through neglect with the sweat of water and saltpetre.

From the depths of the lower subterranean vaults suddenly ascend some Abyssinian priests, who suggest the ancient Magi-Kings, issuing from the bowels of the earth; black faces under large golden tiaras formed like turbans, long robes of cloth of gold sprinkled with imaginary red and blue flowers. Quickly, quickly, with that kind of excited haste which is universal here, they cross the crypts of Saint-Helena and mount towards the other sanctuaries by the big stairway in ruins,—illuminated at first by the light falling from the loop-holes of the vault, splendidly archaic in their golden robes in the midst of the gnomes squatting against the walls,—then, they suddenly disappear above in the distant shadows.

Some distance away, in the sanctuaries at the entrance and near the kiosk of the Sepulchre, the rock of Calvary rises: it supports two chapels to which you ascend by twenty stone steps and which are the veritable place of prostrations and sobs for the crowd.

From the peristyle of these chapels, like an elevated balcony the view commands a confused mass of tabernacles, a maze of churches, where the hypnotized crowd moves about. The most splendid of the two is that of the Greeks; under a nimbus of silver, as resplendent as a rainbow, stand out in human grandeur the pale images of the three crucified ones, Christ and the two thieves; the walls are hidden by icons of silver, gold and precious stones. The altar is erected on the very place of the crucifixion; under the retable a silver lattice lets you see in the black rock the hole where the Cross was planted,—and it is there that you walk on your knees, wetting these sombre stones with tears and kisses, whilst a lulling noise of chants and prayers ascends incessantly from the churches below.

And, for two thousand years, here it has ever been thus; under divers forms, in the different basilicas, with interruptions of sieges, battles, and massacres, but with renewals still more passionate and universal, here the same concert of prayers, the same great chorus of desperate supplications or triumphant thanksgiving have always resounded.

They are somewhat idolatrous, these adorations, for those who say: "God is a Spirit and those who adore Him should adore Him in spirit and in truth." But they are so human, they respond so well to our instincts and our misery. Surely, the first Christians in the purely spiritual flight of their faith, and when the teaching of the master was still fresh in their souls, did not encumber themselves with magnificence, symbols and images. Above all it was not terrestrial memories—the place of a martyr and an empty sepulchre—that preoccupied them; their Redeemer, they did not dream of seeking Him here, as they had seen Him detached forever from transitory things and hovering above in the serene light. But we—all of us, people of the West and North—are some centuries nearer to simple barbarism than the ancient society out of which the early Christians arose; in the Middle Ages, when the new faith penetrated our forests, it overshadowed a thousand primitive beliefs; let us acknowledge it is a small minority that is freed from those accumulated traditions to come again to an evangelical cult in spirit and in truth. And, moreover, when faith is extinguished in our modern souls it is still by that so human veneration for places and memories, that unbelievers like myself are affected with the touching regret for the lost Saviour.

Oh! Christ, for whom all these crowds gather and weep; Christ, for whom this poor old woman, prostrated near me, licks the pavement, leaning against the flags her miserable heart whilst weeping delicious tears of hope; Christ, who holds me, me also, in this place, like her, in a vague, yet very sweet meditation. Oh if He was merely one of our brothers in suffering, now vanished in death, may His memory be adored, even so, for His long illusion of love, meeting again, and eternity. And may this place be also blessed, this unique and strange place which is called the Holy Sepulchre—even contestable, even fictitious if you please—but whither, for fifteen centuries afflicted multitudes have run, where hardened hearts have melted like the snows, and where now my eyes are ready to veil themselves in a last rapture of prayer—very illogical I know—but ineffable and infinite.

In the evening, at nightfall, after I have wandered for a long while in the melancholy little streets, through the Saracen city, where the crowns of fire of the Ramadan begin to flame around the minarets of the mosques,—an attraction draws me slowly towards the Holy Sepulchre.

There reigns here a different darkness to that of the daytime; the rays of white light have ceased to descend by the loop-holes of the vaults; but the lamps that are lighted are more numerous, lamps of silver and lamps of gold, and coloured lamps studding the darkness with little flames of blue, red, or white. A kind of calm rests in this labyrinth of high vaults, like a rest after the exhausting ardour of the day. The noises are nothing more than the buzzing of prayers uttered very low and upon the knee, only the murmurings in the sonorous caves, where dominate the poor raucous voices of the moujiks, and, every now and then their deep coughs. It is nearly time to close the doors and the crowd has melted away; but some groups of people, prostrated in the shadows with faces to the ground, are still kissing the holy flag-stones.

LA GRANDE CHARTREUSE
William Beckford

I rested a moment, and looking against the stout oaken gate, which closed up the entrance to this unknown region, felt at my heart a certain awe, that brought to my mind the sacred terror of those in ancient days going to be admitted into the Eleusinian mysteries.

My guide gave two knocks; after a solemn pause, the gate was slowly opened, and all our horses having passed through it, was again carefully closed.

I now found myself in a narrow dell, surrounded on every side by peaks of the mountains, rising almost beyond my sight, and shelving downwards till their bases were hidden by the foam and spray of the water, over which hung a thousand withered and distorted trees. The rocks seemed crowding upon me, and, by their particular situation, threatened to obstruct every ray of light; but, notwithstanding the menacing appearance of the prospect, I still kept following my guide up a craggy ascent, partly hewn through a rock, and bordered by the trunks of ancient fir-trees, which formed a fantastic barrier, till we came to a dreary and exposed promontory, impending directly over the dell.

The woods are here clothed with darkness, and the torrents rushing with additional violence are lost in the gloom of the caverns below; every object, as I looked downwards from my path, that hung midway between the base and the summit of the cliff, was horrid and woeful. The channel of the torrent sunk deep amidst frightful crags, and the pale willows and wreathed roots spreading over it, answered my ideas of those dismal abodes, where, according to the Druidical mythology, the ghosts of conquered warriors were bound. I shivered whilst I was regarding these regions of desolation, and, quickly lifting up my eyes to vary the scene, I perceived a range of whitish cliffs glistening with the light of the sun, to emerge from these melancholy forests.

On a fragment that projected over the chasm, and concealed for a moment its terrors, I saw a cross, on which was written *Via coeli*. The cliffs being the heaven to which I now aspired, we deserted the edge of the precipice, and, ascending, came to a retired nook of the rocks, in which several copious rills had worn irregular grottoes. Here we reposed an instant, and were enlivened with a few sunbeams, piercing the thickets and gilding the waters that bubbled from the rock, over which hung another cross, inscribed with this short sentence, which the situation rendered wonderfully pathetic, *O Spes unica!* the fervent exclamation of some wretch disgusted with the world whose only consolation was found in this retirement.

We quitted this solitary cross to enter a thick forest of beech trees, that screened in some measure the precipices on which they grew, catching, however, every instant terrifying glimpses of the torrent below. Streams gushed from every crevice in the cliffs, and falling over the mossy roots and branches of the beech, hastened to join the great torrent, athwart which I every now and then remarked certain tottering bridges, and sometimes could distinguish a Carthusian crossing over to his hermitage, that just peeped above the woody labyrinths on the opposite shore.

It was now about ten o'clock, and my guide assured me I should soon discover the convent. Upon this information I took new courage, and continued my route on the edge of the rocks, till we struck into another gloomy grove. After turning about it for some time, we entered again into the glare of daylight, and saw a green valley skirted by ridges of cliffs and sweeps of wood before us. Towards the farther end of this inclosure, on a gentle acclivity, rose the revered turrets of the Carthusians, which extend in a long line on the brow of the hill; beyond them a woody amphitheatre majestically presents itself, terminated by spires of rock and promontories lost among the clouds.

The roar of the torrent was now but faintly distinguishable, and all the scenes of horror and confusion I had passed were succeeded by a sacred and profound calm. I traversed the valley with a thousand sensations I despair of describing, and stood before the gate of the convent with as much awe as some novice or candidate newly arrived to solicit the holy retirement of the order.

As admittance is more readily granted to the English than to almost any other nation, it was not long before the gates opened, and whilst the porter ordered our horses to the stable, we entered a court watered by two fountains and built round with lofty edifices characterized by a noble simplicity.

The interior portal opening discovered an arched aisle, extending till the perspective nearly met, along which windows, but scantily distributed between the pilasters, admitted a pale solemn light, just sufficient to distinguish the objects with a picturesque uncertainty. We had scarcely set our feet on the pavement when the monks began to issue from an arch, about half-way down, and passing in a long succession from their chapel, bowed reverently with much humility and meekness, and dispersed in silence, leaving one of their body alone in the aisle.

The father Coadjutor (for he only remained) advanced towards us with great courtesy, and welcomed us in a manner which gave me far more pleasure than all the frivolous salutations and effected greetings so common in the world below. After asking us a few indifferent questions, he called one of the lay brothers, who live in the convent under less severe restrictions than the fathers whom they serve, and ordering him to prepare our apartment, conducted us to a large square hall with casement windows, and, what was more comfortable, an enormous chimney whose hospitable hearth blazed with a fire of dry aromatic fir, on each side of which were two doors that communicated with the neat little cells destined for our bed-chambers.

Whilst he was placing us round the fire, a ceremony by no means unimportant in the cold climate of these upper regions, a bell rang which summoned him to prayers. After charging the lay brother to set before us the best fare their desert afforded, he retired, and left us at full liberty to examine our chambers.

The weather lowered, and the casements permitted very little light to enter the apartment: but on the other side it was amply enlivened by the gleams of the fire, that spread all over a certain comfortable air, which even sunshine but rarely diffuses. Whilst the showers descended with great violence, the lay brother and another of his companions were placing an oval table, very neatly carved and covered with the finest linen in the middle of the hall; and, before we had examined a number of portraits which were hung in all the panels of the wainscot, they called us to a dinner widely different from what might have been expected in so dreary a situation. Our attendant friar was helping us to some Burgundy, of the happiest growth and vintage, when the Coadjutor returned, accompanied by two other fathers, the Secretary and Procurator, whom he presented to us. You would have been both charmed and surprised with the cheerful resignation that appeared in their countenances, and with the easy turn of their conversation.

In the course of our conversation they asked me innumerable questions about England, where formerly, they said, many monasteries had belonged to their order; and principally that of Witham, which they had learnt to be now in my possession.

The Secretary, almost with tears in his eyes, beseeched me to revere these consecrated edifices, and to preserve their remains, for the sake of St. Hugo, their canonized prior. I replied greatly to his satisfaction, and then declaimed so much in favour of St. Bruno and the holy prior of Witham, that the good fathers grew exceedingly delighted with the conversation, and made me promise to remain some days with them. I readily complied with their request, and, continuing in the same strain, that had so agreeably affected their ears, was soon presented with the works of St. Bruno, whom I so zealously admired.

After we had sat extolling them, and talking upon

much the same sort of subjects for about an hour, the Coadjutor proposed a walk amongst the cloisters and galleries, as the weather would not admit of any longer excursion. He leading the way, we ascended a flight of steps, which brought us to a gallery, on each side of which a vast number of pictures, representing the dependent convents were ranged; for I was now in the capital of the order, where the general resides, and from whence he issues forth his commands to his numerous subjects, who depute the superiors of their respective convents whether situated in the wilds of Calabria, the forests of Poland, or in the remotest districts of Portugal and Spain, to assist at the grand chapter, held annually under him, a week or two after Easter.

Having amused myself for some time with the pictures, and the descriptions the Coadjutor gave me of them, we quitted the gallery and entered a kind of chapel, in which were two altars with lamps burning before them, on each side of a lofty portal. This opened into a grand coved hall, adorned with historical paintings of St. Bruno's life, and the portraits of the generals of the order since the year of the great founder's death (1085) to the present time. Under these portraits are the stalls for the superiors who assist at the grand convocation. In front, appears the general's throne; above, hangs a representation of the canonized Bruno, crowned with stars.

The Coadjutor seemed charmed with the respect with which I looked round on these holy objects; and if the hour of vespers had not been drawing near, we should have spent more time in the contemplation of Bruno's miracles, portrayed on the lower panels of the hall. We left that room to enter a winding passage (lighted by windows in the roof) that brought us to a cloister six hundred feet in length, from which branched off two others, joining a fourth of the same most extraordinary dimensions. Vast ranges of slender pillars extend round the different courts of the edifice, many of which are thrown into gardens belonging to particular cells. We continued straying from cloister to cloister, and wandering along the winding passages and intricate galleries of this immense edifice, whilst the

Coadjutor was assisting at vespers.

In every part of the structure reigned the most death-like calm: no sound reached my ears but the "minute drops from off the eaves." I sat down in a niche of the cloister, and fell into a profound reverie, from which I was recalled by the return of our conductor, who, I believe, was almost tempted to imagine from the cast of my countenance, that I was deliberating whether I should not remain with them forever.

But I soon roused myself, and testified some impatience to see the great chapel, at which we at length arrived after traversing another labyrinth of cloisters. The gallery immediately before its entrance appeared quite gay, in comparison with the others I had passed, and owes its cheerfulness to a large window (ornamented with slabs of polished marble) that admits the view of a lovely wood, and allows a full blaze of light to dart on the chapel door, which is also adorned with marble, in a plain but noble style of architecture.

The father sacristan stood ready on the steps of the portal to grant us admittance; and, throwing open the valves, we entered the chapel and were struck by the justness of its proportions, the solemn majesty of the arched roof and the mild solemn light equally diffused over every part of the edifice. No tawdry ornaments, no glaring pictures disgraced the sanctity of the place. The high altar, standing distinct from the walls which were hung with a rich velvet, was the only object on which many ornaments were lavished; and, it being a high festival, was clustered with statues of gold, shrines, and candelabra of the stateliest shape and most delicate execution. Four of the latter, of a gigantic size, were placed on the steps; which, together with part of the inlaid floor within the choir, were spread with beautiful carpets.

The illumination of so many tapers striking on the shrines, censers and pillars of polished jasper, sustaining the canopy of the altar, produced a wonderful effect; and, as the rest of the chapel was visible only by the faint external light admitted from above, the splendour and dignity of the altar was enhanced by contrast. I retired a moment from it, and seating myself in one of the furthermost stalls of the choir, looked towards it, and fancied the whole structure had risen by "subtle magic," like an exhalation.

Here I remained several minutes breathing nothing but incense, and should not have quitted my station soon, had I not been apprehensive of disturbing the devotions of two aged fathers who had just entered, and were prostrating themselves before the steps of the altar. These venerable figures added greatly to the solemnity of the scene; which as the day declined increased every moment in splendour; for the sparkling of several lamps of chased silver that hung from the roofs, and the gleaming of nine huge tapers which I had not before noticed, began to be visible just as I left the chapel.

Passing through the sacristy, where lay several piles of rich embroidered vestments, purposely displayed for our inspection, we regained the cloister which led to our apartment, where the supper was ready prepared. We had scarcely finished it, when the Coadjutor and the fathers who had accompanied us before, returned, and ranging themselves round the fire, resumed the conversation about St. Bruno.

It grew rather late before my kind hosts had finished their narrations and I was not sorry, after all the exercise I had taken, to return to my cell, where everything invited to repose. I was charmed with the neatness and oddity of my little apartment; its cabin-like bed, oratory and ebony crucifix; in short, everything it contained; not forgetting the aromatic odour of the pine, with which it was roofed, floored and wainscoted. The night was luckily dark. Had the moon appeared, I could not have prevailed upon myself to have quitted her till very late; but, as it happened, I crept into my cabin, and was by "whispering winds soon lulled asleep."

Eight o'clock struck next morning before I awoke; when, to my great sorrow, I found the peaks, which rose above the convent, veiled in vapours, and the rain descending with violence.

After we had breakfasted by the light of our fire (for

the casements admitted but a very feeble gleam), I sat down to the works of St. Bruno; of all medleys one of the strangest. Allegories without end; a theologico-natural history of birds, beast and fishes; several chapters on paradise; the delights of solitude; the glory of Solomon's temple; the new Jerusalem; and numberless other wonderful subjects, full of the loftiest enthusiasm.

I had scarcely finished taking extracts from the writings of this holy and highly-gifted personage when the dinner appeared, consisting of everything most delicate which a strict adherence to the rules of meagre could allow. The good fathers returned as usual before our repast was half over, and resumed as usual their mystic discourse, looking all the time rather earnestly into my countenance to observe the sort of effect their most marvelous narrations produced upon it.

Our conversation, which was beginning to take a gloomy and serious turn, was interrupted, I thought very agreeably, by the sudden intrusion of the sun, which, escaping from the clouds, shone in full splendour above the highest peak of the mountains, and the vapours fleeting by degrees discovered the woods in all the freshness of their verdure. The pleasure I received from seeing this new creation rising to view was very lively, and, as the fathers assured me the humidity of their walks did not often continue longer than the showers, I left my hall.

Crossing the court, I hastened out of the gates, and running swiftly along a winding path on the side of the meadow, bordered by the forests, enjoyed the charms of the prospect, inhaled the perfume of the woodlands, and now turning towards the summits of the precipices that encircle this sacred enclosure, admired the glowing colours they borrowed from the sun, contrasted by the dark hues of the forest. Now, casting my eyes below, I suffered them to roam from valley to valley, and from one stream (beset with tall pines and tufted beech trees) to another. The purity of the air in these exalted regions, and the lightness of my own spirits, almost seized me with the idea of treading in that element.

The tranquillity of the region, the verdure of the lawn,

environed by girdles of flourishing wood, and the lowing of the distant herds filled me with the most pleasing sensations. But when I lifted my eyes to the towering cliffs and beheld the northern sky streaming with ruddy light, and the long succession of misty forms hovering over the space beneath, they became sublime and awful. The dews which began to descend, and the vapours which were rising from every dell, reminded me of the lateness of the hour; and it was with great reluctance that I turned from the scene which had so long engaged my contemplation, and traversed slowly and silently the solitary meadows, over which I had hurried with such eagerness an hour ago.

We had hardly supped before the gates of the convent were shut, a circumstance which disconcerted me not a little, as the full moon gleamed through the casements, and the stars, sparkling above the forests of pines, invited me to leave my apartment again, and to give myself up entirely to the spectacle they offered.

The Coadjutor perceiving that I was often looking earnestly through the windows, guessed my wishes, and calling a lay-brother, ordered him to open the gates, and wait at them till my return. It was not long before I took advantage of this permission, and escaping from the courts and cloisters of the monastery, all hushed in death-like stillness, ascended a green knoll, which several ancient pines strongly marked with their shadows: there, leaning against one of their trunks, I lifted up my eyes to the awful barrier of the surrounding mountains, discovered by the trembling silver light of the moon shooting directly on the woods which fringed their acclivities.

The lawns, the vast woods, the steep descents, the precipices, the torrents, lay all extended beneath, softened by a pale bluish haze, that alleviated, in some measure, the stern prospect of the rocky promontories above, wrapped in dark shadows. The sky was of the deepest azure, innumerable stars were distinguished with unusual clearness from this elevation, many of which twinkled behind the fir-trees edging the promontories. White, grey, and darkish clouds came marching towards the moon that shone full against a range of cliffs, which lift themselves far above the others. The hoarse murmur of the torrent, throwing itself from the distant wilderness into the gloomy vales, was mingled with the blast that blew from the mountains.

It increased. The forests began to wave, black clouds rose from the north, and, as they fleeted along, approached the moon whose light they shortly extinguished. A moment of darkness succeeded; the gust was chill and melancholy; it swept along the desert, and then subsiding, the vapours began to pass away, and the moon returned; the grandeur of the scene was renewed, and its imposing solemnity was increased by her presence. Inspiration was in every wind.

I followed some impulse, which drove me to the summit of the mountains before me; and there, casting a look on the whole extent of wild woods and romantic precipices, thought of the days of St. Bruno. I eagerly contemplated every rock that formerly might have met his eyes; drank of the spring which tradition says he was wont to drink of; and ran to every pine, whose withered appearance bespoke the most remote antiquity, and beneath which, perhaps, the saint had reposed himself, when worn with vigils, or possessed with the sacred spirit of his institutions. It was midnight before I returned to the convent and retired to my quiet chamber, but my imagination was too much disturbed, and my spirits far too active, to allow me any rest for some time.

THE TEMPLES OF HATCHIMAN
Aimé Humbert

The Temples of Hatchiman are approached by long lines of those great cedar-trees which form the avenues to all places of worship in Japan. As we advance along the avenue on the Kanasawa side, chapels multiply themselves along the road, and to the left, upon the sacred hills, we also come in sight of the oratories and commemorative stones which mark the stations of the processions; on the right the horizon is closed by the mountain, with its grottos, its streams, and its pine groves. After we have crossed the river by a fine wooden bridge, we find ourselves suddenly at the entrance of another alley, which leads from the seaside, and occupies a large street. This is the principal avenue, intersected by three gigantic toris, and it opens on the grand square in front of the chief staircase of the main building of the Temple. The precinct of the sacred place extends into the street, and is surrounded on three sides by a low wall of solid masonry, surmounted by a barrier of wood painted red and black. Two steps lead to the first level. There is nothing to be seen there but the houses of the bonzes, arranged like the side-scenes of a theatre, amid trees planted along the barrier-wall, with two great oval ponds occupying the centre of the square. They are connected with each other by a large canal crossed by two parallel bridges, each equally remarkable in its way. That on the right is of white granite, and it describes an almost perfect semicircle, so that when one sees it for the first time one supposes that it is intended for some sort of geometrical exercise; but I suppose that it is in reality a bridge of honour, reserved for the gods and the good genii who come to visit the Temple. The bridge on the left is quite flat, constructed of wood covered with red lacquer, with balusters and other ornaments in old polished copper. The pond crossed by the stone bridge is covered with magnificent white lotus flowers,—the pond crossed by the wooden bridge with red lotus flowers. Among the leaves of the flowers we saw numbers of fish, some red and others like mother of pearl, with glittering fins, swimming about in waters of crystal clearness. The black tortoise glides among the great water-plants and clings to their stems.

The Daïboudhs Of Kamakoura, Japan

After having thoroughly enjoyed this most attractive spectacle, we go on towards the second enclosure. It is raised a few steps higher than the first, and, as it is protected by an additional sanctity, it is only to be approached through the gate of the divine guardians of the sanctuary. This building, which stands opposite the bridges, contains two monstrous idols, placed side by side in the centre of the edifice. They are sculptured in wood, and are covered from head to foot with a thick coating of vermilion. Their grinning faces and their enormous busts are spotted all over with innumerable pieces of chewed paper, which the native visitors throw at them when passing, without any more formality than would be used by a number of schoolboys out for a holiday. Nevertheless, it is considered a very serious act on the part of the pilgrims.

It is the means by which they make the prayer written on the sheet of chewed paper reach its address, and when they wish to recommend anything to the gods very strongly indeed, they bring as an offering a pair of straw slippers plaited with regard to the size of the feet of the Colossus, and hang them on the iron railings within which the statues are enclosed. Articles of this kind, suspended by thousands to the bars, remain there until they fall away in time, and it may be supposed that this curious ornamentation is anything but beautiful.

Here a lay brother of the bonzes approached us, and his interested views were easily enough detected by his bearing. We hastened to assure him that we required nothing from his good offices, except access to an enclosed building. With a shake of his head, so as to make us understand that we were asking for an impossibility, he simply set himself to follow us about with the mechanical precision of a subaltern. He was quite superfluous, but we did not allow his presence to interfere with our admiration. A high terrace, reached by a long stone staircase, surmounted the second enclosure. It is sustained by a Cyclopean wall, and in its turn supports the principal Temple as well as the habitations of the bonzes. The grey roofs of all these different buildings stand out against the sombre forest of cedars and pines. On our left are the buildings of the Treasury; one of them has a pyramidal roof surmounted by a turret of bronze most elegantly worked. At the foot of the great terrace is the Chapel of the Ablutions. On our right stands a tall pagoda, constructed on the principle of the Chinese pagodas, but in a more sober and severe style. The first stage, of a quadrangular form, is supported by pillars; the second stage consists of a vast circular gallery which, though extremely massive, seems to rest simply upon a pivot. A painted roof, terminated by a tall spire of cast bronze, embellished with pendants of the same metal, completes the effect of this strange but exquisitely proportioned building.

All the doors of the buildings which I have enumerated are in good taste. The fine proportions, the rich brown colouring of the wood, which is almost the only material employed in their construction, is enhanced by a few touches of red and dragon green, and the effect of the whole is perfect;—add to the picture a frame of ancient trees and the extreme brilliancy of the sky, for the atmosphere of Japan is the most transparent in the world.

We went beyond the pagoda to visit a bell-tower, where we were shown a large bell beautifully engraved, and an oratory on each side containing three golden images, a large one in the centre, and two small ones on either side. Each was surrounded by a nimbus. This beautiful Temple of Hatchiman is consecrated to a Kami; but it is quite evident that the religious customs of India have supplanted the ancient worship;—we had several proofs of this fact. When we were about to turn back we were solicited by the lay brother to go with him a little further. We complied, and he stopped us under a tree laden with *ex-votos*, at the foot of which stands a block of stone, surrounded by a barrier. This stone, which is probably indebted to the chisels of the bonzes for its peculiar form, is venerated by the multitude, and largely endowed with *ex-voto* offerings. Like all peoples of the extreme East the Japanese are very superstitious; a fact of which we had abundant evidence on this and other occasions.

The Temple towards which we directed our steps on leaving the avenue of the Temple of Hatchiman, immediately diverted our thoughts from the grandeur of this picture. It is admirably situated on the summit of a promontory, whence we overlook the whole Bay of Kamakoura; but it is always sad to come, in the midst of beautiful nature, upon a so-called holy place which inspires nothing but disgust. The principal sanctuary, at first sight, did not strike us as remarkable. Insignificant golden idols stand upon the high altar; and in a side chapel there is an image of the God of Wealth, armed with a miner's hammer. But when the bonzes who received us conducted us behind the high altar, and thence into a sort of cage as dark as a prison and as high as a tower, they lighted two lanterns, and stuck them at the end of a long pole. Then, by this glimmering light, which entirely failed to disperse the shades of the roof, we perceived that we were standing in front of an enormous idol of gilt wood, about twelve yards high, holding in its right hand a sceptre, in its left a lotus, and wearing a tiara composed of three rows of heads representing the inferior divinities. This gigantic idol belongs to the religion of the auxiliary gods of the Buddhist mythology: the Amidas and the Quannons, intercessors who collect the prayers of men and transmit them to heaven. By means of similar religious conceptions, the bonzes strike a superstitious terror into the imaginations of their followers and succeed in keeping them in a state of perpetual fear and folly.

We then went to see the Daïboudhs, which is the wonder of Kamakoura. This building is dedicated to the Daïboudhs, that is to say, to the great Buddha, and may be regarded as the most finished work of Japanese genius, from the double points of view of art and religious sentiment. The Temple of Hatchiman had already given us a remarkable example of the use which native art makes of nature in producing that impression of religious majesty which in our northern climates is effected by Gothic architecture. The Temple of Daïboudhs differs considerably from the first which we had seen. Instead of the great dimensions, instead of the illimitable space which seemed to stretch from portal to portal down to the sea, a solitary and mysterious retreat prepares the mind for some supernatural revelation. The road leads far away from every habitation; in the direction of the mountain it winds about between hedges of tall shrubs. Finally, we see nothing before us but the high road, going up and up in the midst of foliage and flowers; then it turns in a totally different direction, and all of a sudden, at the end of the alley, we perceive a gigantic brazen Divinity, squatting with joined hands, and the head slightly bent forward in an attitude of contemplative ecstasy. The involuntary amazement produced by the aspect of this great image soon gives place to admiration. There is an irresistible charm in the attitude of the Daïboudhs, as well as in the harmony of its proportions. The noble simplicity of its garments and the calm purity of its features are in perfect accord with the sentiment of serenity inspired by its presence. A grove, consisting of some beautiful groups of trees, forms the enclosure of the sacred place, whose silence and solitude are never disturbed. The small cell of the attendant priest can hardly be discerned among the foliage. The altar, on which a little incense is burning at the feet of the Divinity, is composed of a small brass table ornamented by two lotus vases of the same metal, and beautifully wrought. The steps of the altar are composed of large slabs forming regular lines. The blue of the sky, the deep shadow of the statue, the sombre colour of the brass, the brilliancy of the flowers, the varied verdure of the hedges and the groves, fill this solemn retreat with the richest effect of light and colour. The idol of the Daïboudhs, with the platform that supports it, is twenty yards high; it is far from equal in elevation to the statue of St. Charles Borromeo, which may be seen from Arona on the borders of Lake Maggiore, but which effects the spectator no more than a trigonometrical signal-post. The interiors of these two colossal statues have been utilized. The European tourists seat themselves in the nose of the holy cardinal. The Japanese descend by a secret staircase into the foundations of their Daïboudhs, and there they find a peaceful oratory, whose altar is lighted by a ray of sunshine admitted through an opening in the folds of the mantle at the back of the idol's neck. It would be idle to discuss to what extent the Buddha of Kamakoura resembles the Buddha of history, but it is important to remark that he is conformable to the Buddha of tradition.

CATHEDRAL CHURCH OF WELLS, ENGLAND
Edward Augustus Freeman

In every place which boasts of a cathedral church, that cathedral church is commonly the chief object of interest, alike as its present ornament and as the chief centre of its past history. But in Wells the cathedral church and its appurtenances are yet more. Their interest is not only primary, but absorbing. They are not only the chief ornament of the place; they are the place itself. They are not only the centre of the past history of the city; their history is the history of the city. Of our other cities some can trace up a long history as cities independent of their ecclesiastical foundations. Some were the dwelling-places of Kings in days before England became one kingdom. Some have been for ages seats of commerce or manufactures; their history is the history of burghers striving for and obtaining their freedom, a history which repeats in small that same tale of early struggles and later abuses which forms the history of so many greater commonwealths. Others have a long military history; their name at once suggests the memory of battles and sieges, and they can still show walls and castles as the living memorials of the stirring scenes of bygone times. In others even the ecclesiastical pre-eminence of the cathedral church may be disputed by some other ecclesiastical building. The bishoprick and its church may be comparatively modern institutions, and they may be altogether eclipsed by some other institution more ancient in date of foundation, perhaps more ancient in its actual fabric. Thus at Oxford the cathedral church is well-nigh lost among the buildings of the University and its greatest college. At Chester its rank may be disputed by the majestic fragments of the older minster of Saint John. At Bristol the cathedral church, even when restored to its old proportions, will still have at least an equal rival in the stateliest parish church in England. In these cities the bishoprick, its church and its chapter, are institutions of yesterday; the cities themselves were great and famous for ages before they were founded. So at Exeter, though the bishoprick is of far earlier date, yet Exeter was a famous city, which had played its part in history, long before Bishops of Exeter were heard of. Even at Winchester the overwhelming greatness of the old minster has to compete with the earlier and later interests of the royal palace, of the fallen Abbey, of the unique home of noble poverty and of the oldest of the great and still living schools of England. Salisbury alone in our own part of England, and Durham in the far north, have a history which in some measure resembles that of Wells. Like Wells, Salisbury and Durham are cities which have grown up around the cathedral church. Wells stands alone among the cities of England proper as a city which exists only in and through its cathedral church, whose whole history is that of its cathedral church. The bishoprick has been to us what the Abbey has been to our neighbours at Glastonbury, which the church first of Abbots and then of Bishops has been elsewhere to Ely and Peterborough. The whole history of Wells is, I say, the history of the bishoprick and of its church. Of the origin and foundation of the city, as distinguished from that of the church, nothing is known. The name of Wells is first heard of as the place where the church of St. Andrew was standing and its name seldom appears in later history except in connection with the affairs of its church. It was never a royal dwelling-place; it was never a place of commercial importance; it was never a place of military strength. Like other cities, it has its municipal history, but its municipal history is simply an appendage to its ecclesiastical history; the franchises of the borough were simply held as grants from the Bishop. It has its parochial church, a church standing as high among the buildings of its own class as the cathedral church itself. This parochial church has a parochial constitution which is in some points unique. But the parochial church is simply an appendage to the cathedral church; it is the church of the burghers who had come to dwell under the shadow of the minster and the protection of its spiritual lord. And it has ever retained a close, sometimes perhaps a too close, connexion with the cathedral and its Chapter. Thus the history of the church is the history of the city; no battles, no sieges, no parliaments, break the quiet tenor of its way; the name of the city has hardly found its way into our civil and military history. Its name does appear among the troubles of the Seventeenth Century, in the pages of Clarendon and Macaulay, but it appears in connexion with events whose importance was mainly local. And even here the ecclesiastical interest comes in; the most striking event connected with Wells in the story of Monmouth's rebellion is the mischief done to the cathedral, and the way in which further damage and desecration was hindered by Lord Grey. And in our own times, when the parliamentary existence of this city became the subject of an animated parliamentary discussion, even then the ecclesiastical interest was still uppermost. The old battle of the regulars and seculars was fought again over the bodies of two small parliamentary boroughs. I need not remind you that the claims of the old secular foundation were stoutly pressed by one of our own members. But the monastic influence was too strong for us; the mantle of Dunstan and Æthelwald had fallen on the shoulders of Sir John Pakington, and the claims of the fallen Abbey of Evesham were preferred to those of the existing Cathedral of Wells.

The whole interest, then, of the city is ecclesiastical; but its ecclesiastical interest in one point of view surpasses that of every church in England,—I am strongly tempted to say, every church in Europe. The traveller who comes down the hill from Shepton Mallet looks down, as he draws near the city, on a group of buildings which, as far as I know, has no rival either in our island or beyond the sea. To most of these objects, taken singly, it would be easy to find rivals which would equal or surpass them. The church itself, seen even from that most favourable point of view, cannot, from mere lack of bulk, hold its ground against the soaring apse of Amiens, or against the windows ranging, tier above tier, in the mighty eastern gable of Ely. The cloister cannot measure itself with Gloucester or Salisbury; the chapter-house lacks the soaring roofs of York and Lincoln; the palace itself finds its rival in the ruined pile of St. David's. The peculiar charm and glory of Wells lies in the union and harmonious grouping of all. The church does not stand alone; it is neither crowded by incongruous buildings, nor yet isolated from those buildings which are its natural and necessary complement. Palace, cloister, lady chapel, choir, chapter-house, all join to form one indivisible unique bridge which by a marvel of ingenuity connects the church itself with the most perfect of buildings of its class, the matchless Vicars' close. Scattered around we see here and there an ancient house, its gable, its window, or its turret falling in with the style and group of greater buildings, and bearing its part in producing the general harmony of all. The whole history of the place is legibly written on that matchless group of buildings. If we could fancy an ecclesiastical historian to have dropped from the clouds, the aspect of the place would at once tell him that he was looking on an English cathedral church, on a cathedral church which had always been served by secular canons, on a church of secular canons which had preserved its ancient buildings and ancient arrangements more perfectly than any other in the island.

The whole history of Wells before the time of Edward the Elder is excessively obscure, and much of it is undoubtedly fabulous. There is a story about King Ine planting a Bishoprick at Congresbury, which was presently moved to Wells, and a list of Bishops is given between Ine and Edward. There is also a document which professes to be a charter of King Cynewulf in 766, which does not speak of any Bishop at Wells, but which implies the existence of an ecclesiastical establishment of some kind. But unluckily the Congresbury story rests on no good authority, and the charter of Cynewulf is undoubtedly spurious. But because a charter is spurious in form, it does not always follow that its matter is unhistorical and I am the more inclined to attach some value to it, because, while implying the existence of some ecclesiastical establishment, it does not imply the existence of a bishoprick. Putting all things together, and remembering the strong and consistent tradition which connects the name of Ine with the church of Wells, I am inclined to think that there must have been some body of priests, probably of Ine's foundation, existing at Wells before the foundation of the bishoprick by Edward. If then Ine did, somewhere about the year 705, found a church at Wells with a body of priests attached to it, we can well understand why Wells should be chosen as the seat of the new bishoprick in 909.

We have here in Wells the finest collection of domestic buildings surrounding a cathedral church to be seen anywhere. There is no place where so many ancient houses are preserved and are mainly applied to their original uses. The Bishop still lives in the Palace; the Dean still lives in the Deanery; the Canons, Vicars, and other officers still live very largely in the houses in which they were meant to live. But this is because at Wells there always were secular priests, each man living in his own house. In a monastery I need hardly say it was quite different. The monks did not live each man in his own house; they lived in common, with a common refectory to dine in and a common dormitory to sleep in. Thus when, in Henry the Eighth's time, the monks were put out and secular canons put in again, the monastic buildings were no longer of any use, while there were no houses for the new canons. They had therefore to make houses how they could out of the common buildings of the monastery. But of course this could be done without greatly spoiling them as works of architecture. Thus while at Ely, Peterborough, and other churches which were served by monks, there are still very fine fragments of the monastic buildings, there is not the same series of buildings each still applied to its original use which we have at Wells. I wish that this wonderful series was better understood and more valued than it is. I can remember, if nobody else does, how a fine prebendal hall was wantonly pulled down in the North Liberty not many years ago. Some of those whose duty it was to keep it up said that they had never seen it. I had seen it, anybody who went by could see it, and every man of taste knew and regretted it. Well, that is gone, and I suppose the organist's house, so often threatened will soon be gone too. Thus it is that the historical monuments of our country perish day by day. We must keep a sharp eye about us or this city of ours may lose, almost without anybody knowing it, the distinctive character which makes it unique among the cities of England.

It is then in this way that Wells became, what it still is, the seat of the Somersetshire Bishoprick. The Bishop had his throne in the church of St. Andrew, and the clergy attached to church were his special companions and advisers, in a word his Chapter. We have thus the church and its ministers, but the church had not yet assumed its present form, and its ministers had not yet assumed their present constitution. Of the fabric, as it stood in the Tenth Century, I can tell you nothing. There is not a trace of building of anything like such early date remaining: while in other places we have grand buildings of the Eleventh and Twelfth Centuries, at Wells we have little or nothing earlier than the Thirteenth. But it is quite a mistake to fancy that our forefathers in the Tenth Century were wholly incapable of building, or that their buildings were always of wood. We have accounts of churches of that and of still earlier date which show that we then had buildings of considerable size and elaboration of plan. And we know that in the course of the same century Saint Dunstan built a stone church at Glastonbury to the east of the old wooden church of British times. The churches both of Wells and Glastonbury must have been built in the old Romanesque style of England which prevailed before the great improvements of Norman Romanesque were brought in in the Eleventh Century. You must conceive this old church of Saint Andrew as very much smaller, lower, and plainer than the church we now have, with massive round arches and small round-headed windows, but with one or more tall, slender, unbuttressed towers, imitating the bell-towers of Italy. I do not think that we have a single tower of this kind in Somersetshire, but in other parts of England there are a good many. There is a noble one at Earls Barton in Northamptonshire, and more than one in the city of Lincoln.

After about two hundred years from the beginning of the present building in the days of Jocelin, we may look on the cathedral church of Saint Andrew as at last finished. It was finished, in a sense, before the end of the Thirteenth Century, when everything had been built which was needed for its ecclesiastical completeness. But it was in the course of the Fifteenth Century that it finally assumed the shape with which we are all familiar, and which has from that time remained unchanged. Now then we have reached the point at which we can estimate the place which fairly belongs to the church of Wells among the other churches of England and of Christendom. As it seems to me, that position, as I began by saying, is a special and remarkable one; I need not say that in point of size and splendour, the church of Wells has no claim to a place in the first rank of European, or even English churches. Setting aside the Welsh churches, and the churches which have become cathedral without being originally meant for this rank, Wells is one of the very smallest of English episcopal churches. It is hardly fair to compare it with Carlisle, which is a mere fragment, or with Hereford, which has lost its western tower, and with it a part of its nave. But it is, in point of scale, with Carlisle, Hereford, Lincoln, and Rochester, or again with non-cathedral churches like Southwell, Beverley, and Tewkesbury, that Wells must fairly be compared, not with churches like Canterbury and York, or even like Salisbury and Gloucester. And among churches of its own class it certainly ranks high.

I have seen many fine churches both in our own country and abroad, many of them of course on a scale which might seem to put Wells out of all comparison. But I can honestly say that I know of no architectural group which surpasses the harmony and variety of our own cathedral, as seen by the traveller as he first enters the city from Shepton Mallet.

From the outside we turn to that of which the outside is after all the mere shell. When we enter the church we find ourselves in a building which can fairly hold its own against competitors of its own class. The nave has a distinct character of its own: there may be differences of taste as to its merit, but it has a character, and that character is clearly the result of design. The main lines of the interior are horizontal rather than vertical. We can hardly say that there is any division into bays; no vaulting-shafts run up from the ground, nor does the triforium take, as usual, the form of a distinct composition over each arch. In short, we cannot, as we can in most churches, take each arch with the triforium and clerestory over it as a thing existing by itself. One would rather say that three horizontal ranges, one over the other, all converged to the centre, without thinking of what was above or below them. Now tastes may differ as to whether this is a good arrangement or not, but there is no doubt that it is in its way an effective arrangement; there is no nave in which the eye is so irresistibly carried eastward as in that of Wells. And it is worth notice that this arrangement, in its fullness, is confined to the nave; in the transepts the bays are much more clearly marked. The idea of producing this marked horizontal effect was clearly one which came into the heads of the designers as they were working westwards.

It might have been expected that the marked prominence which is thus given to the horizontal line might have gone far to destroy all effect of height in the interior; but it is not so. There is no special feeling of height in Wells Cathedral—not so much, for instance, as there is in the church of St. Mary Redcliff; but there is no such crushing feeling of lowness as there is in Lincoln. This I imagine to be mainly owing to the form of the arch chosen for the vaulting, one boldly but not actually pointed, and to the way in which the lantern-arches fit into the vault. Contrast this with the far larger and loftier nave of York. In that nave the positive height is second only to Westminster among English churches, and the design of the separate bays can hardly be surpassed in its soaring effect. But in the direct eastern or western view the nave of York loses almost its whole effect, partly, no doubt, from the excessive breadth, but partly also from the flat and crushing shape of the vaulting-arch. The nave of Wells makes the most of its small actual height: so do the choir and the presbytery also; for, though I cannot at all admire the kind of vault which is there used, the shape of the arch is as judiciously chosen as it is in the nave. In the presbytery we also get the vaulting-shafts rising from the ground, so as to give the vertical division, and the consequent effect of height, in its highest perfection. Of the exquisite beauty of the Lady Chapel, looked on, as it should be, not as a part of the whole, but as a distinct and almost detached building, I have already spoken. In short, the internal effect of the church, whether looked at as a whole or taken in its several parts if not of the highest order, which its comparatively small scale forbids, may claim a high place among churches of its own class.

I think then on the whole that, even looking at the church by itself, we have every reason to be thankful for what we have got. We have not a church of the first order; but we have a church whose several parts fit very well together, all whose parts have been finished, and of which no part has been destroyed. And I may add that we may be thankful for another thing, for the goodness of the stone of which the greater part of the church is built. The sculpture of the west front indeed has crumbled away; but elsewhere at Wells, as at Glastonbury, wherever the work has not been wantonly knocked away, it is as good as when it was first cut. Now we might have had a church like Chester or Coventry, where the whole surface of the stone has crumbled away, and where the whole ornamental design has become unintelligible. I have said that the church of Wells forms a harmonious whole, that it was perfectly finished, and that no part has been destroyed; and this is a great thing to say. Let me compare the good fortune of

Wells in this respect with the cathedral church of a much more famous city at the other end of England. At Carlisle there is a noble choir, ending in what is probably the grandest window in England. If that choir only had transepts, nave, and towers to match it, the church of Carlisle would be a splendid church indeed. But the choir is built up against a little paltry transept and central tower, and nothing remains by way of nave but two bays of the original small Norman church, the rest having utterly vanished. Here then is a church which does not form a harmonious whole, a church which remains utterly unfinished, and of which one essential part has been destroyed. Or, without taking such an extreme case as this, we may compare our church with some of those of which I have already spoken, with Hereford, Southwell, Beverley and Tewkesbury. In all of these some important feature has either never been finished or has been destroyed at a later time. The Church of Wells then, simply taken by itself, claims a high place among buildings of its own class, that is, among minsters of the second order. But the real charm of Wells does not lie in the church taken by itself, but in the church surrounded by its accompanying buildings. Some of them are inseparably connected both with the fabric and with the foundation of the Cathedral. And it is the preservation of them which gives Wells its peculiar character. Each part may easily be equalled or surpassed, but the whole has no rival in England, and I cannot think that it has many in Christendom.

THE COLISEUM, ITALY
Edward Gibbon

Whatever is fortified will be attacked: and whatever is attacked may be destroyed. Could the Romans have wrested from the popes the Castle of St. Angelo, they had resolved by a public decree to annihilate that monument of servitude. Every building of defence was exposed to a siege; and in every siege the arts and engines of destruction were laboriously employed. After the death of Nicholas the Fourth, Rome, without a sovereign or a senate, was abandoned six months to the fury of civil war. "The houses," says a cardinal and poet of the times, "were crushed by the weight and velocity of enormous stones; the walls were perforated by the strokes of the battering-ram; the towers were involved in fire and smoke; and the assailants were stimulated by rapine and revenge." The work was consummated by the tyranny of the laws; and the factions of Italy alternately exercised a blind and thoughtless vengeance on their adversaries, whose houses and castles they razed to the ground. In comparing the *days* of foreign, with the *ages* of domestic, hostility, we must pronounce, that the latter have been far more ruinous to the city; and our opinion is confirmed by the evidence of Petrarch. "Behold," says the laureat, "the relics of Rome, the image of her pristine greatness! neither time, nor the barbarian, can boast the merit of this stupendous destruction: it was perpetrated by her own citizens, by the most illustrious of her sons, and your ancestors (he writes to a noble Annibaldi) have done with the battering-ram, what the Punic hero could not accomplish with the sword." The influence of the two last principles of decay must in some degree be multiplied by each other; since the houses and towers, which were subverted by civil war, required a new and perpetual supply from the monuments of antiquity.

These general observations may be separately applied to the amphitheatre of Titus, which has obtained the name of the Coliseum, either from its magnitude, or from Nero's colossal statue: an edifice, had it been left to time and nature, which might perhaps have claimed an eternal duration. The curious antiquaries, who have computed the numbers and seats, are disposed to believe, that above the upper row of stone steps, the amphitheatre was encircled and elevated with several stages of wooden galleries, which were repeatedly consumed by fire, and restored by the emperors. Whatever was precious, or portable, or profane, the statues of gods and heroes, and the costly ornaments of sculpture, which were cast in brass, or overspread with leaves of silver and gold, became the first prey of conquest or fanaticism, of the avarice of the barbarians or the Christians. In the massy stones of the Coliseum, many holes are discerned; and the two most probable conjectures represent the various accidents of its decay. These stones were connected by solid links of brass or iron, nor had the eye of rapine overlooked the value of the baser metals; the vacant space was converted into a fair or market; the artisans of the Coliseum are mentioned in an ancient survey; and the chasms were perforated or enlarged to receive the poles that supported the shops or tents of the mechanic trades. Reduced to its naked majesty, the Flavian amphitheatre was contemplated with awe and admiration by the pilgrims of the north; and the rude enthusiasm broke forth in a sublime proverbial expression, which is recorded in the Eighth Century, in the fragments of the venerable

Bede: "As long as the Coliseum stands, Rome shall stand; when the Coliseum falls, Rome will fall; when Rome falls, the world will fall." In the modern system of war, a situation commanded by three hills would not be chosen for a fortress; but the strength of the walls and arches could resist the engines of assault; a numerous garrison might be lodged in the enclosure; and while one faction occupied the Vatican and the Capitol, the other was entrenched in the Lateran and the Coliseum.

The abolition at Rome of the ancient games must be understood with some latitude; and the carnival sports, of the Testacean mount and the Circus Agonalis, were regulated by the law or custom of the city. The senator presided with dignity and pomp to adjudge and distribute the prizes, the gold ring, or the *pallium*, as it was styled, of cloth or silk. A tribute on the Jews supplied the annual expense; and the races, on foot, on horseback, or in chariots, were ennobled by a tilt and tournament of seventy-two of the Roman youth. In the year one thousand three hundred and thirty-two, a bull-feast, after the fashion of the Moors and Spaniards, was celebrated in the Coliseum itself; and the living manners are painted in a diary of the times. A convenient order of benches was restored; and a general proclamation, as far as Rimini and Ravenna, invited the nobles to exercise their skill and courage in this perilous adventure. The Roman ladies were marshalled in three squadrons, and seated in three balconies, which on this day, the third of September, were lined with scarlet cloth. The fair Jacova di Rovere led the matrons from beyond the Tiber, a pure and native race, who still represent the features and character of antiquity. The remainder of the city was divided as usual between the Colonna and Ursini: the two factions were proud of the number and beauty of their female bands: the charms of Savella Ursini are mentioned with praise; and the Colonna regretted the absence of the youngest of their house, who had sprained her ancle in the garden of Nero's tower. The lots of the champions were drawn by an old and respectable citizen: and they descended into the arena, or pit, to encounter the wild bulls, on foot as it should seem, with a single spear. Amidst the crowd, our annalist has selected the names, colours, and devices, of twenty of the most conspicuous knights. Several of the names are the most illustrious of Rome and the ecclesiastical state; Malatesta, Polenta, della Valle, Cafarello, Savelli, Capoccio, Conti, Annabaldi, Altieri, Corsi; the colours were adapted to their taste and situation; the devices are expressive of hope or despair, and breathe the spirit of gallantry and arms. "I am alone, like the youngest of the Horatii," the confidence of an intrepid stranger: "I live disconsolate," a weeping widower: "I burn under the ashes," a discreet lover: "I adore Lavinia or Lucretia," the ambiguous declaration of a modern passion: "My faith is as pure," the motto of a white livery: "Who is stronger than myself?" of a lion's hide: "If I am drowned in blood, what a pleasant death," the wish of ferocious courage. The pride or prudence of the Ursini restrained them from the field, which was occupied by three of their hereditary rivals, whose inscriptions denoted the lofty greatness of the Colonna name: "Though sad I am strong:" "Strong as I am great:" "If I fall," addressing himself to the spectators, "you fall with me:"—intimating (says the contemporary writer) that while the other families were the subjects of the Vatican, they alone were the supporters of the capitol. The combats of the amphitheatre were dangerous and bloody. Every champion successively encountered a wild bull; and the victory may be ascribed to the quadrupeds, since no more than eleven were left on the field, with the loss of nine wounded and eighteen killed on the side of their adversaries. Some of the noblest families might mourn, but the pomp of the funerals, in the churches of St. John Lateran and St. Maria Maggiore, afforded a second holiday to the people. Doubtless it was not in such conflicts that the blood of the Romans should have been shed; yet, in blaming their rashness we are compelled to applaud their gallantry; and the noble volunteers, who display their magnificence, and risk their lives, under the balconies of the fair, excite a more generous sympathy than the thousands of captives and malefactors who were reluctantly dragged to the scene of slaughter.

This use of the amphitheatre was a rare, perhaps a

singular, festival: the demand for the materials was a daily and continual want, which the citizens could gratify without restraint or remorse. In the Fourteenth Century, a scandalous act of concord secured to both factions the privilege of extracting stones from the free and common quarry of the Coliseum; and Poggius laments, that the greater part of these stones had been burnt to lime by the folly of the Romans. To check this abuse, and to prevent the nocturnal crimes that might be perpetrated in the vast and gloomy recess, Eugenius the fourth surrounded it with a wall; and, by a charter long extant, granted both the ground and edifice to the monks of an adjacent convent. After his death, the wall was overthrown in a tumult of the people; and had they themselves respected the noblest monument of their fathers, they might have justified the resolve that it should never be degraded to private property. The inside was damaged; but in the middle of the Sixteenth Century, an æra of taste and learning, the exterior circumference of one thousand six hundred and twelve feet was still entire and inviolate; a triple elevation of fourscore arches, which rose to the height of one hundred and eight feet. Of the present ruin, the nephews of Paul the Third are the guilty agents; and every traveller who views the Farnese Palace may curse the sacrilege and luxury of these upstart princes. A similar reproach is applied to the Barberini; and the repetition of injury might be dreaded from every reign, till the Coliseum was placed under the safeguard of religion by the most liberal of the pontiffs, Benedict the Fourteenth, who consecrated a spot which persecution and fable had stained with the blood of so many Christian martyrs.

When Petrarch first gratified his eyes with a view of those monuments, whose scattered fragments so far surpass the most eloquent descriptions, he was astonished at the supine indifference of the Romans themselves; he was humbled rather than elated by the discovery, that, except his friend Rienzi and one of the Colonna, a stranger of the Rhone was more conversant with these antiquities than the nobles and natives of the metropolis.

THE COLISEUM
Charles Dickens

When we came out of the church again (we stood nearly an hour staring up into the dome: and would not have "gone over" the Cathedral then for any money), we said to the coachman, "Go to the Coliseum." In a quarter of an hour or so, he stopped at the gate, and we went in.

It is no fiction but plain, sober, honest Truth, to say: so suggestive and distinct is it at this hour: that, for a moment—actually in passing in—they who will, may have the whole great pile before them, as it used to be, with thousands of eager faces staring down into the arena, and such a whirl of strife, and blood, and dust, going on there, as no language can describe. Its solitude, its awful beauty, and its utter desolation, strike upon the stranger, the next moment, like a softened sorrow; and never in his life, perhaps, will he be so moved and overcome by any sight, not immediately connected with his own affections and afflictions.

To see it crumbling there, an inch a year; its walls and arches overgrown with green; its corridors open to the day; the long grass growing in its porches; young trees of yesterday, springing up on its ragged parapets, and bearing fruit: chance produce of the seeds dropped there by the birds, who build their nests within its chinks and crannies; to see the Pit of Fight filled up with earth, and the peaceful Cross planted in the centre; to climb into its upper halls, and look down on ruin, ruin, ruin, all about it; the triumphal arches of Constantine, Septimus Severus, and Titus; the Roman Forum; the Palace of the Cæsars; the temples of the old religion, fallen down and gone; is to see the ghost of old Rome, wicked, wonderful old city, haunting the very ground on which its people trod. It is the most impressive, the most stately, the most solemn, grand, majestic, mournful sight, conceivable. Never, in its bloodiest prime, can the sight of the gigantic Coliseum, full and running over with the lustiest life, have moved one heart, as it must move all who look upon it now, a ruin—God be thanked: a ruin!

As it tops the other ruins: standing there, a mountain among graves: so do its ancient influences outlive all other remnants of the old mythology and old butchery of Rome, in the nature of the fierce and cruel Roman people. The Italian face changes as the visitor approaches the city; its beauty becomes devilish; and there is scarcely one countenance in a hundred, among the common people in the streets, that would not be at home and happy in a renovated Coliseum to-morrow.

Here was Rome indeed at last; and such a Rome as no one can imagine in its full and awful grandeur.

GOLDEN TEMPLE OF THE SIKHS, INDIA
G. W. Steevens

The Sikhs are the youngest of the great powers of India. A kind of Hindu Protestants, their Luther arose about 1500 to fulminate against caste and the worship of idols. Instead of Shiva and Kali, they worship their Bible, which is called the Granth. They abhor tobacco, and it is impiety to shave or cut the hair. Sometimes, when a Sikh plays polo, you may see it come undone and wave behind him like a horse-tail. From Puritans they turned to Ironsides, praying and fighting with equal fervour, wearing an iron quoit in their turbans, partly as a sign of grace, and partly as a defence against a chance sword-cut.

For some three hundred years they fought the Musulmans, Mogul or Afghan, for the dominion of the Punjab, and won it in the end. The Musulmans tortured the Sikh teachers to death with their families; the Sikhs sacked and massacred in return. The Musulmans took Amritsar, blew up the temple of the Granth, and washed its foundations in the blood of sacred cows; the Sikhs took Lahore, blew up the mosques, and washed their foundations in the blood of unclean swine. Fanatics and heroes, they lived only for the holy war, and became the barrier of India against the Musulman tribes of the North-West. At last, in 1823, the Sikhs were united under Ranjit Singh into the greatest power of India. But he died in 1839; four wives and seven concubines were burned with him, and you can see their tombs under marble lotuses in Lahore. Ten years later the second Sikh War was over, and the Punjab was British. If the Sikh rule was short, their battles have ever been long.

The later history of the Sikhs—how kindly they accepted British rule, which has still treated their religion with more than tolerant respect; how they supplied and supply to-day noble regiments to our army; the splendid services they rendered in the Mutiny, but a decade after their conquest; the unswerving gallantry and devotion which they have displayed on every field of honour,—all this is part of the military history of the Empire. The very officers of Gurkha and Pathan and Dogra regiments admit that the Sikh is the ideal of all that is soldierly.

Ranjit's capital was Lahore, but the holy city has ever been Amritsar. "The Pool of Immortality," it means, and here in the centre of the pool is the Golden Temple. In its present form it is not yet a century old—quite an infant in India. Amritsar, indeed, is full of new things; for, as it is the Mecca, it is also the Manchester of the Punjab. Carpets and shawls and silks are manufactured there, or brought in by merchants from Persia and Tibet, Bokhara and Yarkand. Here you can see modern native India untainted by Europe.

Amritsar wears an air of solid prosperity. Not in the least like the manufacturing towns we know, lacking the machinery of Bombay or Calcutta, it neither shadows its streets with many-storied factories nor defiles its air with smoke. But it wears a uniform and thriving aspect, as of a town with a present and a future rather than a past. The Bond Street of Delhi is a double row of decayed mansions propped up by tottering booths; the houses of Amritsar are middle-sized, regular, stably built of burned bricks, neither splendid nor ruinous. The looms clatter and whir in the factories, and the merchant bargains between the whiffs of his hookah in his shop, and Amritsar grows rich in a leisurely Indian way, unfevered by Western improvements.

To the Western eye it is unenterprising and rather shabby. The stable comfort of Amritsar stops short at the good brick walls; inside, the shops are bare brick and plaster. There is nothing in the least imposing about it. "Chunder Buksh, Dealer," says one placard, and it would be hard to say what else he could call himself; for his stock seems to consist of one fine carpet, some brass pots, and a towel. Above him is "Ali Mohammed, Barrister-at-Law," in a windowless, torn-blinded office, which you would otherwise take for the attic of Chunder Buksh's assistant. But compared with the rest of India, Amritsar is a model of wellbeing. It is dusty, but otherwise almost clean; the streets, of course, are full of bullocks and buffaloes, but it seems rare that animals share their bed with men; there are plenty of people all but naked, but it is rather from choice or religious enthusiasm than of necessity. The trousered ladies, strolling with trousered babies on their hips or smoking hubble-bubbles on shop counters, wear silver in their blue-black hair, pearls in their noses, gold in their ears; they jingle with locked-up capital. Finally, there is a Jubilee statue of the Queen, and a clock-tower for all the world like an English borough's. But besides these and the Government offices and the railway-station there is hardly a whisper from the West in the town; and in Amritsar you begin to conceive a new respect for India.

The stream in the streets sets steadily towards the Golden Temple. From the heavy-browed city gate to the holy pool the winding alleys are splashed with all the familiar hues—orange outshining lemon and emerald throttling ultramarine. Following the stalwart, bearded pilgrims, in the midst of the city of shopkeepers you suddenly break into a wide square: within it, bordered by a marble pavement—white, black, and umber—a green lake dances in the sunlight; and in the midst of that, mirrored in the pool—you look through your eyelashes, for the hot rays fling back sevenfold-heated, blinding—gleam walls and roofs and cupolas of sheer gold.

A minute or two you blink and stare, then you see that it is a small temple on an island with a causeway leading to it from under an arch. And after the first blink and stare your notions of beauty rise up and protest against it. The temple is neither imposing by size nor winsome by proportion. It has two stories—the lower of marble, inlaid, like the marble of Agra, with birds and beasts and flowers, but with none of Agra's grace and refinement; all above it is of copper-gilt. Above the second story rises something half-cupola, half-dome, but it is not in the middle; there are smaller cupolas at the side overlooking the causeway, and others smaller still at the far side. The whole temple is smaller than St. Clement Danes, and a little building has no right to be irregular. If the Taj Mahal, you say, which is three times this size, can take the trouble to be symmetrical—well, if this is the masterpiece of modern India—as for the gold, it blinds you for the first moment and amuses you for the second; but you might as well ask beauty of a heliograph.

Nevertheless, do not go away, for you will hardly see anything more Indian. Outside the gate they show you a Government ordinance that everybody must either conform to the religious customs of the place or forbear to indulge his curiosity; you bow, and a bearded giant, who might be a high-priest for dignity, takes off your boots and ties on silk slippers instead. You leave your cigar-case behind you: tobacco must not defile the holy place. Then, behind a white-bearded policeman—who performs the triple function of guiding, preventing you from doing anything impious, and clearing worshippers out of the way before you—you start forth to see.

The pilgrims shuffle on eagerly round the pavement to the great gate before the causeway. On a gilt tablet, in English and Punjabi, stands the record of a miracle: how that a great light from heaven fell before the holy book, and then was caught up into heaven again, whence the learned augured much blessing upon the British Raj. Past the gate they press without turning the head, though it is carved and pictured over every inch. On one side of the entrance a marble tablet shows the legend XXXV Sikhs and something in Punjabi. From the gate you issue on to the causeway. It also is flagged with marble, and lined with gilded lamp-posts; but the lamps above the gold are that crass-blue and green-coloured glass of the suburban builder, and more than one hangs broken. So you come to the sanctuary itself—a lofty chamber with four open doors of chased silver. Within sit three priests on the floor, under a canopy of blue and scarlet, before a low ottoman draped in crimson and green and yellow. The high-priest, eagle-eyed and long black-bearded, reads continually in a loud voice from the Granth; beside him sits one with a gilt-handled wisk and fans the sacred book. At another side sit two musicians: one twangs a sort of one-stringed mandoline, one thrums a tom-tom. Before the Granth lies a cloth; and each believer, crouching in, flings on it flowers or cowries or copper coins for his offering. To the white man they bring what looks like a dry half-orange or candied citron, only white; it is made of sugar, and the white man responds with the offering of a rupee. The walls about this strange worship blaze with blue and red and gold in frets and scrolls and flower-tendrils; above are chambers and galleries of the same and studded mirrors; in one more than holy room are brooms made of peacocks' feathers wherewith alone it may be swept.

That is the great shrine of all; but there is much else. All round the lake are palaces of stone and white marble belonging to the great Sikh chiefs who came here to worship. Before them, on the pavement, men squatting under canvas screens hawk flowers—lotus, jasmine, marigold, or scabious—to be offered before the Scripture. In one of the palaces, which matches the temple with a gilt dome of its own, you see a glass case; within it, under crimson silk, rest the sword and mace of some old Sikh Boanerges, mighty in prayer as in battle. Then there is a tower temple of eight stories, dedicated to a bygone saint and miracle-worker, the lower chamber aflame with paint and gold. As the policeman enters he touches the step with his finger; a woman in violet trousers flings a flower on to a cloth and ottoman like that of the central shrine; a woman in green-and-gold trousers places a bread-cake before it and lays her forehead on the marble sill; others grovel and shampoo it with their hands. The next thing you come to is a plain shed with a dynamo that supplies the shrines and gardens with electric light. After that a group of naked fakirs, powdered white with ashes, with long mud-matted hair and mad eyes. Then a door, fast closed and seeming to lead nowhither, with a tiny wreath of marigolds hung on it.

Everywhere the same grotesque contradictions—splendour and squalor, divinity and dirt, superstition and manliness. The Western mind can make nothing of it, cannot bring it into a focus. You simply hold your head, and say that this is the East, and you are of the West. In the treasury above the gate are silver staves and gilt maces, canopies of gold and diadems of pearls and diamonds. In the sacred, putrid lake rot flowers. A fakir standing before an enclosure drones in a full voice words you do not understand, like a psalm without any end to it: the refrain, after every half-dozen words, sounds like "Hullah hah leay." Inside the shrine the high-priest never ceases to intone the Granth, nor the other priest to fan it, nor the musicians to tinkle and thrum; and in and out that holy place fly clouds of pigeons, perching on the canopy and fouling the growing pile of offerings before the ottoman. At every turn you come on little shrines with books on silken cushions and prostrate adorers. A calf, unchecked, is trying to lick the gold off the great gateway.

THE GIRALDA, SEVILLE, SPAIN
Théophile Gautier

The Giralda, which serves as a campanila to the cathedral, and rises above all the spires of the town, is an old Moorish tower, erected by an Arabian architect, named Geber or Guever, who invented algebra, which was called after him. The appearance of the tower is charming, and very original; the rose-coloured bricks and the white stone of which it is built, give it an air of gaiety and youth, which forms a strange contrast with the date of its erection, which extends as far back as the year 1000, a very respectable age, at which a tower may well be allowed to have a wrinkle or two and be excused for not being remarkable for a fresh complexion. The Giralda in its present state is not less than three hundred and fifty feet high, while each side is fifty feet broad. Up to a certain height the walls are perfectly even; there are then rows of Moorish windows with balconies, trefoils, and small white marble columns, surrounded by large lozenge-shaped brick panels. The tower formerly ended in a roof of variously coloured varnished tiles, on which was an iron bar, ornamented with four gilt metal balls of a prodigious size. This roof was removed in 1568 by the architect Francisco Ruiz, who raised the daughter of the Moor Guever one hundred feet higher in the pure air of heaven, so that his bronze statue might overlook the sierras, and speak with the angels who passed. The feat of building a belfry on a tower was in perfect keeping with the intentions of the members composing that admirable chapter who wished posterity to imagine they were mad. The additions of Francisco Ruiz consist of three stories; the first of these is pierced with windows, in whose embrasures are hung bells; the second, surrounded by an open balustrade, bears on the cornice of each of its sides, these words—*Turris fortissima nomen Domini*; and the third is a kind of cupola or lantern, on which turns a gigantic gilt bronze figure of Faith, holding a palm in one hand and a standard in the other, and serving as a weathercock, thereby justifying the name of Giralda given to the tower. This statue is by Bartholomew Morel. It can be seen at a very great distance; and when it glitters through the azure atmosphere, really looks like a seraph lounging in the air.

You ascend the Giralda by a series of inclined ramps, so easy and gentle, that two men on horseback could very well ride up to the summit, whence you enjoy an admirable view. At your feet lies Seville, brilliantly white, with its spires and towers, endeavouring, but in vain, to reach the rose-coloured brick girdle of the Giralda. Beyond these stretches the plain, through which the Guadalquiver flows, like a piece of watered silk, and scattered around are Santiponce, Algaba, and other villages. Quite in the background is the Sierra Morena, with its outlines sharply marked, in spite of the distance, so great is the transparency of the air in this admirable country. On the opposite side, the Sierras de Gibram, Zaara and Moron, raise their bristling forms, tinged with the richest hues of lapis lazuli and amethyst, and completing this magnificent panorama, which is inundated with light, sunshine and dazzling splendour.

A great number of fragments of columns, shaped into posts and connected with each other by chains, except where spaces are left for persons to pass, surround the cathedral. Some of these columns are antique, and come either from the ruins of Italica, or from the remains of the ancient mosque, whose former site is now occupied by the cathedral, and of which the only remaining vestiges are the Giralda, a few old walls, and one or two arches, one of which serves as the entrance to the courtyard *de los Nanjeros*. The *Longa* (Exchange) is a large and perfectly regular edifice, built by the heavy and wearisome Herrera, that architect of *ennui*, to whom we owe the Escurial, which is decidedly the most melancholy building in the world; the Longa, also, like the cathedral, is surrounded by the same description of posts. It is completely isolated and presents four similar façades; it stands between the cathedral and the Alcazar. In it are preserved the archives of America, and the correspondence of Christopher Columbus, Pizarro and Fernando Cortez; but all these treasures are guarded by such savage dragons, that we were obliged to content ourselves with looking at the outside of the pasteboard boxes and portfolios, which are stowed away in mahogany compartments, like the goods in a drapers' shop. It would be a most easy thing to place five or six of the most precious autographs in glass cases, and thus satisfy the very legitimate curiosity of travellers.

THE CATHEDRAL OF MONREALE, ITALY
John Addington Symonds

Sicily under the Normans offered the spectacle of a singularly hybrid civilization. Christians and Northmen, adopting the habits and imbibing the culture of their Musulman subjects, ruled a mixed population of Greeks, Arabs, Berbers, and Italians. The language of the princes was French; that of the Christians in their territory, Greek and Latin; that of their Mahommedan subjects, Arabic. At the same time the Scandinavian Sultans of Palermo did not cease to play an active part in the affairs, both civil and ecclesiastical, of Europe. The children of the Vikings, though they spent their leisure in harems, exercised, as hereditary Legates of the Holy See, a peculiar jurisdiction in the Church of Sicily. They dispensed benefices to the clergy, and assumed the mitre and dalmatic, together with the sceptre and the crown, as symbols of their authority in Church as well as State. As a consequence of this confusion of nationalities in Sicily, we find French and English ecclesiastics mingling at court with Moorish freedmen and Oriental odalisques, Apulian captains fraternizing with Greek corsairs, Jewish physicians in attendance on the person of the prince, and Arabian poets eloquent in his praises. The very money with which Roger subsidized his Italian allies, was stamped with Cuphic letters, and there is reason to believe that the reproach against Frederick of being a false coiner arose from his adopting the Eastern device of plating copper pieces to pass for silver. The commander of Roger's navies and his chief minister of state was styled, according to Oriental usage, Emir or Ammiraglio. George of Antioch, who swept the shores of Africa, the Morea, and the Black Sea, in his service, was a Christian of the Greek Church, who had previously held an office of finance under Temim Prince of Mehdia. The workers in his silk factories were slaves, from Thebes and Corinth. The pages of his palace were Sicilian or African eunuchs. His charters ran in Arabic as well as Greek and Latin. His jewelers engraved the rough gems of the Orient with Christian mottoes in Semitic characters.[5] His architects were Musulmans who adapted their native style to the requirements of Christian ritual, and inscribed the walls of cathedrals with Catholic legends in the Cuphic language. The predominant characteristic of Palermo was Orientalism. Religious toleration was extended to the Musulmans, so that the two creeds, Christian and Mahommedan, flourished side by side.

At Palermo, Europe saw the first instance of a court not wholly unlike that which Versailles afterwards became. The intrigues which endangered the throne and liberty of William the Bad, and which perplexed the policy of William the Good, were court-conspiracies of a kind common enough at Constantinople. In this court life men of letters and erudition played a part three centuries before Petrarch taught the princes of Italy to respect the pen of a poet. King Roger, of whom the court geographer Edrisi writes that "he did more sleeping than any other man

---

[5] The embroidered skullcap of Constance of Aragon, wife of Frederick II, in the sacristy of the Cathedral at Palermo, is made of gold thread thickly studded with pearls and jewels—rough sapphires and carbuncles, among which may be noted a red cornelian engraved in Arabic with this sentence, "In Christ, God, I put my hope."

waking," was surrounded during his leisure moments, beneath the palm-groves of Favara, with musicians, historians, travelers, mathematicians, poets, and astrologers of Oriental breeding.

The architectural works of the Normans in Palermo reveal the same ascendancy of Arab culture. San Giovanni degli Eremiti, with its low white rounded domes, is nothing more or less than a little mosque adapted to the rites of Christians. The country palaces of the Zisa and the Cuba, built by the two Williams, retain their ancient Moorish character, standing beneath the fretted arches of the hall of the Zisa, through which a fountain flows within a margin of carved marble, and looking on the landscape from its open porch, we only need to reconstruct in fancy the green gardens and orange-groves, where fair-haired Normans whiled away their hours among black-eyed odalisques and graceful singing boys from Persia. Amid a wild tangle of olive and lemon trees overgrown with scarlet passion-flowers the pavilion of the Cubola, built of hewn stone and open at each of its four sides, still stands much as it stood when William II paced through flowers from his palace of the Cuba, to enjoy the freshness of the evening by the side of its fountain. The views from all these Saracenic villas over the fruitful valley of the Golden Horn, and the turrets of Palermo, and the mountains and the distant sea, are ineffably delightful. When the palaces were new—when the gilding and the frescoes still shone upon their honeycombed ceilings, when their mosaics glittered in noonday twilight, and their amber-coloured masonry was set in shade of pines and palms, and the cool sound of rivulets made music in their courts and gardens, they must have well deserved their Arab titles of "Sweet Waters" and "The Glory" and "The Paradise of Earth."

But the true splendour of Palermo, that which makes this city one of the most glorious of the South, is to be sought in its churches—in the mosaics of the Cappella Palatina founded by King Roger, in the vast aisles and cloisters of Monreale built by King William the Good at the instance of his Chancellor Matteo,[6] in the Cathedral of Palermo begun by Offamilio, and in the Martorana dedicated by George the Admiral. These triumphs of ecclesiastical architecture, none the less splendid because they cannot be reduced to rule or assigned to any single style, were the work of Saracen builders assisted by Byzantine, Italian, and Norman craftsmen. The genius of Latin Christianity determined the basilica shape of the Cathedral of Monreale. Its bronze doors were wrought by smiths of Trani and Pisa. Its walls were incrusted with the mosaics of Constantinople. The woodwork of its roof, and the emblazoned patterns in porphyry and serpentine and glass and smalto, which cover its whole surface, were designed by Oriental decorators. Norman sculptors added their dog-tooth and chevron to the mouldings of its porches; Greeks, Frenchmen, and Arabs may have tried their skill in turn upon the multitudinous ornaments of its cloister capitals. "The like of which church," says Lucius III in 1182, "hath not been constructed by any king even from ancient times, and such an one as must compel all men to admiration." These words remain literally and emphatically true. Other cathedrals may surpass that of Monreale in sublimity, simplicity, bulk, strength, or unity of plan. None can surpass it in the strange romance with which the memory of its many artificers invests it. None again can exceed it in richness and glory, in the gorgeousness of a thousand decorative elements subservient to one controlling thought. "It is evident," says Fergusson in his history of architecture, "that all the architectural features in the building were subordinate in the eyes of the builders to the mosaic decorations, which cover every part of the interior, and are in fact the glory and the pride of the edifice, and alone entitle it to rank among the finest of mediæval churches." The whole of the Christian history is depicted in this series of Mosaics; but on first entering, one form alone compels attention. The semi-dome of the eastern apse above the high altar is

---

[6] Matteo of Ajello induced William to found an archbishopric at Monreale in order to spite his rival Offamilio.

entirely filled with a gigantic half-length figure of Christ. He raises His right hand to bless, and with His left holds an open book on which is written in Greek and Latin, "I am the Light of the World." His face is solemn and severe, rather than mild or piteous; and round His nimbus runs the legend Ἰησους χριστὸς ὁ παντοκράτωρ. Below Him on a smaller scale are ranged the archangels and the mother of the Lord, who holds the child upon her knees. Thus Christ appears twice upon this wall, once as the Omnipotent Wisdom, the Word by whom all things were made, and once as God deigning to assume a shape of flesh and dwell with men. The magnificent image of supreme Deity seems to fill with a single influence and to dominate the whole building. The house with all its glory is His. He dwells there like Pallas in her Parthenon or Zeus in his Olympian temple. To left and right over every square inch of the cathedral blaze mosaics, which portray the story of God's dealings with the human race from the Creation downwards, together with those angelic beings and saints, who symbolize each in his own degree some special virtue granted to mankind. The walls of the fane are therefore an open book of history, theology, and ethics for all men to read.

The superiority of mosaics over fresco as an architectural adjunct on this gigantic scale is apparent at a glance at Monreale. Permanency of splendour and glowing richness of tone are all on the side of the mosaics. Their true rival is painted glass. The jeweled churches of the south are constructed for the display of coloured surfaces illuminated by sunlight falling on them from narrow windows, just as those of the north—Rheims, for example, or Le Mans—are built for the transmission of light through a variegated medium of transparent hues. The painted windows of a northern cathedral find their proper counterpart in the mosaics of the south. The Gothic architect strove to obtain the greatest amount of translucent surface. The Byzantine builder directed his attention to securing just enough light for the illumination of his glistening walls. The radiance of the northern church was similar to that of flowers or sunset clouds or jewels. The glory of the southern temple was that of dusky gold and gorgeous needlework. The north needed acute brilliancy as a contrast to external greyness. The south found rest from the glare and glow of noonday in these sombre splendours. Thus Christianity, both of the south and of the north, decked her shrines with colour. Not so the Paganism of Hellas. With the Greeks, colour, though used in architecture, was severely subordinated to sculpture; toned and modified to a calculated harmony with actual nature, it did not, as in a Christian church, create a world beyond the world, a paradise of supersensual ecstasy, but remained within the limits of the known. Light falling upon carved forms of gods and heroes, bathing clear-cut columns and sharp bas-reliefs in simple lustre, was enough for the Phœbian rights of Hellas. Though we know that red and blue and green and gilding were employed to accentuate the mouldings of Greek temples, yet neither the gloomy glory of mosaics nor the gemmed fretwork of storied windows was needed to attune the souls of Hellenic worshippers to devotion.

THE LUXEMBOURG PALACE
Augustus J. C. Hare

The Rue de la Seine will bring us to the Palace of the Luxembourg, now the Palace of the Senate (open from nine to four in winter, nine to five in summer), built by Marie de' Medici on the site of a hotel erected by Robert de Harlay de Saucy early in the Sixteenth Century, which was bought by the Duc de Pincy-Luxembourg. The queen employed Jacques Debrosses as her architect in 1615, and his work was completed in 1620. The ground floor, in the Tuscan style, was intended to convey a reminiscence of the Florentine Palazzo Pitti, in which Marie de' Medici was born: the upper stories are Grecian.

The queen intended to call the palace Palais Medicis, though the name has always clung to it which is derived from François de Luxembourg, Prince de Tingry, who owned the site in 1570. The palace was bequeathed by Marie de' Medici to her youngest son Gaston, Duc d'Orléans, from whom it came to his two daughters, who each held half of the Luxembourg—"La Grande Mademoiselle," and the pious Duchesse de Guise (whose mother, sister of the Duc de Lorraine, had clandestinely become the second wife of Monsieur), who was terribly tyrannized over by her rich half sister. It was here that Mademoiselle received the visits of M. de Lauzun, whilst La Fosse was painting the loves of Flore and Zephyr, and here that she astonished Europe by the announcement of her intended marriage, to which—for a few days—Louis XIV. was induced to give his consent.

At her death, Mademoiselle bequeathed her right in the Luxembourg to her Cousin Philippe, Duc d'Orléans, brother of Louis XIV. During the Regency, the palace was the residence of the Duchesse de Berry (daughter of the Regent Philippe d'Orléans), who by her orgies here rivalled those of her father at the Palais Royal. The Luxembourg was bought by Louis XV., and given by Louis XVI. to his brother "Monsieur," who resided in it till his escape from Paris at the time of the flight to Varennes.

Treated as national property during the Revolution, the Luxembourg became one of the prisons of the Reign of Terror. Amongst other prisoners, comprising the most illustrious names in France, were the Vicomte de Beauharnais and his wife Josephine, afterwards Empress of the French: *"De quoi se plaignent donc ces damnés aristocrates?"* cried Montagnard; *"nons les logeons dans les châteaux royaux."* David, the painter, designed his picture of the Sabines during his imprisonment at the Luxembourg, in a little room on the second floor. Here also in a different category, were imprisoned Hébert, Danton, Camille Desmoulins, Philippeaux, Lacroix, Hérault de Séchelles, Payne, Bazire, Chabot, and Fabre d'Eglantine. In 1793, people used to come and stand for hours in the garden in the hope of being able to have a last sight of their friends, from their being allowed to show themselves at the windows.

It was at the Luxembourg that (December 10, 1797), Bonaparte presented the treaty of the peace of Campo Formio to the Directory, after returning from his first campaign in Italy. At the end of 1799, the palace became for a time *Le Palais du Consulat*: *Le Palais du Sénat*, then *de la Pairie*. Marshal Ney was condemned to death here, under the Restoration (November 21, 1815), and was executed in the Allée de l'Observatoire, at the end of the garden on December 7. The iron wicket still remains in the door of his prison, opening west at the end of the great gallery of archives. The ministers of Charles X. were also judged at the Luxembourg, and Fieschi and the other conspirators of July, 1835, were condemned here; as was Prince Louis Napoleon Bonaparte, after the attempt at Bologne in 1840.

The Luxembourg is only shown when the Senate is not sitting. The apartments best worth seeing are the Chapel of 1844, decorated with modern paintings; and *the Ancienne Salle du Livre d'or*, where the titles and arms of peers were preserved under the Restoration and Louis Philippe, adorned with the decorations of the apartment of Marie de' Medici. The ceiling of the gallery, which forms part of the hall, represents the Apotheosis of Marie. The arabesques in the principal hall are attributed to Giovanni da Udine: the ceiling represents Marie de' Medici reestablishing the peace and unity of France. The first floor is reached by a great staircase which occupies the place of a gallery once filled with the twenty-four great pictures of the life of the Regent Marie by Rubens, now in the Louvre. The oratory of the queen and another room are now united to form the *Salle des Gardes*, her bedroom is the *Salle des Messagers d'état* and her reception-room is known as the *Salon de Napoléon I*. The cupola of the *Salle du Trône* by Alaux represents the Apotheosis of the first Emperor.

The *Hôtel du Petit Luxembourg* is a dependency of the greater palace, and was erected about the same time by Richelieu, who resided here till the Palais Royal was built. When he moved thither, he gave this palace to his niece, the Duchesse d'Aiguillon, from whom it passed to Henri Jules de Bourbon-Condé, after which it received the name of *Petit Bourbon*. Anne, Palatine of Bavaria, lived here, and added a hôtel towards the Rue Vaugirard to accommodate her suite. Under the First Empire the Luxembourg was occupied for some time by Joseph Bonaparte. It is now the official residence of the President of the Senate. The cloister of the former convent of the *Filles du Calvaire*, whom Marie de Medici established near her palace, is now a winter garden attached to the Petit

Luxembourg. The chapel, standing close to the grill of the Rue de Vaugirard, is an admirable specimen of the end of the Sixteenth Century; on the summit of its gable is a symbolical Pelican nourishing its young.

Beyond the Petit Luxembourg is a modern building containing the Musée du Luxembourg. The collection now in the galleries of the Louvre was begun at the Luxembourg and only removed in 1779, when Monsieur came to reside here. In 1802 a new gallery was begun at the Luxembourg, but, in 1815, its pictures were removed to the Louvre to fill the places of those restored to their rightful owners by the Allies. It was Louis XVIII. who ordered that the Luxembourg should receive such works of living artists as were acquired by the State. The collection, recently moved from halls in the palace itself, is always interesting, but as the works of each artist are removed to the Louvre ten years after his death, the pictures are constantly changing.

THE GREAT LAMA TEMPLE
C. F. Gordon-Cumming

This morning soon after 5 A.M. Dr. Dudgeon took me to see the Yung-ho-kung, a very fine old Lama temple, just within the wall, at the north-east corner of the Tartar city. It contains about 1,300 monks of all ages, down to small boys six years old, under the headship of a Lama, who assumes the title of "The Living Buddha."

These monks are Mongol Tartars of a very bad type, dirty and greedy of gain; and, moreover, are known to be grossly immoral. They are generally offensively insolent to all foreigners, many of whom have vainly endeavoured to obtain access to the monastery,—even the silver key, which is usually so powerful in China, often failing to unlock the inhospitable gates.

That I had the privilege of entrance was solely due to the personal influence of Dr. Dudgeon, whose medical skill has happily proved so beneficial to the "Living Buddha," and several of the priests, as to ensure him a welcome from them. It was not, however, an easy task to get at these men, as a particularly insolent monk was acting as door-keeper, and attempted forcibly to prevent our entrance. That, however, was effected by the judicious pressure of a powerful shoulder, and after a stormy argument, the wretch was at length overawed, and finally reduced to abject humility by threats to report his rudeness to the head Lama.

At long last, after wearisome expostulation and altercation, every door was thrown open to us, but the priest in charge of each carefully locked it after us, lest we should avoid giving him an individual tip, or *kum-sha*, as it is here called. Happily I had a large supply of five and ten cent silver pieces, which the Doctor's knowledge of Chinese custom compelled our extortioners to accept. At the same time, neither of us could avoid a qualm as each successive door was securely locked, and a vision presented itself of possible traps into which we might be decoyed.

Every corner of the great building is full of interest, from the brilliant yellow china tiles of the roof to the yellow carpet in the temple. The entrance is adorned with stone carvings of animals, and the interior is covered with a thousand fantastic figures carved in wood—birds, beasts, and serpents, flowers and monstrous human heads mingle in grotesque confusion. It is rich in silken hangings, gold embroidery, huge picturesque paper lanterns of quaint form, covered with Chinese characters and grotesque idols, canopied by very ornamental baldachinos.

Conspicuous amongst these idols is Kwang-ti, who was a distinguished warrior at the beginning of the Christian era, and who about eight hundred years later was deified as the God of War, and State temples were erected in his honour in every city of the Empire. So his shrine is adorned with all manner of armour, especially bows and arrows—doubtful votive offerings. He is a very fierce looking god, and is attended by two colossal companions, robed in the richest gold embroidered silk. Another gigantic image is that of a fully armed warrior leading a horse. I believe he is Kwang-ti's armour bearer. In various parts of the temple hang trophies of arms and military standards, which are singular decorations for a temple wherein Buddha is the object of supreme worship.

But the fact is, that though Kwang-ti is the God of War, he is also emphatically "Protector of the Peace," and his aid is invoked in all manner of difficulties, domestic or national. For instance, when the great salt wells in the Province of Shansi dried up, the sorely perplexed Emperor was recommended by the Taouist High Priest to lay the case before Kwang-ti. The Emperor, therefore, wrote an official despatch on the subject, which was solemnly burnt, and thus conveyed to the spirit-world, when, lo! in answer to the Son of Heaven, the Warrior-god straightway appeared in the clouds, mounted on his red war-horse, and directed the Emperor to erect a temple in his honour. This was done, and the salt springs flowed as before.

Kwang-ti again appeared in 1855, during the Taiping rebellion, to aid the Imperial troops near Nankin, for which kind interposition, Hien-feng, the reigning Emperor (whose honour-conferring power extends to the spirit-world), promoted him to an equal rank with Confucius! So here we find him reverenced alike by Taouists and Buddhists!

All the altar-vases in this temple are of the finest Pekin enamel—vases, candlesticks, and incense-burners, from which filmy clouds of fragrant incense float upward to a ceiling paneled with green and gold. Fine large scroll paintings tempted me to linger at every turn, and the walls are encrusted with thousands of small porcelain images of Buddha.

In the main temple, which is called the Foo-Koo, or Hall of Buddha, stands a cyclopean image of Matreya, the Buddha of Futurity. It is seventy feet in height, and is said to be carved from one solid block of wood, but it is coloured to look like bronze. Ascending a long flight of steps, we reached a gallery running round the temple about the level of his shoulders. I found that this gallery led into two circular buildings, one on each side, constructed for the support of two immense rotating cylinders, about seventy feet in height, full of niches, each niche containing the image of a Buddhist saint.

They are rickety old things, and thickly coated with dust, but on certain days worshippers come and stick on strips of paper, bearing prayers. To turn these cylinders is apparently an act of homage to the whole saintly family, and enlists the good-will of the whole lot. Some Lama monasteries deal thus with their 128 sacred books and 220 volumes of commentary, placing them in a huge cylindrical bookcase, which they turn bodily, to save the trouble of turning individual pages—the understanding having apparently small play in either case.

It was nearly 6 A.M. ere we reached the Lama Temple, so that we were too late to see the grand morning service, as that commences at 4 A. M., when upwards of a hundred mats are spread in the temple, on each of which kneel ten of the subordinate Lamas, all wearing their yellow robes and a sort of classical helmet of yellow felt, with a very high crest like that worn by Britannia. They possess red felt boots, but can only enter the temple barefooted. The Great Lama wears a violet-coloured robe and a yellow mitre. He bears a sort of crozier, and occupies a gilded throne before the altar: a cushion is provided for him to kneel upon. The whole temple is in darkness or dim twilight save the altar, which is ablaze with many tapers.

When the copper gong sounds its summons to worship, they chant litanies in monotone, one of the priests reading prayers, from a silken scroll, and all joining in a low murmur, while clouds of incense fill the temple. A peculiarity of this chant is, that while a certain number of the brethren recite the words, the others sing a continuous deep bass accompaniment. Again the gong marks the change from prayer to sacred chants, and after these comes a terrible din of instrumental music—a clatter of gongs, bells, conch-shells, tambourines, and all manner of ear-splitting abominations. Then follows a silence which may be felt, so utter is the stillness and so intense the relief.

HADDON HALL, ENGLAND
John Leyland

When the Derbyshire Wye has pursued its winding way from its source in the millstone grit, and between the wooded steeps and precipitous limestone cliffs that curb and shape its course towards Bakewell, the hills on either bank recede, and the river flows through pleasant alluvial meadows, overlooked by occasional rocky scars, and by woods of fir, ash, beech, and oak, to its confluence with the Derwent at Rowsley. Some two miles below Bakewell, shortly before the stream of the Lathkil comes down from its enchanting valley on the right, with its narrow tributary, the Bradford, to swell the waters of the Wye, the limestone crops out as a platform on the opposite bank, and there, half-concealed by the umbrageous woodland, stand the time-worn towers and walls of Haddon. Whether we approach the spot from the direction of Rowsley or of Bakewell, the prospect can scarcely be surpassed in its kind, either for the wondrous grouping of the grey towers and battlements on the slope of the hill, or for the rich beauties of the varied foliage on the height beyond, and the flower-decked meads and pellucid stream below. These charms of a truly English landscape, and an old English mansion, have long had, and must continue to have, a spell of fascination for the artist and lover of the picturesque; but it is not only for them that visitors come in a ceaseless stream to Haddon. What other place can wake such impressions of old-time greatness touched by the witchery of bygone romance? It is here—better, perhaps, than any other spot in England—that we can grasp the conditions of life of the mediæval and Tudor gentlemen. The long line of the Vernons passes before us. We witness them, generation by generation adding to the majestic pile; the vacant chambers are peopled with stately ladies and mail-clad knights, the bowmen are ranged in the courtyard, and the sentinel keeps watch from the tower. We see the knight in anxious deliberation on questions of State and wonder what answer shall be returned to the King-maker's letter. We partake of the bounteous hospitality of the Knight of the Peak, as many strangers have done before, bethinking ourselves anon of his daughter, fair Dorothy, and how that Manners is concealed in the woods, watching the light in her chamber. Then the sounds of revelry strike upon the ear, the door opens and she steals down the steps, and presently we hear the clang of hoofs upon the road. It is, indeed, such impressions as these that have given to the external beauties of Haddon Hall the additional charm of legend, poetry and romance, and have contributed to make it a place to which visitors from afar will always delight to come.

Although the various parts of the celebrated hall have been built at widely different periods, and upon a sloping and irregular rocky platform, its plan is very easy to understand, and it may be well, at the outset, to explain the disposition of the buildings as clearly as may be. They surround two courtyards—the lower one, to the west, on the river front, and the upper one, separated from the first by the great hall and domestic offices, rising up to the east on the hill-side behind it. The visitor enters the lower quadrangle at its north-western angle, placing his foot, as he passes the postern, in a hole which has been worn deeply by unnumbered strangers before him. He notices, on his right, beneath the archway, the porter's room, with a bedstead that may well have kept that functionary wakeful;

and beyond it, still on the right hand and western side, the so-called Chaplain's Room—with its hunting-horn, old musket, Seventeenth Century boots, service of pewter platters, and other miscellaneous contents—as well as two other chambers, before the domestic chapel is reached. This edifice occupies the south-western angle, and extends about half-way up the southern side of the lower courtyard. Being not at right angles with the other portions of this quadrangle, it gives, with its picturesque bell-turret, a pleasing variety to the buildings within; and, externally, its east window and the angles of its chancel and southern aisle, with the heavy buttress at the western end, add materially to the picturesque effect of the hall. The chapel, moreover, contains, with some of the foundation walls, the oldest portions of the edifice, and the round column and chalice-like font are anterior, perhaps, to the coming of the Vernons to Haddon. The south side of the western quadrangle is completed by a range of constructions, including passages to the private apartments, and a turret stair to the battlemented wall; and leading up to the doorway is a flight of steps—added in the Sixteenth Century—which projects into the area of the courtyard. This space is further broken up by the three steps which extend across it from north to south, dividing it into an upper and a lower platform. Standing upon the slight elevation thus gained, the chapel, the buildings opposite on the western side, the entrance gateway, with the very curious corbelling and constructive ties over it in the angle, and the offices on the western side, with the turret, have a most pleasing and varied effect.

The main block of buildings, lying between the two quadrangles, is now entered by the porch, which leads into a lobby or passage separating the great hall on the right from the kitchen and its offices on the left. This arrangement was general in mediæval dwelling-places, and may be seen in many of the timber manor-houses of Lancashire and Cheshire, where, as we see it at Haddon, the Minstrel's Gallery is usually over the entrance passage, at the end of the hall opposite to the daïs. At Haddon, the table at the upper end still remains, supported on its three pedestal legs, and we think of the time when the King of the Peak held festival there, as we look upon its time-worn board. It is to be observed that the constructional conditions of the hall rendered it impossible to add the great bay, which was a chief feature of mediæval banqueting-rooms—one that may be seen in its perfection in the magnificent, but roofless hall of Wingfield, a few miles away. In the manor-houses of Lancashire and Cheshire, to which allusion has been made, the withdrawing-room lies in general immediately behind the great hall, and adjacent to the daïs, but at Haddon we find, in that position, a private dining-room, with a fine recessed window; and the drawing-room, which is above it, is approached by a flight of stone steps. The drawing-room at Haddon is a beautiful tapestried chamber, with fine views from its bay window over the gardens and down the valley of the Wye; and from it access is had to the Earl's Bedroom and the Page's Room. On the other side of the lobby from which the hall is entered is a sloping passage leading down to the kitchen, with its huge fireplace and curious culinary appliances, and other doors from the same passage open into the buttery, wine-cellar, add sundry offices. The great hall, and the domestic offices described, complete the enclosure of the first courtyard and form the western side of the second. The northern side of this upper quadrangle is formed of a series of small chambers; and a staircase from the hall-passage leads up to the quaint tapestried rooms above them, which, if tradition may be believed, were the nursery and the rooms of Dorothy Vernon, of Lady Cranborne, daughter of John Manners, eighth Earl of Rutland, and of Roger Manners. By the same staircase from the passage, access is had to the Minstrel's Gallery, as well as to the gallery on the eastern side of the hall (a later addition), which brings the visitor to the top of the stone steps by which the drawing-room is reached. At that place are the segmental steps of solid oak, whereby the magnificent Long Gallery or Bedroom is entered. This great chamber, which is a chief glory of Haddon, will be alluded to later. It occupies the whole length of the southern side of the upper courtyard, and projects picturesquely at its eastern end upon the terrace, where a window affords a view of the winter garden towards Dorothy Vernon's Walk. From the Long Gallery a door leads into the range of buildings enclosing the second quadrangle on its eastern side. These are the anteroom, with Dorothy Vernon's Steps leading down to the Terrace; the State Bedroom, with its Gobelin tapestry, its strange bas-relief of *Orpheus taming the Beasts*; its huge bed and ancient hangings, and its mirror called "Queen Elizabeth's Looking-glass;" the Ancient Stateroom, a chamber coeval with the angle tower; and the little passage-room over the gateway—the original entrance to the castle—whence the winding-stair is reached, leading up to the Peveril Tower, which dominates the whole range of buildings. From this elevation the visitor sees the two courtyards below him, with the woods and terraces, and the upper and lower gardens on the south side, as well as the way leading down to the footbridge over the Wye, and a fine prospect of the winding vale of that river, and of many a distant hill.

Having thus before us the general plan of the buildings of Haddon Hall, we may proceed to consider the historical, legendary, and other considerations to which the venerable edifice very naturally leads us. There have been those who have chosen to see, in the lower parts of its construction, the evidences of Saxon work, and, indeed, very likely Haddon was a location in Saxon times. However, that may be, we find it mentioned in Domesday Book as a berewick of the Manor of Bakewell, and the first possessor of whom we have authentic knowledge was that same William Peveril, a natural son of the Conqueror, to whom he granted "Peveril's Place in the Peke," and who also had custody of the Manor of Chatsworth. Thus, at this very early period, we find Haddon associated in ownership with two of the most interesting places in the Peak district. The Peverils did not long enjoy their possessions, for William Peveril, probably a grandson of the first possessor, having, it was alleged, poisoned Ranulph, Earl of Chester, who supported Matilda, took to ignominious flight in order to avoid punishment, and his possessions fell to Henry II. It is possible that some parts of the foundations of Haddon belong to the time of the Peverils, but, at any rate, the memory of their association with it is preserved in the name of the north-eastern tower. At the date of their fall, Haddon—or, to speak more precisely, Nether Haddon, for Over Haddon lies some two miles away on the hills—was held by William de Avenell in knight's-service, and the King thus became direct lord of his fee. Towards the close of the Twelfth Century, Haddon came to the Vernons by the marriage of Richard de Vernon with Avicia, a daughter and one of the co-heiresses of William de Avenell, the other being married to Sir Simon Bassett. This Richard de Vernon was descended from the Barons of Shipbroke, the first of whom, William de Vernon, came over with the Conqueror, and received his barony at the hands of Hugh Lupus, Earl of Chester. The Vernon name is derived from the Lordship which the family held in what is now the Department of the Eure and Arrondissement of Evreux.

We now reach the celebrated episode of Dorothy Vernon, upon which the fate of Haddon hung and which has lent the glamour of romance to the scenes in which she moved. Sir George Vernon, her father, the last heir male of the Haddon line, was twice married, and his effigy now lies in Bakewell Church, with those of his two wives, Margaret, daughter of Sir Gilbert Tayleboys, and Maude, daughter of Sir Ralph Langford. Of his two daughters, Margaret, the elder, was married to Sir Thomas Stanley of Winwick, in Lancashire, son of the third Earl of Derby; and Dorothy, the younger—who ultimately became sole heiress—to John Manners, the second son of Sir Thomas Manners, first Earl of Rutland. It is not easy to say at this date what could have been the strong objection which the "King of the Peak" is averred to have had to his daughter's marriage with John Manners, whose father was of high descent, and died, covered with honours, in 1543, having had a royal augmentation granted to his arms, by reason of his descent from Anne Plantagenet, sister of Edward IV. It may, indeed, be that Sir George had planned some great alliance for his daughter, and was ill content with a younger son, or perhaps differences of religion were at the root of his objection, or, we may suppose again, that some personal antipathy, of which there is no record, was felt by the knight to his daughter's lover. However this may be, tradition tells us that the attachment was a secret one, or, at least, that the meeting of Manners and Dorothy Vernon was under her father's ban. Legend has grown up about the episodes, and it is related that Manners lingered in the woods of Haddon disguised as a forester or a hunter, gaining speech at times with the lady, and watching the light in her window. As to the actual circumstances of the elopement—if elopement there was, which seems probable—we have tradition alone to guide us. It is said that, on the occasion of certain festivities at the Hall—held, as some aver, in honour of the marriage of her elder sister—Dorothy stole away from the gay scene, ran down to the terrace by the steps from the anteroom which now bear her name, and joined her lover, who had horses waiting near. The pair then mounted, and galloped, as the story goes, all through the night, until they reached Aylston, in Leicestershire, where they were married on the morrow. The memory of Dorothy Vernon will linger long about the tapestried chambers and sweet-scented gardens of Haddon, and whatever there may be of truth or falsehood in the story of her elopement, the visitor who passes down the steps and walks beneath the low-hanging boughs of the yew-trees on the terrace, or is shadowed by the limes and sycamores in Dorothy Vernon's Walk, where the banks are carpeted with flowers in the spring-time, will do well to cherish this legendary history, which has given an unfailing charm to Haddon. In Bakewell Church, moreover, where both Dorothy and her husband lie buried, he may see her kneeling effigy, and, if her features should strike him as homely, and somewhat unattractive withal, he will bethink him what profound depths of feeling, and what strange capacities for romance, exist unsuspected in the life of every day. It will be of interest here to record the fact that, in the year 1841, when the church of Bakewell was being restored, excavations were made on the site of the monument of John Manners and his wife, and remains believed to be theirs were found in wooden coffins. "The head of the female," we read, "was still covered with hair, cut short on the forehead, but long behind, extremely friable, remarkably soft, and of a beautiful auburn colour, and in it were found six brass pins." The wife of John Manners died on Midsummer Day, 1584, but her husband survived many years, and died on the 4th of June, 1611. He continued to reside at Haddon, and showed no lack of interest in the great house that had become his own. There can be no reasonable doubt that the Long Gallery was built by him, and thus one of the chief beauties of the Hall is attributed to its first possessor of the Manners' name. Both within and without, the three great bays relieve it from all monotony, and the first impression on entering it is of its grandeur and dignity. The Long Gallery or Ball-Room was a customary feature in great houses of Tudor and Stuart times, and may yet be seen in many places—as, for example, in very stately form at Belvoir, and characteristically at Astley Hall, in Lancashire, but nowhere more attractively than at Haddon. There its length is more than one hundred and nine feet, its width eighteen feet, and its height fifteen feet. The heavy steps of solid oak by which it is entered, and the whole flooring of the room are said to have been cut from one gigantic oak which grew in the woods. The wainscot is divided by fluted pilasters into panels, which have arched tops, and, above, the boar's-head crest of the Vernons, and the Manners' peacock, with roses and thistles, are alternated. In the windows also there is blazonry of the arms of Rutland and Shrewsbury, with the royal shield of England; and over the mantel hangs a very remarkable picture, representing Thomyris, Queen of the Massagetae, victorious over Cyrus, whose head is being presented to her.

The subsequent relation of the Manners family with Haddon Hall need not occupy us very long, for the building itself was completed, and the addition of the terraces and some features of the gardens left it as we see it now, save that its chambers were not yet bare. John, the eighth Earl, who lived at Belvoir and Haddon alternately, espoused the cause of the Parliament, and took the Solemn League and Covenant. Belvoir Castle was captured by the Royalists, and suffered sadly in the subsequent troubles, the Earl meanwhile living mostly at Haddon, where his magnificence, it would seem, rivalled that of the "King of the Peak." He shared in the Restoration; and, as we read in Lysons, between 1660 and 1670, although the family were then living mostly at Belvoir, there was a prodigious consumption of beeves and sheep at Haddon, and particularly that an open Christmas was held there in 1663, when, as appears by the bailiff's charges, outlay was made for much work in the kitchen, and for pipers and dancers to make the guests merry withal. John, the ninth Earl, was created Marquis of Granby and Duke of Rutland by Queen Anne, and was succeeded, upon his death at Belvoir in 1711, by his son John, the second Duke, who died in 1721, and he again by his son, also named John, the third Duke, who lived occasionally at Haddon. It was, however, during his lifetime that the family finally quitted their ancient home by the Wye, and the Hall was dismantled about the year 1740. Yet, ever since that time, the successive Dukes of Rutland have safeguarded the venerable edifice, and, without attempting restoration, by structural supports and careful watching, have preserved it from decay. It is to them that the public owe the inestimable privilege of being allowed to linger within the time-worn walls and chambers, which, besides being of abounding interest in themselves, awaken so many delightful memories of history and romance.

When the Hall ceased to be a place of residence not all its adornments were removed. The tapestry deserves special attention, there being, in several of the rooms, some fine remains of Gobelins and other work. The graceful drawing-room is partially hung with it, as was customary, in such manner as to conceal the entrance to the Earl's dressing-room, and there are curious iron hooks for holding it back. The Earl's bedroom itself is tapestried with representations of the chase. One of the rooms in the western range, as well as several small chambers on the north side, including Dorothy Vernon's room, and others not usually shown to visitors, contain much good work of Flemish and French manufacture. In addition to the large picture in the Long Gallery, and the portraits in the dining-room which have been alluded to, there are many paintings in various parts of the house. A number of them are in the anteroom leading from the Long Gallery, including portraits of Queen Elizabeth and Charles I. There is a portrait, also, in the drawing-room, of the sixth Earl of Rutland, who died in 1632, and several of less importance are in the great hall. Many of the pictures are Italian, and little seems to be known about them; but they are thought to have been brought or sent to England by Sir Oliver Manners, a younger brother of Dorothy's husband.

The visitor to Haddon will notice some other objects of curiosity and interest, and he will do well not to hurry through the vacant rooms, for, if the plan of the house be understood, and something of the several dates of its erection, very much may be learned of the ways, manners, and surroundings of mediæval and Tudor gentlemen. Then, passing down through the pleasant gardens, and recrossing the River Wye, the stranger will look back gratefully upon the grey towers, lighted perchance by the setting sun, and will bear away with him an impression of beauty, grandeur, and romance which surely will never fade.

CATHEDRAL OF PALERMO, ITALY
John Addington Symonds

While treating of Palermo, we are bound to think again of the Emperor who inherited from his German father the ambition of the Hohenstauffens and from his Norman mother the fair fields and Oriental traditions of Sicily. The strange history of Frederick—an intellect of the Eighteenth Century born out of date, a cosmopolitan spirit in the age of Saint Louis, the Crusader who conversed with Moslem sages on the threshold of the Holy Sepulchre, the Sultan of Lucera who presented Paterini while he respected the superstition of Saracens, the anointed successor of Charlemagne, who carried his harem with him to the battle-fields of Lombardy, and turned Infidels loose upon the provinces of Christ's Vicar—would be inexplicable, were it not that Palermo still reveals in all her monuments the *genius loci* which gave spiritual nurture to this phœnix among kings. From his Mussulman teachers Frederick derived the philosophy to which he gave a vogue in Europe. From his Arabian predecessors he learned the arts of internal administration and finance, which he transmitted to the princes of Italy. In imitation of Oriental courts, he adopted the practice of verse composition, which gave the first impulse to Italian literature. His Grand Vizier, Piero Delle Vigne, set an example to Petrarch, not only by composing the first sonnet in Italian, but also by showing to what height a low-born secretary versed in art and law might rise. In a word, the zeal for liberal studies, the luxury of life, the religious indifferentism, the bureaucratic system of state government, which mark the age of the Italian Renaissance, found their first manifestation within the bosom of the Middle Ages in Frederick. While our King John was signing the Magna Charta, Frederick had already lived long enough to comprehend, at least in outline, what is meant by the spirit of modern culture. It is true that the so-called Renaissance followed slowly and by tortuous paths upon the death of Frederick. The Church obtained a complete victory over his family, and succeeded in extinguishing the civilization of Sicily. Yet the fame of the Emperor who transmitted questions of sceptical philosophy to Arab sages, who conversed familiarly with men of letters, who loved splendour and understood the arts of refined living, survived both long and late in Italy. His power, his wealth, his liberality of soul and lofty aspirations, formed the theme of many a tale and poem. Dante places him in hell among the heresiarchs; and truly the splendour of his supposed infidelity found for him a goodly following. Yet Dante dates the rise of Italian literature from the blooming period of the Sicilian Court. Frederick's unorthodoxy proved no drawback to his intellectual influence. More than any other man of mediæval times he contributed, if only as the memory of a mighty name, to the progress of civilized humanity.

Let us take leave both of Frederick and of Palermo, that centre of converging influences, which was his cradle, in the cathedral where he lies gathered to his fathers. This church, though its rich sun-browned yellow[7] reminds one of the tone of Spanish buildings, is like nothing one has

---

[7] Nearly all cities have their own distinctive colour. That of Venice is a pearly white, suggestive of every hue in delicate abeyance, and that of Florence is a sober brown. Palermo displays a rich yellow ochre passing at the deepest into orange, and at the lightest into primrose. This is the tone of the soil, of sun-stained marble, and of the rough ashlar masonry of the chief buildings. Palermo has none of the glaring whiteness of Naples, nor yet of that parti-coloured gradation of tints, which adds gaiety to the grandeur of Genoa.

seen elsewhere. Here even more than at Monreale, the eye is struck with a fusion of styles. The western towers are grouped into something like the clustered sheafs of the Caen churches: the windows present Saracenic arches; the southern porch is covered with foliated incrustations of a late and decorative Gothic style; the exterior of the apse combines Arabic inlaid patterns of black and yellow with the Greek honeysuckle; the western door adds Norman dog-tooth and chevron to the Saracenic billet. Nowhere is any one tradition firmly followed. The whole wavers and yet is beautiful—like the immature eclecticism of the culture which Frederick himself endeavoured to establish in his southern kingdoms. Inside there is no such harmony of blended voices: all the strange tongues, which speak together on the outside, making up a music in which the far North, and ancient Byzance, and the delicate East sound each a note, are hushed. The frigid silence of the Palladian style reigns there—simple indeed and dignified, but lifeless as the century in which it flourished. Yet there, in a side chapel near the western door, stand the porphyry sarcophagi which shrine the bones of the Hautevilles and their representatives. There sleeps King Roger—"*Dux Strenuus et primus Rex Siciliæ*"—with his daughter Constance in her purple chest beside him. Henry VI. and Frederick II. and Constance of Aragon complete the group, which surpasses for interest all sepulchral monuments—even the tombs of the Scaligers at Verona—except only, perhaps, the statues of the nave of Innsprück. Very sombre and stately are these porphyry resting-places of princes born in the purple, assembled here from lands so distant—from the craggy heights of Hohenstauffen, from the green orchards of Cotentin, from the dry hills of Aragon. They sleep, and the centuries pass by. Rude hands break open the granite lids of their sepulchres, to find tresses of yellow hair and fragments of imperial mantles, embroidered with the hawks and stags the royal hunter loved. The church in which they lie, changes with the change of taste in architecture and the manners of successive ages. But the huge stone arks remain unmoved, guarding their freight of mouldering dust beneath gloomy canopies of stone, that temper the sunlight as it streams from the chapel windows.

THE FORTRESS AND PALACE OF GWALIOR, INDIA
Louis Rousselet

The ancient city of Gwalior, which must not be confounded with the modern town of that name, nor with the Mahratta camp of the Scindias, is situated on the summit of a steep and isolated rock, 342 feet in height at the north end, where it is highest, and a mile and a half in length; its greatest breadth is 300 yards. Its position and the exterior appearance of its fortifications, behind which rise numerous monuments, remind one of Chittore, the famous capital of Meywar.

This rock, which is a block of basalt topped with sandstone, stands like a sentinel at the entrance of a valley; and above the slopes at its foot rise pointed cliffs, forming natural ramparts, on which are built the fortifications of the town.

Tradition places the date of the founding of Gwalior several centuries before the Christian era. The attention of the Aryan colonists from the valley of the Chumbul probably was early attracted by the admirable position of this rock. The first to establish themselves here were no doubt the Anchorites, who were sent forth in such numbers by the Indian schools of philosophy in the Sixteenth and Seventeenth Centuries before the Christian era, as is attested by the numerous caverns, formed by man, in the sides of the rock. In 773, Rajah Sourya Sena completed a system of defence round the plateau by constructing ramparts. The Kâchwas held the fortress until the reign of Tej Pal Doula, who, upon being expelled by the Chohans in 967, founded the dynasty of Ambîr. Sultan Shahab Oudin's generalissimo, Koutub Eibeck, took it from the Chohans in 1196; and thirty-eight years later it was again taken by the Emperor Altamsh after a long siege. In 1410, the Touar Rajpoots got possession of it, and held it until 1519, when it was finally attached to the crown of Delhi by Ibrahim Lodi. At the dismemberment of the Mogul Empire, it fell alternately into the hands of the Jâts and Mahrattas. In 1779, it was garrisoned by Scindia, from whom it was taken by a British force under Major Popham, and it was again made over to Scindia by the treaty of 1805.

But the vicissitudes of the ancient fortress did not end here. In 1857, the Maharajah Scindia having refused to countenance the revolt, the rebels, under the command of one of Nana Sahib's captains, took the place; but General Sir Hugh Rose dislodged them by planting his batteries on the surrounding heights, and, for the purpose of protecting the young king from his rebellious subjects, the English kept possession of the plateau.

The present town of Gwalior extends to the north and east of the fortress, being hemmed in between the rock and the river Sawunrika. It was a large and handsome settlement, containing thirty or forty thousand inhabitants; but the founding of a new capital by the Scindias, at a distance of about two miles was a death-blow to its grandeur, the higher branches of trade and the nobility having followed the Court to Lashkar. The architecture of its stone houses is, for the most part, handsome; but the streets are narrow and crooked. It is probable that at one time there was a large suburb round the foot of the ascent leading to the fortress, but it was not until the Sixteenth Century that the town assumed its present proportions. There are no monuments to be found of an earlier date; and the two worthy of remark are the Jummah Musjid, a handsome mosque, flanked by two lofty minarets, and the Hatti Durwaza, or "Gate of the Elephants," a curious triumphal arch, situated on a mound at the entrance to the town.

The bazaars of Gwalior contain several manufactures peculiar to the place, such as silken fabrics, embroidered in gold, for turbans; *saris*, or cotton scarfs for women, and curious stuffs in the most brilliant colours. A very fair trade is carried on in these articles.

Two flights of steps, one on the east and the other on the west, lead up to the fortress; of which that on the east is a notable achievement, since it had to be cut out of the solid rock. It is the more ancient of the two; and, although on a very steep incline, it is practicable for horses and elephants.

In order to reach this elevation, you must traverse the whole length of the lower town; and the entrance to it is guarded by an embattled fortification and guard-houses. Hidden among the trees, at a short distance, stands a large palace, the exterior of which is ornamented with bright blue enamel. Five monumental gates, placed at intervals, and still armed with portcullis and heavy iron doors, guard the access to the fortress. From the first, which is a splendid triumphal arch with a Saracenic archway, and surmounted by a tier of small columns, commences the causeway, which, although wide and well kept, is a long and fatiguing ascent; and thence also commences a series of monuments, bas-reliefs, caverns, and cisterns, forming a natural museum of great interest to the archæologist. Even the rocks which overhang the road merit his attention, for they contain numerous chambers, altars and statues, which are reached by narrow paths, requiring a steady head and a sure and practised foot.

Between the third and fourth gate are some huge tanks, excavated out of the solid rock, and fed by springs. The capitals of the pillars which support the ceiling appear above the water, and one can scarcely distinguish the bottom in the obscurity. Near these tanks the surface of the rock, which has been made smooth and even, is covered with numerous bas-reliefs; one of the largest of which, representing an elephant and rider, still is easily distinguishable in spite of considerable mutilation; and further on is a head of Siva.

Opposite the fourth gate is a small monolith of great antiquity, supposed to date from the Fifteenth Century. It is a temple cut out of a single block of stone, and consists of a small square room, entered by a peristyle and crowned with a pyramidal spire. The upper portion of the latter, having been destroyed, has been replaced by a small dome in stonework; and a few sculptures surround the entrance to the sanctuary and the altar.

On the summit of the hill stands King Pal, which springs from the very brink of the precipice. It is supported by six towers, and pierced by only a few large windows ornamented with balconies and pilasters. Sculptured bands, Jaïn arches, and indented cordons relieve the monotony of the massive exterior, and give it a peculiarly light and graceful appearance. The spaces between the Jaïn arches of the gallery are filled in and covered with mosaics in enamelled bricks, representing palm-trees on a blue ground; and each tower is surmounted by a lantern with a double row of columns. It is difficult to imagine a grander or more harmonious effect than that produced by this gigantic edifice, combining rampart and palace in one.

At the south angle of the palace is a gateway, which gives access to the interior of the fortress, and through which you enter a narrow street that overlooks the lateral frontage of the palace. This is built on the same plan as the exterior, but here the stone is completely hidden by enamel. Bands of mosaics, representing candelabra, Brahma ducks, elephants and peacocks in blue, rose-colour, green and gold, give this immense blank wall an incomparably beautiful appearance. The bricks of which these mosaics are composed still retain their primitive brilliancy of colour and delicacy of shading, though ten centuries have passed over them. I know of no country in the world where an architect has succeeded so well in giving a graceful appearance to a heavy blank wall.

The exact date of the construction of these facings is unknown, though it is certain that they were the work of a

Rajpoot prince of the name of Pal; but, as several Chandela and Kâchwa chiefs bore this name, it is difficult to fix the date more precisely than between the Eighth and Ninth Centuries.

The palace of the kings of Gwalior covers an immense area on the east of the plateau; but it was not the work of a single prince; the most ancient portions of it date back to the Sixteenth Century. Each dynasty enlarged the mass of buildings, and the Moguls themselves made considerable additions to it. The interior of the Palace of Pal is extremely simple in style. The various stories, which you enter through rows of square pillars, overlook the large paved courts; and the rooms are low with flat ceilings.

Among these ruins a portion of the ancient palace of the Vaïshnava kings may still be seen. The thick walls, pierced with triangular openings, are somewhat in the same style as the corridors of the Mexican temples. It is to be regretted that so much of this part of the Palace has already been destroyed.

The northern extremity of the plateau, which gradually becomes narrower and narrower, was entirely covered by the palaces of the Emperors Akbar and Jehanghir; but you do not find here the magnificent buildings of Agra or of Delhi. It is evident that these were mere provincial residences. There are nevertheless, a graceful dewani-khas and a small zenanah, containing some fine galleries.

THE HOLY HOUSE OF LORETTO, ITALY
Arthur Penrhyn Stanley

On the slope of the eastern Apennines, overlooking the Adriatic gulf, stands what may be called (according to the belief of the Roman Catholic Church) the European Nazareth. Fortified as if by the bastions of a huge castle, against the approach of Saracenic pirates, a vast church, even now gorgeous with the offerings of the faithful, contains the "Santa Casa," the "Holy House," in which the Virgin lived, and (as is attested by the same inscription as that at Nazareth) received the Angel Gabriel. Everyone knows the story of the House of Loretto. The devotion of one-half the world, and the ridicule of the other half, has made us all acquainted with the strange story, written in all the languages[8] of Europe round the walls of that remarkable sanctuary: how the house of Nazareth was, in the close of the Thirteenth Century, conveyed by angels,

---

[8] Of these numerous versions of the story, made in 1635, one is in English, one in Lowland Scotch, containing all the peculiarities of diction with which every one is so familiar from the nearly contemporary conversations of King James I, in *The Fortunes of Nigel*; showing clearly that at that time these two dialects of English were regarded as two distinct languages, each unintelligible to the speaker of the other.

first to the heights above Fiume, at the head of the Adriatic gulf, then to the plain and lastly to the hill, of Loretto. But this "wondrous flitting" of the Holy House is not the feature in its history which is most present to the pilgrims who frequent it. It is regarded by them simply as an actual fragment of the Holy Land, sacred as the very spot on which the mystery of the Incarnation was announced and begun. In proportion to the sincerity and extent of this belief is the veneration which attaches to what is undoubtedly the most frequented sanctuary of Christendom. The devotion of pilgrims even on week-days exceeds anything that is seen at any of the holy places in Palestine, if we except the Church of the Holy Sepulchre at Easter.

Before the dawn of day the worship begins. Whilst it is yet dark, the doors are opened—a few lights round the sacred spot break the gloom, and disclose the kneeling Capuchins, who have been here throughout the night. Two soldiers, sword in hand, take their place by the entrance of the "House," to guard against all injury. One of the hundred priests who are in daily attendance immediately begins mass at the high altar of the church, the first of a hundred and twenty that are repeated daily within its precincts. The "Santa Casa" itself is then opened and lighted, the pilgrims flock in; and, from that hour till sunset, come and go in a perpetual stream. The "House" is thronged with kneeling or prostrate figures, the pavement round it is deeply worn with the passage of pilgrims, who, from the humblest peasant of the Abruzzi up to the King of Naples, crawl round it on their knees; the nave is filled with the bands of worshippers, who, having visited the sacred spot, are retiring backwards from it, as from some royal presence.

On the "Santa Casa" alone depends the sacredness of the whole locality in which it stands. Loretto—whether the name is derived from the sacred grove (Lauretum) or the lady (Loreta) under whose shelter the house is believed to have descended—had no existence before the rise of this extraordinary sanctuary. The long street with its venders of rosaries, the palace of the governor, the strong walls built by Pope Sixtus IV., are all mere appendages to the humble edifice which stands within the Church. The "Santa Casa" is spoken of by them as a living person, a corporation sole on which the whole city depends, to which the whole property far and near over the rich plain which lies spread beneath it belongs forever.

No one who has ever witnessed the devotion of the Italian people on this singular spot, can wish to speak lightly of the feelings which it inspires. But a dispassionate statement of the real facts of the case may not be without use. Into the general question of the story we need not enter here. It has been ably proved elsewhere,[9] first, that of all the pilgrims who record their visit to Nazareth from the Fourth to the Sixteenth Century, not one alludes to any house of Joseph as standing there, or as having stood there, within human memory or record; secondly, that the records of Italy contain no mention of the House till the Fifteenth Century; thirdly, that the representation of the story as it now stands, with the double or triple transplantation of the sanctuary, occurs first in a bull of Leo X., in the year 1518. But it is the object of these remarks simply to confront the House as it stands at Loretto with the House as it appears at Nazareth. It has been already said that each professes to contain the exact spot of the Angelic visitation, to be the scene of a single event which can only have happened in one; each claims to be the very House of the Annunciation, and bases its claim to sanctity on that especial ground. But this is not all: even should either consent to surrender something of this peculiar sacredness, yet no one can visit both sanctuaries without perceiving that by no possibility can one be amalgamated with the other. The House of Loretto is an edifice of thirty-six feet by seventeen; its walls, though externally cased in marble, can be seen in their original state from the inside, and these appear to be of a dark red polished stone. The west wall has one square window, through which it is said the Angel flew; the east wall contains a rude chimney, in front of which is a mass

---

[9] See an elaborate and conclusive Essay on the origin of the story of the Holy House of Loretto, which appeared in the *Christian Remembrancer*, April, 1855.

of cemented stone, said to be the altar on which St. Peter said mass, when the Apostles, after the Ascension, turned the house into a church. On the north side is (or rather was) a door, now walled up. The monks of Loretto and of Nazareth have but a dim knowledge of the sacred localities of each other. Still, the monks of Nazareth could not be altogether ignorant of the mighty sanctuary which, under the highest authorities of their Church, professes to have once rested on the ground they now occupy. They show, therefore, to any traveller who takes the pains to inquire, the space on which the Holy House stood before its flight. That space is a vestibule immediately in front of the sacred grotto; and an attempt is made to unite the two localities by supposing that there were openings from the house into the grotto. Without laying any stress on the obvious variation of measurements, the position of the grotto is, and must always have been incompatible with any such adjacent building as that at Loretto. Whichever way the house is supposed to abut on the rock, it is obvious that such a house as has been described, would have closed up, with blank walls, the very passages by which alone the communication could be effected. And it may be added, that there is no traditional masonry of the "Santa Casa" left at Nazareth, there is the traditional masonry close by of the so-called workshop of Joseph of an entirely different character. Whilst the former is of a kind wholly unlike anything in Palestine, the latter is, as might be expected, of the natural grey limestone of the country, of which in all times, no doubt, the houses of Nazareth were built.

It may have seemed superfluous labour to have attempted any detailed refutation of the most incredible of Ecclesiastical legends. But Loretto is so emphatically the "Holy Place" of one large branch of Christendom—its claim has been so strongly maintained by French and Italian writers of our own times—and is, moreover, so deeply connected with the alleged authority of the Papal See—that an interest attaches to it far beyond its intrinsic importance. No facts are insignificant which bring to an issue the general value of local religion—or the assumption of any particular Church to direct the conscience of the world—or the amount of liberty within such a Church left on questions which concern the faith and practice of thousands of its members.

But the legend is also curious as an illustration of the history of "Holy Places" generally. It is difficult to say how it originated—or what led to the special selection of the Adriatic gulf as the scene of such a fable; yet, generally speaking, the explanation is easy and instructive. Nazareth was taken by Sultan Khalil in 1291, when he stormed the last refuge of the Crusaders in the neighbouring city of Acre. From that time, not Nazareth only, but the whole of Palestine, was closed to the devotions of Europe. The Crusaders were expelled from Asia, and in Europe the spirit of the Crusades was extinct. But the natural longing to see the scenes of the events of the Sacred History—the superstitious craving to win for prayer the favour of consecrated localities—did not expire with the Crusades. Can we wonder that, under such circumstances, there should have arisen the feeling, the desire, the belief, that if Mahomet could not go to the mountain, the mountain must come to Mahomet? The House of Loretto is the petrifaction, so to speak, of the "Last Sigh of the Crusades"; suggested possibly by the Holy House of St. Francis at Assisi, then first acquiring its European celebrity. It is indeed not a matter of conjecture that in Italy—the country where the passionate temperament of the people would most need such stimulants—persons in this state of mind did actually endeavour, so far as circumstances permitted, to reproduce the scenes of Palestine within their own immediate neighbourhood. One such is the Campo Santo of Pisa—"the Holy Field," as this is "the Holy House"—literally a cargo of sacred earth from the Valley of Hinnom, carried, as is well known, not on the wings of angels, but in the ships of the Pisan Crusaders. Another example is the remarkable Church of St. Stephen's at Bologna, within whose walls are crowded together various chapels and courts, representing not only, as in the actual Church of the Sepulchre, the several scenes of the Crucifixion, but the Trial and Passion also; and which is entitled, in a long inscription affixed to its cloister, the

"Sancta Sanctorum"; nay, literally, "the *Jerusalem*" of Italy. A third still more curious instance may be seen at Varallo, in the kingdom of Piedmont. Bernardino Caimo, returning from a pilgrimage to Palestine at the close of the Fifteenth Century, resolved to select the spot in Lombardy most resembling the Holy Land, in order to give his countrymen the advantage of praying at the Holy Place without undergoing the privations which he had suffered himself. Accordingly, in one of the beautiful valleys leading down from the roots of Monte Rosa, he chose (it must be confessed that the resemblance is of the slightest kind) three hills, which should represent respectively Tabor, Olivet, and Calvary; and two mountain-streams, which should in like manner personate the Kedron and Jordan. Of these the central hill, Calvary, became the "Holy Place" of Lombardy. It was frequented by S. Carlo Barromeo; under his auspices the whole mountain was studded with chapels, in which the scenes of the Passion are represented in waxen figures of the size of life; and the whole country round now sends its peasants by thousands as pilgrims to the sacred spot. We have only to suppose these feelings existing as they naturally would exist in a more fervid state two centuries earlier, when the loss of Palestine was more keenly felt—when the capture of Nazareth especially was fresh in every one's mind—and we can easily imagine that the same tendency, which by deliberate purpose produced a second Jerusalem at Bologna and a second Palestine at Varallo, would, on the secluded shores of the Adriatic, by some peasant's dream, or the return of some Croatian chief from the last Crusade, or the story of some Eastern voyager landing on their coasts, produce a second Nazareth at Fiume and Loretto. What, in a more poetical and ignorant age was in the case of the Holy House ascribed to the hands of angels, was actually intended by Sixtus V. to have been literally accomplished in the case of the Holy Sepulchre by a treaty with the Sublime Porte for transferring it bodily to Rome, so that Italy might then have the glory of possessing the actual sites of the conception, the birth, and the burial of our Saviour.

THE ALCAZAR OF SEVILLE, SPAIN
Edmundo De Amicis

The Alcazar, an old palace of the Moorish kings, is one of the best preserved buildings in Spain. From the outside, it looks like a fortress, as it is completely surrounded by high walls, battlemented towers and old houses, which structures form two spacious courts in front of the façade. Like the other parts of this building, the façade is plain and severe. The door is ornamented with arabesques that are painted and gilded, and there is also a Gothic inscription recording the time when the Alcazar was restored by the order of the king Don Pedro.

In fact, although the Alcazar is an Arabian palace, it is the work of Christian rather than Arabian monarchs. The date that it was begun is not known, but it was rebuilt towards the end of the Twelfth Century by King Abdelasio. King Ferdinand took possession of it about the middle of the Thirteenth Century; it was altered again by Don Pedro in the next century, since when it was inhabited by nearly all the kings of Castile. Finally it was chosen by Charles V. for the celebration of his marriage with the Infanta of Portugal.

The Alcazar has witnessed the loves and crimes of

three races of kings, and every one of its stones awakens some memory or holds some secret. After entering, you cross two or three rooms, in which there is nothing Arabian left except the ceiling and some mosaics upon the walls, and find yourself in a court that strikes you dumb with wonder. A gallery composed of elegant arches supported by small marble columns arranged in pairs runs along the four sides. The arches, walls, windows and doors are covered with mosaics, carvings and arabesques. The latter are delicate and intricate, in some places perforated like a veil, in others thick and close as woven carpets and elsewhere again hanging and jutting out like garlands and bunches of flowers. With the exception of the brilliantly coloured decorations everything is as white, clean and glistening as ivory. Four large doors, one in each side, lead into the royal rooms. Here you no longer wonder; you are enchanted. Everything that the most ardent fancy could imagine in the way of wealth and splendour is to be found in these rooms. From the ceiling to the floor, around the doors, around the windows in the distant recesses, wherever the eye may please to wander, such a multitude of gold ornaments and precious stones, such a close network of arabesques and inscriptions, such a marvelous blending of designs and colours appear that, before you have gone twenty steps, you are overpowered and confused, and you glance here and there as if trying to find a piece of bare wall upon which to rest your eye.

In one of the rooms, the custodian pointed out a reddish spot upon the marble pavement, and said very solemnly:

This is the stain caused by the blood of Don Fadrique, Grand Master of the Order of Santiago, who was killed here in the year 1358, by the order of the King Don Pedro, his brother.

When I heard this, I remember looking at the custodian as if to say: "Let us move on," and the good man answered dryly:

"Caballero, if I were to tell you to believe this on my word you would be perfectly right to doubt it; but when you see the thing with your own eyes, it seems to me—I may be mistaken,—but——"

"Yes," I hastily replied, "yes it is blood, I have no doubt of it; but don't let us talk about it any more."

Even if you are able to joke about a spot of blood, you cannot do so about the story of the crime. The place awoke in my mind all the most horrible facts. I seemed to hear Don Fadrique's step echoing through these gilded rooms, as he was being pursued by the soldiers armed with clubs. The palace is shrouded in darkness; no noises are heard but those of the executioners and their victim. Don Fadrique tries to enter the court. Lopez de Padilla seizes him and he breaks away. Now he is in the court; he grasps his sword; he utters maledictions upon it for the cross of the hilt is entangled in the mantle of the Order of Santiago. Now the archers arrive; he cannot draw it from its sheath; he flies hither and thither as best he may. Fernandez de Roa overtakes him and fells him with a blow from his mace; the others approach and wound him and he expires in a pool of blood.

This sad memory soon vanishes amidst the thousand fancies of the delicious life of the Moorish kings. These lovely little windows at which the dreamy face of an Odalisk ought to appear at any moment; these secret doors before which you pause, despite yourself, as if you heard the rustling of a dress; these sleeping-rooms of princes enveloped in a mysterious gloom, where you fancy you hear the sighing of girls who lost in them their virginal purity; and the prodigious variety of colours and friezes resembling an ever-changing symphony excite your senses to such a degree that you are like one in a dream. The delicate and very light architecture, the little columns (which suggest the arms of a woman), the capricious arches, and the ceilings covered with ornaments that hang in the form of stalactites, icicles, and bunches of grapes,— all rouse in you the desire to seat yourself in the centre of one of these rooms, pressing to your heart a beautiful dark Andalusian head which will make you forget the world and lose all sense of time, and with one long kiss that drinks away your life, put you to sleep forever.

The most beautiful room on the ground floor is that of

the ambassadors, formed by four great arches supporting a gallery of forty-four smaller arches, and above, a lovely cupola which is sculptured, painted and ornamented with an inimitable grace and a fabulous magnificence. On the next floor which contained the winter apartments, nothing remains but an oratory of Ferdinand and Isabella the Catholic, and a small room which is said to be the one where the King Don Pedro slept. You descend from here, by a narrow, mysterious staircase, into the rooms inhabited by the famous Maria di Padilla, a favourite of Don Pedro, whom popular tradition accuses of having instigated Don Pedro to the murder of his brother.

The gardens of the Alcazar are not large, nor extraordinarily beautiful; but the fancies that they engender are more precious than size or beauty. Beneath the shade of those oranges and cypresses, near the soft sound of those fountains when a great brilliant moon shone in the clear Andalusian sky and the host of courtiers and slaves lay down to rest, how many sighs of lovelorn sultanas were heard! how many humble words of proud kings! what mighty loves and embraces!

"Itimad! my love!" I murmured, thinking of the famous favourite of King Al-Motamid, as I roamed from path to path as if following her spirit: "Itimad! Do not leave me alone in this quiet paradise! Stop! Give me one hour of delight to-night. Don't you remember? You came to me and your lovely locks fell over my shoulders like a mantle; and as the warrior seizes his sword, I seized your neck, softer and whiter than a swan's! How beautiful you were! How my parched heart satisfied its thirst on thy blood-coloured lips. Your beautiful body issued from your splendidly embroidered robe like a gleaming blade from its scabbard; and then I pressed with both hands your large hips and slender waist in all the perfection of their beauty. How dear you are, Itimad! Your kiss is as sweet as wine, and your glance, like wine, makes me lose my reason!"

While I was uttering this declaration of love in the phrases and imagery of the Arabian poets, I entered a pathway bordered with flowers and suddenly felt a jet of water on my legs; I jumped back and had a dash of it in my face; I turned to the right, and felt a spray on my neck; turning to the left, I got another on the nape of my neck; then I began to run and there was water under me, over me, and all around me, in jets, sprays, and showers, so that in a moment I was as wet as if I had been plunged in a tub. Just at the moment I was about to shout I heard a loud laugh at the end of the garden, and, turning, I saw a young man leaning against the wall and looking at me, as if to say: "Did you enjoy it?" Then he showed me the spring he had touched in order to play the trick and comforted me by saying that the Seville sun would not leave me long in that wet condition, into which I had passed so brusquely, ah me! from the amorous arms of my sultana.

THE TOWER OF BELEM, PORTUGAL
Arthur Shadwell Martin

The place where Vasco da Gama spent the night before starting on his voyage of discovery, and where he was received by Emmanuel I., on his triumphant return in 1499, was called Bairro de Restello, and here stood a small *Ermida*, or hermitage, which had been founded for the use of navigators by the great pioneer of maritime discovery, Prince Henry the Navigator.

Osorio, Bishop of Sylves, thus describes the embarcation of the successful expedition which Belem specially commemorates: There was a chapel by the seaside, about four miles from Lisbon, built by Emmanuel in honour of the Virgin Mary; thither Gama resorted the day before he went aboard, and spent the whole night in offering up prayers, and performing other religious duties. Next day he was followed by vast crowds of people to take leave of him and the rest who embarked in the expedition. Not only those in holy orders, but all present, with one voice put up their petitions to the Almighty that he would grant them a prosperous voyage and a safe return. Many of those who came to see them aboard were deeply concerned, and expressed their sorrow as if they had come to the funeral of their friends. "Behold," said they, "the cursed effects of avarice and ambition! What greater punishment could be devised for these men, if guilty of the blackest crimes? To be thrown upon the merciless ocean, to encounter all the dangers of such a voyage, and venture their lives in a thousand shapes. Would it not be more eligible to suffer death at home than be buried in the deep at such a distance from their native country? These, and many other things did their fears suggest. But Gama, though he shed some tears at departure from his friends, was full of hope, and went aboard with great alacrity. He sailed on the 9th of July, 1497. Those who stood on the shore followed the ships with their eyes; nor did they move from thence till the fleet was under full sail, and quite out of sight." A few weeks after the return of Vasco da Gama, the foundation-stone of the edifice was laid by the thankful monarch. Boutaca, who was responsible for some of the work at Setubal, supplied the general design, and its details were worked out by the famous Joao de Castilho, who assumed the superintendence of the work in 1517. John III. discontinued the work in 1551, and it is still incomplete. The first stone was laid in 1500 by the Fortunate King with great ceremony, and the construction progressed very rapidly. The limestone of which the buildings were constructed was procured from the Alcantara valley in the vicinity, and lends itself readily to exquisite carving. Originally white when it came from the quarry, it has now mellowed into tints of rich brown, and it is very durable.

The architectural style of the building is what is called

the *Arte Manoelina*, called after the king, Emmanuel I., the Fortunate, (1495–1521) under whose reign it flourished. It is a transitional style, or rather a luxuriant medley of Gothic, Renaissance and Mauresque. Its wealth of detail often borders on the extravagant and fantastic, but its interest cannot be denied. Belem has been said to be the last struggle between Christian and Pagan art in Portugal, and it shows the scars of both in its excessive ornamentation. Its barbaric splendour of enriched stonework cannot fail to fascinate the art-lover, though it is inferior even in these characteristics to the beautiful *Capella Imperfeita* at Batalha.

There is a strange story told of the building of the church of Belem. The architect had made some miscalculation, so that when the scaffolding of the nave was removed, the vaulted roof fell, killing a number of the workmen. When the damage was repaired, the architect was so nervous that he fled to France. The king consequently gave orders for the removal of the scaffolding by criminals under sentence of death, with a promise of pardon in case they escaped death. It is related that the walls and roof stood the strain this time, and the criminals received the timbers of the scaffolding as perquisites, used them in building houses for themselves, and later became pillars of society. When the architect heard that his plans were justified, he returned and was rewarded for his work with a pension. He also was honoured by having his bust carved on one of the pillars.

The entire building is erected on a foundation of pine piles, and suffered scarcely any damage in the great earthquake of 1755.

The great church contains many features of interest, several chapels, magnificent arches, pulpits and choir stalls, and numberless statues. Of the lifelike figure of St. Jerome, Philip II. said: "I am waiting for it to speak to me." The stalls are delicately carved with intricate Arabesque tracery. There are two organs, one of which shows traces of former magnificence. The capella-mór (death chapel) of Renaissance decoration is entered through a magnificent arch flanked by two richly carved pulpits. On the North in recesses are the tombs of King Emmanuel and his Queen Maria, and on the South are similar ones of Joao III. and his Queen Catharina. These sarcophagi are borne by elephants. In the chapel beyond are tombs of other royal personages, including that of King Sebastian, who mysteriously disappeared at the battle of Al-Kasr al-Kebîr (1578); the eight children of Joao III., and a natural son of his, Don Duarte, Archbishop of Braga. Close by is the tomb of Catherine of Braganza, the neglected wife of the Merry Monarch, Charles II. of England; and others of the Cardinal King Henrique and other Infantes. Behind the high altar is a chapel containing the tombs of Alfonso VI., his brother Theodosio and a sister. The king is attired in the costume of the period in which he lived, and his body is said to be in perfect preservation.

The chief glory of the convent, however, is its superb cloisters, the masterpiece of Joao de Castilho. They are about 180 feet square, surrounded by a two-storied arcade. Other features are the Casa Pia, the Refectory, the Sacristy and the Capella dos Jeronymos. The Sala dos Reis contains (some imaginary) portraits of the kings of Portugal down to John VI. The Spanish usurpers are omitted.

At the Eastern extremity of the suburb of Belem, on the banks of the Tagus, are the constructions of the Belem tower, a massive building rather more than 100 feet square, flanked on the corners by Gothic turrets. It shelters a telegraph station and battery that defends the port.

This tower (Torre de Sao Vicente) is generally regarded as one of the most interesting structures in Lisbon. It stands really on a rocky islet in the Tagus, but the silting up of the channel between it and the shore renders its position less imposing than it used to be. Moreover its picturesque effect has been further marred by the erection of factories in the immediate vicinity.

In the castle of Belem is kept a registry-office for all vessels that enter or leave the Tagus; as well as an establishment of custom-house officers, health officers and naval police for the protection of property.

The Torre de Belem is of three stories, and its commanding situation affords a splendid view of the beautiful Tagus. Belem now forms a suburb of Lisbon, and the vineyards that formerly adorned the intervening banks of the river have been largely utilized for building purposes, but the tower still forms a striking object in the landscape and dominates the vicinity. The rhapsodies of travellers who visited Lisbon half a century ago are still justified. One of them writes: "From this point, the view up the river, to the East, is grand beyond all conception; and, to do the magnificent opening of the scenery justice, the most elaborate description would be perfectly inadequate. The breadth of the mighty river crowded with the vessels of every nation; men-of-war at anchor, and in various stages of equipment; the heights to the South crowned with batteries, villages and vineyards, descending down their sides to the very skirts of the water; the numerous fishing and pleasure-boats gliding swiftly across the river in various directions; the long uninterrupted line of palaces, convents and houses, running along the shore from Belem to Lisbon, under the elevated ridge upon which the splendid residence of the Portuguese sovereigns, the Ajuda, is erected, and then the beauteous city itself, with its domes and towers and gorgeous buildings, extended over its many hills; and, above all, the deep blue of the heaven's dazzling canopy above,—form a combination of objects, the striking interest of which can scarcely be represented to a northern imagination."

The tower is said to be modelled on an old design by Garcia da Resende. The lower part adjoins a sort of platform projecting over the river, and is enclosed by a parapet with battlements and the shields of the Knights of Christ. Six ornate turrets copied from Indian originals adorn the corners. The decoration of the square tower itself on the front facing the river consists of a balcony with traceried parapet and round-headed windows. The other sides have bow-windows. Higher up, the tower is girt with a passage for the use of its defenders. Four Indian turrets ornament the flat roof. The interior contains several square rooms which have suffered many restorations. One of them, the Sala Regia is celebrated for its peculiar acoustic properties. The basement is divided into dungeons that have seldom been vacant in the past. The prisoners immured there received light and air only through gratings in the floor of the casemates. They were constantly filled with political offenders under Miguel.

VENETIAN PALACES
Théophile Gautier

The Grand Canal is to Venice what the Strand is to London, the Rue Saint-Honoré to Paris, and the Alcala to Madrid,—the principal artery for the circulation of the whole city. Its form is that of a double S, reversed, the sweep of which bounds the city around St. Mark's while the upper point borders upon the isle of Santa-Chiara, and the lower point at the Custom-House, near the canal of the Giudecca. This S is cut about the middle by the bridge of the Rialto.

The Grand Canal of Venice is the most marvelous thing in the world. No other city can present so beautiful, so bizarre and so fairy-like a spectacle: perhaps you may find elsewhere remarkable specimens of architecture, but never placed in such picturesque conditions. Here, every palace has a mirror in which to admire her own beauty, just like a feminine coquette. The superb reality is repeated in a charming reflection. The water lovingly caresses the feet of those beautiful façades whose brows are kissed by a clear light and are rocked in two skies. The little boats and the large barks which can come up close to them seem moored on purpose to produce effective dark spots, or foregrounds for the convenience of scene-painters and water-colourists.

In drifting along by the Custom-House, which, with the Palace Giustiniani (to-day the *Hôtel de l'Europe*) marks the entrance of the Grand Canal, throw a glance at those skeleton-like heads of horses sculptured in the square and dumpy cornice which supports the globe of Fortune. Does this peculiar ornament mean that the horse was useless in Venice (you get rid of him at the Custom-House) or rather is it not a pure caprice of ornamentation? This explanation seems to me the best, for I do not wish to fall into the symbolical exaggeration with which I have been reproaching others. I have already described the Salute, which I can see from my window and which does not require any attention after having seen Canaletto's picture, which is, perhaps, the painter's masterpiece. But here I experience embarrassment. The Grand Canal is the true Golden Book in which all the Venetian nobility has signed its name upon the monumental façades.

The Foscari Palace, Italy

Each stone of the walls has a story to tell; each house is a palace; each palace, a masterpiece with a legend: at each stroke of the oar, the gondolier mentions a name which was as well-known at the time of the Crusades as it is to-day; and this on the right and left for a length of more than half a league.

I have written a list of these palaces, not quite all but the most remarkable of them, and I dare not insert it on account of its length. It takes up five or six pages: Pietro Lombardo, Scamozzi, Vittoria, Longhena, Andrea Tremignan, Giorgio Massari, Sansovino, Sebastiano Mazzoni, Sammichelli, the great architect of Verona, Selva, Domenico Rossi, and Visentini designed and superintended the construction of these princely dwellings,—without counting the marvellous unknown artists of the Middle Ages who erected the most picturesque and romantic ones, those that gave to Venice her distinction and originality.

Upon these two banks, façades, all charming and variously beautiful, succeed each other without interruption. After a specimen of Renaissance architecture, with its columns and superimposed orders comes a mediæval palace of the Gothic-Arabian style, of which the Ducal palace is the prototype, with its open-work, balconies, its ogives, its trefoils and its lace-like acrotera. A little farther is a façade encased in coloured marbles, ornamented with medalions and consoles; then comes a great rose-coloured wall, where a large window with little columns is cut out. Every style is found here: Byzantine, Saracen, Lombard, Gothic, Roman, Greek, and even Rococo; the column and the small column, the ogive and the cincture and the capricious capital filled with birds and flowers that has come from Acre or Jaffa; the Greek capital found amidst Athenian ruins, the mosaic and the bas-relief; the classic severity and the elegant fantasy of the Renaissance. It is an immense gallery in the open air, where one can study from his gondola the art of seven or eight centuries. What genius, talent and money have been expended in this space that can be traversed in less than an hour! What wonderful artists! But also what intelligent and magnificent lords! What a pity that the patricians who knew how to have such beautiful things made should exist no longer save in the canvasses of Titian, Tintoretto and Il Moro!

Just before arriving at the Rialto, you have to the left, in ascending the Canal, the Dario Palace, Gothic style; the Venier Palace, which reveals itself by one corner with its ornaments, its precious marbles and its medalions, Lombard style; the Fine-Arts, classic façade by the side of the ancient School of Charity and surmounted by a figure of Venice riding on a lion; the Contarini Palace, of Scamozzi's architecture; the Rezzonico Palace, with three orders superimposed; the triple Giustiniani Palace, in the taste of the Middle Ages, inhabited by Signor Natale Schiavoni, a descendant of the celebrated painter Schiavoni, who has a picture-gallery and a beautiful daughter, the living reproduction of a picture painted by her ancestor; the Foscari Palace, recognizable by its lower door, its two rows of little columns supporting the ogives and the trefoils, where formerly lived those sovereigns who visited Venice, and now abandoned; the Balbi Palace, from the balcony of which the princes leaned to watch the regatta which took place on the Grand Canal with so much pomp and brilliancy during the heyday of the Republic; the Pisani Palace, in the German style of the beginning of the Fifteenth Century; and the Tiepolo Palace, quite smart and relatively modern, with its two elegant pyramids. To the right, very near the European Hotel, there stands between two large buildings a delicious little palace, composed of a window and a balcony; but what a window and what a balcony! a lace-work of stone: scrolls, guilloches, and open-work that one would not believe it possible to execute except by a cutting-machine and a piece of paper. I regretted that I did not have 25,000 francs about me to buy it, for that is all they asked.

A little farther, still ascending, you find the Palace Corner della Cà Grande, which dates from 1532, one of Sansovino's best; Grassi, to-day the Emperor's inn, the marble stairway of which is garnished with handsome orange trees in pots; Corner-Spinelli, whose marble base is surrounded by a double fretwork of fine effect and which is to-day the Post Office; and Farsetti, with its columned peristyle and its long gallery with little columns occupying all the façade, where the municipality is lodged. We could say, as Don Ruy-Gomez da Silva says to Charles V. in *Hernani*, when he shows him the portraits of his ancestors: "*J'en passe, et des meilleurs.*" We ask, however, attention for the Loredan Palace and the ancient dwelling of Enrico Dandolo, the conqueror of Constantinople. Between these palaces there are some worthy houses, whose chimneys in the form of turbans, towers, and vases of flowers, break the great lines of architecture very appropriately.

Ascending always, you meet on the left the Corner della Regina Palace, so named on account of the Queen Conaro, whom Parisians know through Halévy's opera, *La Reine de Chypre*, in which Madame Stoltz played such a fine *rôle*. I do not remember if the scenery of MM. Séchan, Dieterle and Despléchin resembled it; it could have been without sacrificing anything, because the architecture of Domenico Rossi is of great elegance. The sumptuous palace of Queen Cornaro is now a pawn shop, and the humble rags of misfortune and the jewels of improvidence come to heap themselves here beneath the rich decorations which should not fall into ruins: for to-day it does not suffice to be beautiful, it is necessary to be useful.

The College of the Armenians, which is a short distance from here, is an admirable building by Baldassare de Longhena, of a rich, solid and imposing architecture. It is the ancient Pesaro Palace.

To the right there rises the Palazzo della Cà d'Oro, one of the most charming of the Grand Canal. It belonged to Mademoiselle Taglioni, who had it restored with the most intelligent care. It is all embroidered, all denticulated, all cut out in a Grecian, Gothic and Barbarian style, so fantastic, so light and so aërial that you would say it must have been made for the nest of a sylph. Mademoiselle Taglioni took pity upon these poor abandoned palaces. She rented several of them that attracted her out of pure commiseration for their beauty; three or four were pointed out to me upon which she had bestowed this charity of repairs.

Look at those blue and white stakes sprinkled with golden *fleur-de-lis*; they will tell you that the ancient palace Vendramini Calergi has become a quasi-royal habitation. It is the dwelling of Her Highness the Duchesse de Berry, and certainly she is better lodged than at the pavilion Marsan; for this palace, the most beautiful one in Venice, is a masterpiece of architecture and its carvings are of a marvelous delicacy. Nothing could be more beautiful than the groups of children who are supporting shields upon the arches of the windows. The interior is filled with precious marbles: you admire above all two porphyry columns of such rare beauty that their value would pay for the palace.

Although I have been a long time about it, I have not told all. I see that I have not yet spoken of the Mocenigo palace, where the great Byron lived; our gondolier however has grazed the marble stairway, where with her hair flying in the wind, her foot in the water, in the rain and tempest, the daughter of the people and mistress of Lord Byron welcomed him upon his return with these tender words: "Great dog of the Madonna, is it time to go to the Lido?"

The Barbarigo Palace also deserves mention. I have not seen the twenty-two Titians that are contained within it and which are held under seal by the Russian consul who has bought them for his master; but it still possesses some very beautiful pictures, and the carved and gilded cradle destined for the heir of this noble family,—a cradle which might be converted into a tomb, for, like most of the ancient families of Venice, the Barbarigo family is extinct: of the nine hundred patrician families inscribed in the Golden Book, only about fifty now remain.

The old caravansary of the Turks, so crowded at the time that Venice held all the commerce of the Orient and the Indies, presents now two rows of Arabian arcades, littered and obstructed by hovels that have pushed themselves up there like unhealthy mushrooms.

Saint Ouen, Rouen, France
L. De Fourcaud

The Fourteenth Century erected in France four churches of a peculiar grandeur and magnificence: the Cathedral of Saint Quentin; the abbey of Saint Bertin, Saint Omer; Saint Nazaire of Carcassonne and Saint Ouen of Rouen. The first two have disappeared, but the two others have come down to us almost intact, and both of them derive their disconcerting basilicas from the end of the Thirteenth Century; Saint Urbain of Troyes is a piece of stone jewelry.

We shall have less trouble in characterizing briefly the marvelous building of Saint Ouen, than in describing Notre-Dame (Rouen). The edifice is longer, less ample, clearer, and more of a unity as far as the structure is concerned, and it is deprived of those brilliant accessories which engross the attention. It is, by all odds, superior in harmony and compactness of the execution and inferior in size. The one attracts poets, the other is preferred by men of learning. Everybody will appreciate the subtlety.

Now, first of all and very briefly, here is the history of this abbey. Upon the ruins of an oratory constructed in this very place by the indefatigable Saint Victrice about 535, Clotaire erected a large church dedicated to Saint Peter and Saint Paul. In the last years of the Seventh Century, Saint Ouen restored it and wished it to be his sepulchre. According to the *Life* of that great bishop attributed to Fridegode, a monk of Canterbury, it was a building of noble appearance, constructed of square stones in the *Gothic style*. It is useless to discuss these words, quoted on account of their curiosity, but which might well be accounted for by some alteration in the text, and, in any case, have but little meaning for us. After the appearance of the Northmen, the abbey experienced varied fortunes: it was sacked and demolished in 841, repaired in 1046 by the Abbé Nicholas of Normandy, son of Duke Richard III., and it was burned to the ground several times. A fragment of Nicholas's apsis at the end of the nave is preserved under the name of *Chambre aux clercs*: a portion of the hemicycle arched cul-de-four is ornamented very coarsely, but it is strongly built.

But to resume: there was no glory for the monks of Saint Benoît here until the beginning of the Fourteenth Century and the advent of the Abbé Jean Roussel. This Jean Roussel, born in Quincampoix, near Rouen, and known, nobody knows why, by the nick-name of Marc d' Argent, was a very original personage. Active, discreet, prudent, energetic, and devoted to everything under his charge, he re-established the monastic discipline and by the wisdom of his administration doubled the revenues; and, as Suger did before him at Saint Denis, he resolved to rebuild his abbey according to the latest developments in architecture. We do not know who was his master in this work; but certainly it must have been some clever man who had carefully studied Amiens, Beauvais, Troyes and Séez. Within a few years, the work was sufficiently advanced for his conception to have become definitive. His successors had nothing more to do than to follow out his ideas. Materials were not stinted. The quarries of Chaumont, Vernon and Saint-Leu furnished their magnificent calcareous stone, of fine grain mixed with silex. As the Abbé was never at a loss for funds, it was popularly imagined that he coined gold, and many a legend exists upon this subject. The truth is, he knew how to economize with large sums, obtained from the King important rights regarding the cutting of wood in the forest Verte and created disinterested good-will around him. In the year 1318, the first stone was laid, and in the year 1339, when he died, more than 79,936 livres (2,600,000 francs of our money) were paid to the stone-cutters. The inscription placed on his tomb, destroyed in 1562 by the Calvinists, described the state in which he left the church, the choir and the eleven transept chapels comprising the large terminal chapel were finished: the large pillars of the transept were only lacking the tower, the two arms of the transept were approaching completion, and doubtless also the nave was quite advanced.

The Hundred Years' War retarded the work without actually interrupting it. We find Charles VI. in 1380 allowing 3,000 livres to the Abbé Arnaud du Breuil to hasten the work. The portal called *des Marmousets* at the south arm of the transept is now given over to the sculptors. However the hour for rapid achievement has passed. It is not until 1439 that the two roses of Master Alexandre de Berneval and his legendary pupil unfold at the extremities of the transept. Under Admiral d' Estouteville, Archbishop of Rouen and Abbé of the monastery, the entrance to the choir was closed by a precious Gothic rood-screen; but the nave had yet to be finished, and the central tower and the façade had yet to be done. The Abbé Bohier at the very last of the Fifteenth Century, finished the building. The delicious square tower, eighty-two metres high, set off with bays, with gables and corner buttresses upon which are grafted the flying-buttresses of the octagonal belfry with the open-worked crown, is of the same date, the same style, and, perhaps, of the same hand as the *Tour de Beurre*. We possess the plan of the façade, drawn at this time by an unknown artist. It recalls the taste of the Normans for the porches under bell-towers of which few examples are to be found outside of their province after the Thirteenth Century. This master conceived two large, square towers placed diagonally, of a most original effect of perspective, and beneath which opened two lateral porches whose sheltered arches broke the draughts and were very converging and very convenient for the entrance and exits in and out of the church of the several filing processions. We are astonished to think that such a picturesque arrangement was never carried into effect. The execution of the plan was never commenced. The two bell-towers had been carried up to twenty metres and then abandoned. Their dimensions frightened the architect Grégoire, who in 1840 was charged with enriching Marc d' Argent's façade, and he pulled down the stumps to build those two towers with their thin spires and that commonplace façade with its dry lines that we now see.

A glance at the general plan of the building is necessary. Nothing could be simpler than this general arrangement: a polygonal choir and chapels between the buttresses; a lantern in the centre; some rather narrow branches of the transept; a large nave moderately wide, but very long with some quite narrow tributaries. The total length amounts to 138 metres; the width of the nave is restricted to twenty-six. What does this matter if these proportions are well united? What astonishes us beyond everything is the evident charming intention. There are no walls beyond those that are necessary; it is all tracery with support. The second impression is received from the forms; with the exception of a few architectural details in the bay near the porch, the style is perfectly homogeneous. There is no spirit of creation here; it is that admirable spirit of refinement and adaptation of the Fourteenth Century. As at Saint Urbain de Troyes, all the arches spring from pillars and all the ribs return to them, where, to employ the synthetic formula of Viollet-le-Duc, "the piers are nothing more than projections in clusters of the different profiles of the arches." What then is the use of capitals under such conditions? They are more detrimental than useful. Moreover, you find no trace of them except in the oldest parts of the choir. The ribs of the arches instead of being strictly fastened against the walls cross the mass to leap outside in bracing arches and archivolts. Exactly as at Séez, the triforium drops very low and ends, not in a massive ledge but in a gallery of lace-work, in order to allow you to see from the nave across its spaces between the arches the dazzling lucidity of the windows of the gallery. And everywhere is manifested this threefold intention: elevation, ease and open-work.

And what windows to adorn these masses of filagree work! The most varied, the finest and the richest of the period of Louis XII. at its apogee. Patriarchs and martyrs, prophets and holy abbés, kings and sibyls stand out on all sides in the hues of brilliant and soft jewels. We have no longer the frank mosaic of former days giving life to the light, and bestowing upon it a certain mystical impression; they are not the simple large figures under sumptuous baldaquins brightened with silver gilt; they are, most frequently, the glass pictures of the Renaissance. We are astonished at the perfection of their treatment. Several subjects are those that the Thirteenth Century took pleasure in evoking; witness the legend of the pilgrim of Saint-Jacques, whose son, unjustly hung, is kept on the gibbet by the saint himself and recognized as innocent. Nothing seems to me, however, so memorable here, as much on account of the subject as for the treatment, as the series of sibyls—those pagans to which the Middle Ages had begun to give a Christian fate and which the Sixteenth Century treated so voluptuously. This is why they assume a new importance at Saint Ouen. The artist took pleasure in painting them under the adornments of elegant ladies, in landscapes bristling with buildings. Above all, I cannot forget the charming sibyl of Samos, in her embroidered robe covered with *orfèvrerie* and jewels, two doves pecking at her feet in the midst of a piece of country scenery, and treated so to speak, in the manner of a portrait. This series of glass extending from one end of the church to the other and almost from top to bottom, forms an immense, translucent and radiant tapestry. It seems as if a breath might annihilate it. But no, it remains hard, rigid and as if incorporate with the very wall. Solid bars of iron, cutting the bays, give it an indestructible armature. The evanescent dream of the period has eternalized itself in a fairy-like vision.

What beautiful roses are cut out in the transept! On the central one, God the Father appears on his throne of gold, above the adoring kings. The other, with its more complicated outlines, shows us the Glory of Paradise. You know the tradition attached to these two architectural flowers with the resplendent lobes? Alexandre de Berneval having designed the first, became jealous of one of his disciples who traced the second, and in anger, killed him. To expiate the crime he had to die by the hands of the hangman. Who invented this story? The master lies yonder, in the second chapel down the nave to the right, by the side of one of his pupils, or, perhaps with his son Colin. Can any one believe that the monks would admit under any pretext beneath the holy vaults the body of an assassin and honour him with a superb sepulchral stone? Upon the stone the two architects live again in their long robes lined with vair, and their large hats. The older, his compass in his hand carving out a quarter-round, the younger one making a plan, the feet of both resting on a lion, and above them a Gothic daïs. The older is Berneval who died in 1440: the inscription tells us this. Of the younger we know nothing, for the inscription concerning him was never made.

There is no fine carving to note in the interior of the abbey. Many of the pillars in the nave were ornamented with statues in the style of the Fourteenth Century, but placed in niches that retreat a little. Broken in 1794, when the building was used as a forge, they have never been restored. The destruction of the rood-screen dates from 1791, at the time of the departure of the monks and the erection of the parish church. This rood-screen must assuredly have spoiled the perspective of a building so frankly conceived for the effect in perspective. But if one wants to delight in sculptured scenes, it is before the *portail des Marmousets* that he must betake himself. Beneath a finely arched porch, is a door that is condemned to-day. The statue of Saint Ouen, decapitated by the Reformers, and the pier covered with little bas-reliefs, relates in detail the life and miracles of the holy bishop. On the tympanum, three zones of perfect figures describe the death of the Virgin, her funeral, her assumption and her entrance into heaven between two angels who are playing the organ and the rebeck. A curious popular invention has found its place in the funeral scene, where an impious Jew trying to make an attempt upon the coffin has to see the Archangel Michael cut off his hands and St. Peter give them back to him, whilst converting him. This decoration is of an exceptional vivacity and delicacy of carving.

From the public garden, we can take in the development of the apsis. The elegance of design and the working-out are seen in all their grandeur from here. From the pinnacled buttresses spring the graceful double flying-buttresses responding exactly to the spring of the arches that are distributed and repeated with such wise judgment. Above the chapels with their pyramidal roofs runs a balustrade of quatrefoils inscribed in a curved quadrangle reproduced at the base of the top. These charming galleries whose stone rivals ironwork, in its extraordinary precision of the cutting, define the essential lines of the plan through the bristling lines of the secondary forms. They represent calm and order surrounded by agitation.

But from whatever point of view you survey Saint Ouen, you will recognize the most exemplary refinement of construction. It is not merely the frame which should be taken as a model with its square and chamfred wood, its suspended binding-pieces, its Saint Andrew's cross, and its double sabliere plates gathered at the base of the chevrons. In the eyes of architects, the Abbey of the wise Abbé Marc d' Argent will always be regarded as one of the *chefs d'œuvre* of the art of building in France.

CARISBROOKE CASTLE, ENGLAND
Sir James D. Mackenzie

The Isle of Wight, like Kent, was peopled by Jutes, who, coming in under the wing of the actual conquerors, Cerdic and Cynric, exterminated the existing Romano-British inhabitants at the bloody battle of Wihtgaresbyrg (Saxon Chron.), a name which, omitting the primary syllable, became "Carisbrooke." The later castle, whose site is actually that of the battlefield of 530, was conferred by the conquerors on their relative Wihtgar. But whereas the Jutes of Kent were the first, those of the Isle of Wight were the last among the English to embrace Christianity, and in the Seventh Century the fine proselytizing zeal of the West Saxons led them to invade and annihilate with their murderous knives the heathen islanders, whose land they annexed to the Wessex diocese.

The island was already found to give the shortest passage between England and Normandy, and for this reason was used in Saxon times, as also by William the Conqueror on some of his journeys to and from Normandy. It was here that he arrested his half-brother, Bishop Odo, as he was on his way to Rome, and here he tarried on quitting England for his last journey to France. William granted the Isle of Wight to William Fitz Osborne, Earl of Hereford, who, it is believed, reared the castle of Carisbrooke, in which Odo was arrested, as he likewise founded the priory adjoining. He had accompanied his leader from Normandy, and was one of his army marshals. Besides having the lordship of this isle, he was made constable of the newly built castles of York and Winchester, and justiciary for the King in the North. On the great mound of the Saxon burh at Wihtgaresbyrg he built a Norman keep, but as he was killed in France four years after coming to the isle, it is probable that the work he began was completed by his son, Roger de Bretteville, who was imprisoned for life by William for levying war against him, all his estates being forfeited to the Crown.

Henry I. next gave the lordship of the isle, with the castle and honour of Carisbrooke, to Richard de Redvers, whose son succeeding him (temp. Stephen) was made Earl of Devon; large additions were made by this family to the castle, which was held by the Redvers until that race ended in an heiress, Isabella de Fortibus, so called from her marriage with an Earl of Albemarle of that name. This lady lived here (1262–1293) and built a large part of the castle, which, at her death, she bequeathed to King Edward I. Afterwards, in the Fourteenth Century, the castle was held by Piers Gaveston, William Montague, the chivalrous Earl of Salisbury, and by Edward, Earl of Rutland, son of Edmund of Langley, fifth son of Edward III. who inherited his father's title of Duke of York, and fell at Agincourt, when, after his widow, Philippa's death, the castle and island fell to Humphrey, the Good Duke of Gloucester, in the reign of Henry VI. After him the lordship was enjoyed by several royal and other personages, and lastly by Anthony, Earl Rivers, and his brother, Sir Edward Woodville, who, together with a large force he had raised in the island, fell at the battle of St. Anbyn, in a foolish expedition against the King of France. Since that time Carisbrooke has always been held by the Crown. In Elizabeth's reign, when preparations were made on the south coast to repel the Spanish Armada, very elaborate outworks were planned and executed at this castle, entirely surrounding it with fortifications of the then new type, escarp and ditch and ravelin and redan, which exist at the present time: but they were never wanted, and only served usefully as a promenade for the royal victim, King Charles, in his imprisonment.

Charles having escaped from his durance with the army at Hampton Court (November 11, 1647), rode to Titchfield, the Earl of Southampton's place, where he might have sailed by Portsmouth Harbour to the Continent, as his intention was; but, by a mistake, Colonel Hammond, the Governor of the Isle of Wight, was brought to Titchfield, and he conducted the King to Carisbrooke, where he became again a prisoner. Here three attempts seem to have been made, chiefly by some gentlemen of the island, to give him freedom during the twelve months of his detention. On the first of these occasions it was arranged that Charles should pass through the window of his room, and let himself down to the ramparts, below which a guide with a horse was waiting, and a boat was ready to take him to a ship in the offing; but an iron bar in the window prevented his getting through, and so the King had to wave off his friends. The window in question is discernible from the outside of the King's lodgings; it adjoins the only buttress of the wall, and is walled up. On another occasion implements having been provided for him, Charles managed to saw through and remove the bar which impeded him, and all arrangements were made for his flight, but a rascally officer, one Major Rolfe, was entrusted with the secret and betrayed it. So, when the King was about to make the attempt, he observed below more people than were expected, and wisely decided to remain where he was. It was said that Rolfe intended to have shot the King as he descended. After being there for a year, Charles was removed, with scant ceremony or respect from Carisbrooke. At daybreak one morning a party of soldiers were sent, who, rousing him from bed, took him off to Hurst Castle, a fort on the mainland, standing at the extremity of the spit of land, near Lymington, which stretches across the Solent Strait to within a mile of the opposite island. Here the King was detained for a month, when he was taken to Windsor. To Carisbrooke were sent the two royal children, the year succeeding their father's judicial murder, but in less than a month the Princess Elizabeth was found dead in her room, her face resting on the Bible given her by her father at their last interview. Prince Henry remained there nearly two years. An attack was made on the castle at the outbreak of the civil war by the mayor and people of Newport, in obedience to the instructions of the Parliament, in order to get rid of the King's captain, the Earl of Portland, and his successor, Lord Pembroke; and the fortress was yielded on honourable terms. After the Restoration, the governor, Lord Cutts, made great and lamentable alterations in the old fabric, quite modernizing a part of it; but at a recent date the Government have restored the work in a judicious manner, and brought to light some hidden and interesting features.

The Norman keep of Richard de Redvers stands on the ancient English mound at the north-east angle of the inner ward, surrounded by its moat; it is an irregular polygon in shape, a shell keep sixty feet across, with walls of great strength and thickness, the access to which is by a long flight of stairs, the postern being protected by double gates and a portcullis. One room only remains, in which is a deep well, the others are destroyed, but there remains a small staircase to the top, whence a very fine view is obtained; at the foot was a sally-port defended by a bastion, which has disappeared. The entrance is on the west by a fine machicolated gateway, flanked by two round embattled towers, through a high pointed archway with portcullis grooves; all this was built by Anthony, Lord Scales, who had the lordship in 1474, and whose arms are on the gatehouse, as they are on Middleton Tower near Lynn with the Rose of York. Inside are the older gates, with latticed ironwork, and on the right the ruins of the guardhouse, and the chapel of St. Nicholas, built in 1738 on the site of the ancient chapel. On the north are the ruins of the buildings occupied by King Charles, a small room being shown as his bedroom. The governor's quarters, barracks and other buildings are all of different periods. In the centre of the south wall are remains of a mural tower, and there are the ruins of the Mountjoy, a Norman tower in the south-east corner, the walls here being eighteen feet thick: east are two other towers. Anciently there must have been some outworks, as in the Domesday Survey, the area of this castle is said to be one virgate, or twenty acres.

THE PANTHEON, ITALY
Augustus J. C. Hare

The Pantheon, the most perfect pagan building in the city, was built B.C. 27, by Marcus Agrippa, the bosom friend of Augustus Cæsar, and the second husband of his daughter Julia. The inscription, in huge letters, perfectly legible from beneath, "M. Agrippa, L. F. Cos. Tertium Fecit," records its construction. Another inscription on the architrave, now almost illegible, records its restoration under Septimius Severus and his son Caracalla, *c.* 202, who, *"Pantheum vetustate corruptum cum omni cultur restitverunt."* Some authorities have maintained that the Pantheon was originally only a vast hall in the baths of Agrippa, acknowledged remains of which exist at no great distance; but the name "Pantheum" was in use as early as A.D. 59.

In A.D. 399 the Pantheon was closed as a temple in obedience to a decree of the Emperor Honorius, and in 608 was consecrated as a Christian church by Pope Boniface IV., with the permission of the Emperor Phocas, under the title of Sta. Maria ad Martyres. To this dedication we owe the preservation of the main features of the building, though it has been terribly maltreated. In 663, the Emperor Constans, who had come to Rome with great pretense of devotion to its shrines and relics, and who only stayed there twelve days, did not scruple, in spite of its religious dedication to strip off the tiles of gilt bronze with which the roof was covered, and carry them off with him to Syracuse, where, upon his murder, a few years after, they fell into the hands of the Saracens. In 1087, it was used by the anti-pope Guibert as a fortress, whence he made incursions upon the lawful pope, Victor III., and his protector, the Countess Matilda. In 1101, another anti-pope, Sylvester IV., was elected here. Pope Martin V., after the return from Avignon, attempted the restoration of the Pantheon by clearing away the mass of miserable buildings in which it was encrusted, and his efforts were continued by Eugenius IV., but Urban VIII. (1623–1644), though he spent 15,000 scudi upon the Pantheon, and added the two ugly campaniles, called in derision "the asses' ears," of their architect, Bernini, did not hesitate to plunder the gilt bronze ceiling of the portico, 450,250 lbs. in weight, to make the baldachino of St. Peter's, and cannons for the Castle of Saint Angelo. Benedict XIV. (1740–1758) further despoiled the building by tearing away all the precious marbles which lined the attic to ornament other buildings.

The Pantheon was not originally, as now, below the level of the piazza, but was approached by a flight of five steps. The portico, which is one hundred and ten feet long and forty-four feet deep, is supported by sixteen grand Corinthian columns of oriental granite, thirty-six feet in height. The ancient bronze doors remain. On either side are niches, once occupied by colossal statues of Augustus and Agrippa.

The Interior is a rotunda, 143 feet in diameter, covered by a dome. It is only lighted by an aperture in the centre, twenty-eight feet in diameter. Seven great niches around the walls once contained statues of different gods and goddesses, that of Jupiter being the central figure. All the surrounding columns are of giallo-antico, except four, which are of pavonazzetto, painted yellow. It is a proof of the great value and rarity of the giallo-antico, that it was always impossible to obtain more to complete the set.

Some antiquarians have supposed that the aperture at the top of the Pantheon was originally closed by a huge "Pigna," or pine-cone of bronze, like that which crowned the summit of the mausoleum of Hadrian, and this belief has been encouraged by the name of a neighbouring church being S. Giovanni della Pigna.

The Pantheon has become the burial-place of painters, Raphael, Annibale Caracci, Taddeo Zucchero, Baldassare Peruzzi, Pierino del Vaga, and Giovanni da Udine, are all buried here.

The third chapel on the left contains the tomb of Raphael (born April 6, 1483; died April 6, 1520). From the pen of Cardinal Bembo is the epigram:

"Ille hic est Raphael, timuit quo sospite vinci

Rerum magna parens, et moriente mori."

Taddeo Zucchero and Annibale Caracci are buried on either side of Raphael. Near the high altar is a monument to Cardinal Gonsalvi (1757–1824), the faithful secretary and minister of Pius VII., by Thorwaldsen. This, however, is only a cenotaph, marking the spot where his heart is preserved. His body rests with that of his beloved brother Andrew in the church of S. Marcello.

During the Middle Ages the Pope always officiated here on the day of Pentecost, when, in honour of the descent of the Holy Spirit, showers of white rose-leaves were continually sent down through the aperture during service.

In the Piazza della Rotunda is a small obelisk found in the Campus Martius. Following the Via della Rotunda from hence, in the third street on the left is the small semicircular ruin called, from a fancied resemblance to the favourite cake of the people, Arco di Ciambella. This is the only remaining fragment of the baths of Agrippa, unless the Pantheon itself was connected with them.

Behind the Pantheon is the Piazza della Minerva, where a small obelisk was erected in 1667 by Bernini, on the back of an elephant. It is exactly similar to the obelisk in front of the Pantheon, and they were both found near this site, where they formed part of the decorations of the Campus Martius. The hieroglyphics show that it dates from Hophres, a king of the 25th dynasty.

St. Laurence, Nuremberg, Germany
Linda Villari

Once in the train bound for Nuremberg, every sight on the road seems to bring one nearer to Mediæval Germany, and is a fitting prelude to its charms. The storied prettiness of the Rhine district left behind, ripening vines give way to festoons of hops and plots of tobacco; you pass through forests of fir and larch, and come to fields of gold brocade where the lupines are in bloom. Woodlands merge into pleasant meadows watered by swiftly-running streams; every village is crowned by a ruined castle; and there are storks' nests on clustered roofs about the red church spires. Flaxen-haired children are driving flocks of fat geese; here and there is a battlemented monastery; then come tracts of moorland flushed pink and purple with heather; you dive into hill-sides; you sight dark masses of pine-trees beyond a winding river crossed by an occasional ferry; you halt at mediæval towns capped by crumbling yellow walls of palace and prison, and before long at the spick and span station of manufacturing Fürth (where most of the toys and wood-carvings are now made). And then you see a confusion of dusky, jagged roofs pierced by lofty spires and high walls; massive towers loom above the greenery of a steep hill-side, and you know that your goal is reached. This is Nuremberg, the "jewel-casket of the German Empire." Your first impression is that it should rather be named the city of wonderful roofs. Mighty roofs heave their four and five rows of dormers high in air above a forest of lower dwellings, with roofs of every degree of steepness, covered for the most part with small inverted tiles of reddish-brown hue. This arrangement gives them a soft and curious shagginess that greatly adds to their effect. Driving first round the town, before passing its gates, you see that it is almost entirely surrounded by dark-red walls, studded by numerous steeple-crowned watch-towers, and further guarded by a dry moat a hundred feet wide and fifty deep, now draped with vines and planted with vegetables and fruit-trees. The River Pegnitz runs through the city, and issues from it in two arms at either end; its islands and covered bridges, with smaller bridges (*hinterbrücke*) swung underneath, supply deliciously pictorial incidents of towers and sheds and mills and timber-yards, with fascinating peeps up and down stream into the interior of the town.

St. Sebald is the patron saint of the older part of the city near the castle, St. Laurence of the portion across the river, dating from the Thirteenth Century.

Passing through the "Lady Gate," with its massive Sixteenth Century fortifications, the König's Strasse lies before us, and we are in the Germany of the Middle Ages. What matter modern shop-fronts or gliding trams? We hardly see them; can only look at the wonderful houses on either hand, their steep, jagged roofs, their gables and stepped gables, their pepper-caster towers, projecting casements, bays and oriels and mullions, carved doors and eaves and balconies, fantastic gargoyles and cross-timbered fronts. In short, all the exquisite irregularities and details of mediæval domestic architecture. And, as we look, we think of Grimm's household tales, the beloved dog's eared treasure of our childish days. Yonder broad-shouldered inn, *Zum grünen Weinstock* (the Green Vine) might well be the lodging where the soldier with the blue light played his naughty pranks on the king's daughter.

But now the street widens; other gabled avenues branch off from it, and we are face to face with the red-brown bulk of St. Laurence. There it is, the beautiful church of the twin towers, with its sculptured portals and grand wheel windows! It almost seems to fill the square in which it stands, and where ancient red houses, deep-porched with jutting galleries and many-storied roofs are set about the stones of the precincts.

We wandered round the church to admire its exterior, and dally as it were with the wonderland within, but a fierce easterly wind gave an edge to our desire, and we speedily knocked at the side entrance appointed to sightseers. A wonderland indeed—rather a perfect symphony of form and colour! St. Laurence is certainly one of the most beautiful, perhaps one of the finest Gothic interiors in Europe, with a special charm of its own, that makes your first moments in it moments breathless with delight. Presently you begin to analyze your sensations, and study the details of the lovely scene that has stirred your sense of beauty to so reverent a joy. St. Laurence is very lofty and admirably proportioned, being 322 feet long by 104 broad. Its pointed Gothic arches spring from their tall, slender shafts with the grace and somewhat the effect of a grove of palms. Windows of richest stained glass lend a magic glow to the delicate avenues of stone, and on all sides are picturesque details: monuments, statues, paintings, and relics of ancient days. Midway up the nave is suspended the coloured group in wood carved by the famous Veit

Stoss, and known as the "Angel's Greeting." Sculptured saints and virgins project from the columns, and make you in love with the naïve realism of early German art. One wooden Madonna is absolutely romping with her babe. The side chapels are lined with quaint, rich tapestries from the designs of Albert Dürer, representing Scriptural scenes. There are many pictures of the Nuremberg school, of which the best are those of Wohlgemuth, Dürer's master; several interesting mural tombs and curious crucifixes. But the chief art treasure of the church is, of course, the Ciborium, or "Sacraments Hauslein" of Adam Krafft, erected against one of the pillars of the choir. It is a poem in stone. Its leading motive is the crown of thorns, but all the scenes of the passion are represented on small tablets in high relief; its base is supported by the kneeling figures of the sculptor and his two assistants. It is in the shape of a five-sided tower, gradually tapering to a curled finial sixty-four feet from the ground. Every detail is a marvel of grace and delicacy, and the faces of Krafft and his men are full of life and expression. They had worked on this masterpiece for four years.

In this beautiful church you are grateful to the happy tolerance that has preserved the art relics of Catholicism in the temple of a purer faith. Nuremberg was one of the first cities to protest against the sale of indulgences, to adopt the tenets of Luther and Melancthon, and in 1530 it subscribed to the Augsburg Confession.

This great change was accomplished in the most peaceable way. One by one, the convents and monasteries were suppressed, and when the Catholic bishop of Bamberg called on the Swabian Bund to oppose these measures by force, he was told that the Bund had no concern in the matter, and that the free city claimed the right of freedom of conscience.

So much for the history, but we cannot leave St. Laurence without relating some of the old-world legends attached to its walls. The cathedral was begun in 1278, but the Fifteenth Century was growing old before its completion; and when the north tower (finished in 1498) was commenced there was a great squabble among the builders. The master mason was unjustly dismissed by the intrigues of two of his men, who were jointly promoted to his post. But the accomplices soon quarrelled, and, vowing a mortal hate, each sought the other's destruction. One day they had to mount the half-built tower together to inspect the works, and as one leant forward from a window the other rushed on him and tried to throw him out. But the first man turned on his assailant, gripped him hard; both fell and both were dashed to pieces on the stones below. It chanced that their ill-treated predecessor was crossing the square at the time, and was standing still gazing at the tower he was to have built just when his two enemies came crashing down within an inch of him. The town council heard of his miraculous escape, and likewise how the dead men had ousted him from his post. So they reinstated him as master builder, and decreed him the right of recording on the tower stones in what manner God had chastised the guilty and preserved the life of the innocent. But the master builder refused to exercise this privilege, and only craved permission to destroy all trace of the dreadful event. He had the window walled up, and it remained so for centuries. And even after the gilded roof was struck by lightning in 1865, and half the tower had to be rebuilt, the blank window was still left untouched. Only in 1874 public opinion was roused on the subject, and satirical rhymes circulated on the offence to taste of this blind window. So now, north and south towers have an equal number of openings.

Another legend recounts how in the Thirteenth Century a monk was solemnly walled up in the south-western corner of the church, where the bell-ropes hang. The criminal was young, his offence slight, and general horror and pity were excited by his dreadful doom. People shuddered as they passed that darksome corner, but for the sacristan's pretty daughter it seemed to have a curious attraction. She had wept bitterly on hearing the fate of the young monk whom she had so often seen praying at the altar, but her pity did not affect her appetite, for it was noticed that this had suddenly increased. One day the bell-ringers of St. Laurence were surprised to see a rat spring from a hole in the wall with a fresh cabbage-leaf in his mouth. They talked of the strange sight; a watch was set, search made. And when the hole was enlarged, behold! it led to the niche of the condemned monk, who was found not only alive, but well nourished, after having been buried for weeks! The sacristan's daughter had supplied him with food through the crack in the wall. The affair made a great noise. It was the hand of Providence cried the townsfolk. And so the prisoner was pardoned, and allowed to go free. There the story ends, but we hold to the idea that he did not go alone.

But the most picturesque of the many legends, of which the cathedral is the scene, is that of the "Mass of the Dead."

A lady of the Imhoff family, being left a widow in her youth, could in no way resign herself to God's will, remained sunk in grief and attended every service at St. Laurence in the vain hope of obtaining relief by prayer. Even in the coldest winter season she was always to be seen at early mass. One All Saint's Eve she was awakened from her first sleep by the sound of the church-bells. The moon was still shining, but the lady thought it was the first break of day, and, rising from her bed, wrapped herself in a thick cloak and hastened across the square to the church. Its doors stood wide open, and an unusually large congregation was already assembled. Kneeling in her accustomed place, she saw that the priest was already bending before the altar, and the candles burnt with so strange a light that the faces of her fellow-worshippers appeared ghastly pale. And when the priest turned she recognized him as one who had died and been buried during the past year. She glanced right and left with terrified eyes, and on all sides were persons she had once known but who were no longer living. As she sank back in her chair in mortal dismay, there glided close to her an old friend whose death she had recently mourned and whose body she had helped to clothe in the garments of the grave. In faint, far-away tones the friend whispered in her ear: "Beloved Clara, as soon as the bell rings for the elevation of the Host fly thou quickly from the church, or Death will chastise thee for disturbing by thy presence the souls of the dead." And having uttered these words, the form vanished from her side, and Widow Clara fled towards the door as fast as her trembling limbs could carry her. She heard a dreadful rustling and clattering behind; it seemed as though the whole ghostly company were in full pursuit at her heels. As she hurried through the churchyard she saw that all the graves were gaping, and fell fainting on her own threshold. There she was found by her attendants, who, alarmed by hearing her rise and go out in the middle of the night, were coming to seek her just as the church-bell struck one. The moon had gone down, and the deepest stillness reigned in the cathedral precincts. The next day the cloak, which had slipped from the lady's shoulders in her terrified flight, was found torn into tiny fragments and scattered among the gravestones.

THE TORRE DEL ORO, SPAIN
Edmundo De Amicis

I arrived at a hotel, threw my valise into a *patio*, and went to roam about the city. It seemed to me to be a larger, a more beautiful and an enriched Cordova. The streets are wider, the houses taller, and the *patios* more spacious; but the general appearance of the city is the same. Here is the same spotless whiteness, the same intricate network of small streets, the general odour of oranges, the delightful feeling of mystery and that strange Oriental look that produces in the heart that sweet sentiment of melancholy and in the mind the thousand fancies, desires and visions of a far-away world, a strange life, an unknown people and an earthly paradise full of love, delight and peace. In these streets you read the history of the city: every balcony, fragment of sculpture and solitary cross-road recall the nocturnal adventures of a king, the dreams of a poet, the adventures of a beauty, a love-scene, a duel, an abduction, a fable, and a feast. Here is a reminiscence of Maria de Pedilla, there of Don Pedro, farther away one of Cervantes and elsewhere of Columbus, Saint Theresa, Velasquez and Murillo. A column reminds you of the Roman rule; a tower, the magnificence of the monarchy of Charles V.; an Alcazar recalls the splendours of the Arabian courts. Superb marble palaces stand beside modest white houses; the tiny, winding streets lead to immense squares filled with orange-trees; from lonely and silent cross-streets you emerge, after a sharp turn, into a street filled with a noisy crowd. Wherever you go, through the graceful gratings of the *patios*, you see flowers, statues, fountains, rooms, walls covered with arabesques, Arabian windows and slender columns of precious marble; and at every window and in every garden there are women dressed in white half hidden, like shy nymphs, behind the grapevines and rose-bushes.

Passing from one street to another, at last I come to a promenade on the banks of the Guadalquiver, called the Christina, which bears the same relation to Seville that the Lungarno does to Florence. Here you may enjoy a sight that is simply enchanting.

First I went to the famous Torre del Oro. This tower, called The Golden Tower, was so-named from the fact that in it was placed the gold that the Spanish ships brought from America, or because the King Don Pedro hid his treasures there. Its form is octagonal with three receding storeys, crowned by battlements and washed by the river. According to tradition, this tower was built by the Romans and here the most beautiful favourite of the King dwelt until the tower was joined to the Alcazar by a building that was destroyed to make room for the Christina promenade.

This promenade extends from Torre del Oro to the Duke of Montpensier's palace. It is thickly shaded by oriental plane-trees, oaks, cypresses, willows, poplars, and other northern trees which the Andalusians admire as we should admire the palms and aloes in the fields of Piedmont and Lombardy. A large bridge spans the river and leads to the suburb of Triana from which one sees the first houses on the opposite bank. A long line of ships, *golettas* (a species of light boat) and barks are on the river; and between the Torre del Oro and the Duke's palace there is a constant coming and going of boats. The sun was setting. A crowd of ladies swarmed through the streets, troops of workmen crossed the bridge, the ships showed more signs of life, a band hidden among the trees began to play, the river became rose-coloured, the air was filled with the perfume of flowers, and the sky seemed to be aflame.

Cathedral of Orvieto, Italy
John Addington Symonds

On the road from Siena to Rome, half-way between Ficulle and Viterbo, is the town of Orvieto. Travellers often pass it in the night-time. Few stop there, for the place is old and dirty and its inns are indifferent. But none who see it even from a distance can fail to be struck with its imposing aspect, as it rises from the level plain upon its mass of rock among the Apennines.

Orvieto is built upon the first of those huge volcanic

blocks which are found like fossils, embedded in the more recent geological formations of Central Italy, and which stretch in an irregular but unbroken line to the Campagna of Rome. Many of them, like that on which Civita Castellana is perched, are surrounded by rifts and chasms and fosses, strangely furrowed and twisted by the force of fiery convulsions. But their advanced guard, Orvieto, stands up definite and solid, an almost perfect cube, with walls precipitous to the north and south and east, but slightly sloping to the westward. At its foot rolls the Paglia, one of those barren streams which swell in winter with the snows and rains of the Apennines, but which in summertime shrink up and leave bare beds of sand and pestilential canebrakes to stretch irregularly round their dwindled waters.

The weary flatness and utter desolation of this valley present a sinister contrast to the broad line of the Apennines swelling tier on tier, from their oak-girdled basements set with villages and towers, up to the snow and cloud that crown their topmost crags. The time to see this landscape is at sunrise; and the traveler should take his stand upon the rising ground over which the Roman road is carried from the town—the point, in fact, which Turner has selected for his vague and misty sketch of Orvieto in our Gallery. Thence he will command the whole space of the plain, the Apennines, and the river creeping in a straight line at the base; while the sun, rising to his right, will slant along the mountain flanks and gild the leaden stream, and flood the castled crags of Orvieto with a haze of light. From the centre of this glory stand out in bold relief old bastions built upon the solid tufa, vast gaping gateways black in shadow, towers of churches shooting up above a medley of deep-corniced tall Italian houses, and, amid them all, the marble front of the Cathedral, calm and solemn in its unfamiliar Gothic state. Down to the valley from these heights there is a sudden fall; and we wonder how the few spare olive-trees that grow there can support existence on the steep slope of the cliff.

The great Duomo was erected at the end of the Thirteenth Century to commemorate the Miracle of

Bolsena. The value of this miracle consisted in its establishing unmistakably the truth of transubstantiation. The story runs that a young Bohemian priest who doubted the dogma was performing the office of the mass in a church at Bolsena, when, at the moment of consecration, blood issued from five gushes in the wafer, which resembled the five wounds of Christ. The fact was evident to all the worshippers, who saw blood falling on the linen of the altar; and the young priest no longer doubted, but confessed the miracle, and journeyed straightway with the evidence thereof to Pope Urban IV. The Pope, who was then at Orvieto, came out with all his retinue to meet the convert and do honour to the magic-working relics. The circumstances of this miracle are well known to students of art through Raphael's celebrated fresco in the Stanze of the Vatican. And it will be remembered by the readers of ecclesiastical history that Urban had in 1264 promulgated by a bull the strict observance of the Corpus Christi festival in connection with his strong desire to re-establish the doctrine of Christ's presence in the elements. Nor was it without reason that, while seeking miraculous support for this dogma, he should have treated the affair of Bolsena so seriously as to celebrate it by the erection of one of the most splendid cathedrals in Italy; for the peace of the church had recently been troubled by the reforming ardour of the Fraticelli and by the promulgation of Abbot Joachim's Eternal Gospel. This new evangelist had preached the doctrine of progression in religious faith, proclaiming a Kingdom of the Spirit which should transcend the Kingdom of the Son, even as the Christian dispensation had superseded the Jewish supremacy of the Father. Nor did he fail at the same time to attack the political and moral abuses of the Papacy, attributing its degradation to the want of vitality which pervaded the old Christian system, and calling on the clergy to lead more simple and regenerate lives, consistently with the spiritual doctrine which he had received by inspiration. The theories of Joachim were immature and crude; but they were among the first signs of that liberal effort after self-emancipation which eventually stirred all Europe at the time of the Renaissance. It was, therefore, the obvious policy of the Popes to crush so dangerous an opposition while they could; and by establishing the dogma of transubstantiation, they were enabled to satisfy the growing mysticism of the people, while they placed upon a firmer basis the cardinal support of their own religious power.

In pursuance of his plan, Urban sent for Lorenzo Maitani, the great Sienese architect, who gave designs for a Gothic church in the same style as the Cathedral of Siena, though projected on a smaller scale. Fergusson in his *Handbook of Architecture*, remarks that these two churches are perhaps, taken altogether, the most successful specimens of "Italian pointed Gothic." The Gottico Tedesco had never been received with favour in Italy. Remains of Roman architecture, then far more numerous and perfect than they are at present, controlled the minds of artists, and induced them to adopt the rounded rather than the pointed arch. Indeed, there would seem to be something peculiarly Northern in the spirit of Gothic architecture: its intricacies suit the gloom of Northern skies, its massive exterior is adapted to the severity of Northern weather, its vast windows catch the fleeting sunlight of the North, and the pinnacles and spires which constitute its beauty are better expressed in rugged stone than in the marbles of the South. Northern cathedrals do not depend for their effect upon the advantages of sunlight or picturesque situations. Many of them are built upon broad plains, over which for more than half the year hangs fog. But the cathedrals of Italy owe their charm to colour and brilliancy: their gilded sculpture and mosaics, the variegated marbles and shallow portals of their façades, the light aërial elegance of their campanili, are all adapted to the luminous atmosphere of a smiling land, where changing effects of natural beauty distract the attention from solidity of design and permanence of grandeur in the edifice itself.

The Cathedral of Orvieto will illustrate these remarks. Its design is very simple. It consists of a parallelogram, from which three chapels of equal size project, one at the east end, and one at the north and south. The windows are small and narrow, the columns round, and the roof displays none of that intricate groining we find in English churches. The beauty of the interior depends on surface decoration, on marble statues, woodwork, and fresco-paintings. Outside, there is the same simplicity of design, the same elaborated local ornament. The sides of the Cathedral are austere, their narrow windows cutting horizontal lines of black and white marble. But the façade is a triumph of decorative art. It is strictly what Fergusson has styled a "frontispiece"; for it bears no relation whatever to the construction of the building. Its three gables rise high above the aisles. Its pinnacles and parapets and turrets are stuck on to look agreeable. It is a screen such as might be completed or left unfinished at will by the architect. Finished as it is, the façade of Orvieto is a wilderness of beauties. Its pure white marble has been mellowed by time to a rich golden hue, in which are set mosaics shining like gems or pictures of enamel. A statue stands on every pinnacle; each pillar has a different design; round some of them are woven wreaths of vine and ivy; acanthus leaves curl over the capitals, making nests for singing-birds or Cupids; the doorways are a labyrinth of intricate designs, in which the utmost elegance of form is made more beautiful by incrustations of precious agates and Alexandrine glasswork. On every square inch of this wonderful façade have been lavished invention, skill, and precious material. But its chief interest centres in the sculptures executed by Giovanni and Andrea, sons and pupils of Nicola Pisano. The names of these three men mark an era in the history of art. They first rescued Italian sculpture from the grotesqueness of the Lombard and the monotony of the Byzantine styles. Sculpture takes the lead of all the arts. And Nicola Pisano, before Cimabue, before Duccio, even before Dante, opened the gates of beauty, which for a thousand years had been shut up and overgrown with weeds. As Dante invoked the influence of Virgil when he began to write his mediæval poem, and made a heathen bard his hierophant in Christian mysteries, just so did Nicola Pisano draw inspiration from a Greek sarcophagus, which had been cast upon the shore at Pisa.

He studied the bas-relief of Phædra and Hippolytus, which may still be seen upon the tomb of Countess Beatrice, in the Campo Santo, and so learned by heart the beauty of its lines, and the dignity expressed in its figures, that in all his subsequent works we trace the elevated tranquillity of Greek sculpture. This imitation never degenerated into servile copying; nor, on the other hand, did Nicola attain the perfect grace of an Athenian artist. He remained a truly mediæval carver, animated with a Christian, instead of a Pagan spirit, but caring for the loveliness of form which art in the Dark Ages failed to realize.

Whether it was Nicola or his sons who designed the bas-reliefs at Orvieto is of little consequence. Vasari ascribes them to the father; but we know that he completed his pulpit at Pisa in 1230, and his death is supposed to have taken place fifteen years before the foundation of the Cathedral. At any rate, they are imbued with his genius, and bear the strongest affinity to his sculptures at Pisa, Siena, and Bologna. To estimate the influence they exercised over the arts of sculpture and painting in Italy would be a difficult task. Duccio and Giotto studied here; Ghiberti closely followed them. Signorelli and Raphael made drawings from their compositions. And the spirit which pervades these sculptures may be traced in all succeeding works of art. It is not classic; it is modern, though embodied in a form of beauty modelled on the Greek.

The bas-reliefs are carved on four marble tablets placed beside the porches of the church, and corresponding in size and shape with the chief doorways. They represent the course of Biblical history, beginning with the creation of the world, and ending with the Last Judgment. If it were possible here to compare them in detail with the similar designs of Ghiberti, Michel Angelo, and Raphael, it might be shown that the Pisani established modes of treating sacred subjects from which those mighty masters never deviated, though each stamped upon them his peculiar genius, making them more perfect as time added to the power of art. It would also be not without interest to show that in their primitive conceptions of the earliest events in history, the works of the Pisan artists closely resemble some sculptures executed on the walls of Northern cathedrals, as well as early mosaics in the south of Italy. We might have noticed how all the grotesque elements which appear in Nicola Pisano, and which may still be traced in Ghiberti, are entirely lost in Michel Angelo, how the supernatural is humanized, how the symbolical receives an actual expression, and how intellectual types are substituted for mere local and individual representations. For instance, the Pisani represent the Creator as a young man, standing on the earth, with a benign and dignified expression, and attended by two ministering angels. He is the Christ of the Creed, "by whom all things were made." In Ghiberti we find an older man, sometimes appearing in a whirlwind of clouds and attendant spirits, sometimes walking on the earth, but still far different in conception from the Creative Father of Michel Angelo. The latter is rather the Platonic Demiurgus than the Mosaic God. By every line and feature of his face and flowing hair, by each movement of his limbs, whether he ride on clouds between the waters and the firmament, or stand alone creating by a glance and by a motion of his hand Eve, the full-formed and conscious woman, he is proclaimed the Maker who from all eternity has held the thought of the material universe within his mind. Raphael does not depart from this conception. The profound abstraction of Michel Angelo ruled his intellect, and received from his genius a form of perhaps greater grace. A similar growth from the germinal designs of the Pisani may be traced in many groups.

But we must not linger at the gate. Let us enter the Cathedral and see some of the wonders it contains. Statues of gigantic size adorn the nave. Of these the most beautiful are the work of Ippolito Scalza, an artist whom Orvieto claims with pride as one of her own sons. The long line of saints and apostles whom they represent, conduct us to the high altar surrounded by its shadowy frescoes, and gleaming with the work of carvers in marble and bronze and precious metals. But our steps are drawn towards the chapel of the south transept, where now a golden light from the autumnal sunset falls across a crowd of worshippers. From far and near the poor people are gathered. Most of them are women. They kneel upon the pavement and the benches, sunburnt faces from the vineyards and the canebrakes of the valley. The old look prematurely aged and withered—their wrinkled cheeks bound up in scarlet and orange-coloured kerchiefs, their skinny fingers fumbling on the rosary, and their mute lips moving in prayer. The younger women have great listless eyes and large limbs used to labour. Some of them carry babies trussed up in tight swaddling-clothes. One kneels beside a dark-browed shepherd, on whose shoulder falls his shaggy hair; and little children play about, half-hushed, half heedless of the place, among old men whose life has dwindled down into a ceaseless round of prayers. We wonder why this chapel alone in the empty Cathedral, is so crowded with worshippers. They surely are not turned towards that splendid Pietà of Scalza—a work in which the marble seems to live a cold, dead, shivering life. They do not heed Angelico's and Signorelli's frescoes on the roof and walls. The interchange of light and gloom upon the stalls and carved work of the canopies can scarcely rivet so intense a gaze. All eyes seem fixed upon a curtain of red silk above the altar. Votive pictures and glass cases full of silver hearts, wax babies, hands and limbs of every kind, are hung around it. A bell rings. A jingling organ plays a little melody in triple time; and from the sacristy comes forth the priest. With much reverence, and with a show of preparation, he and the acolytes around him mount the altar steps, and pull a string which draws the curtain. Behind the curtain we behold Madonna and her child—a faint, old, ugly picture, blackened with the smoke and incense of five hundred years, a wonder-working image, cased in gold, and guarded from the common air by glass and draperies. Jewelled crowns are stuck upon the heads of the mother and the infant. In the efficacy of Madonna di San Brizio to ward off agues, to deliver from the pangs of childbirth or the fury of the storm, to keep the lover's troth and make the husband faithful to his home, these pious women of the marshes and the mountains put a simple trust.

While the priest sings, and the people pray to the dance-music of the organ, let us take a quiet seat unseen, and picture to our minds how the chapel looked when Angelico and Signorelli stood before its plastered walls, and thought the thoughts with which they covered them. Four centuries have gone by since those walls were white and even to their brushes; and now you scarce can see the golden aureoles of saints, the vast wings of the angels, and the flowing robes of prophets through the gloom. Angelico came first, in monk's dress, kneeling before he climbed the scaffold to paint the angry Judge, the Virgin crowned, the white-robed army of the Martyrs, and the glorious company of the Apostles. These he placed upon the roof, expectant of the Judgment. Then he passed away, and Luca Signorelli, the rich man who "lived splendidly and loved to dress himself in noble clothes," the liberal and courteous gentleman, took his place upon the scaffold. For all the worldliness of his attire and the delicacy of his living, his brain teemed with stern and terrible thoughts. He searched the secrets of sin and of the grave, of destruction and of resurrection, of heaven and hell. All these he has painted on the walls beneath the saints of Fra Angelico. First come the troubles of the last days, the preaching of Antichrist, and the confusion of the wicked. In the next compartment we see the Resurrection from the tomb; and side by side with that is painted Hell. Paradise occupies another portion of the chapel.

After viewing these frescoes, we muse and ask ourselves why Signorelli's fame is so inadequate to his deserts? Partly, no doubt because he painted in obscure Italian towns, and left few easel pictures. Besides the artists of the Sixteenth Century eclipsed all their predecessors, and the name of Signorelli has been swallowed up in that of Michel Angelo. Vasari said that "*esso Michel Angelo imitò l'andar di Luca, come può vedere ognuno.*" Nor is it hard to see that what the one began at Orvieto the other completed in the Vatican. These great men had truly kindred spirits. Both struggled to express their intellectual conceptions in the simplest and most abstract forms. The works of both are distinguished by contempt for adventitious ornaments and for the grace of positive colour. Both chose to work in fresco, and selected subjects of the gravest and most elevated character. The study of anatomy, and the correct drawing of the naked body, which Luca practised, were carried to perfection by Michel Angelo. Sublimity of thought and self-restraint pervade their compositions. He who would understand Buonarotti must first appreciate Signorelli. The latter, it is true, was confined to a narrower circle in his study of the beautiful and the sublime. He had not ascended to that pure idealism superior to all the accidents of place and time, which is the chief distinction of Michel Angelo's work. At the same time, his manner had not suffered from too close a study of the antique. He painted the life he saw around him, and clothed his men and women in the dress of Italy.

Such reflections, and many more, pass through our mind as we sit and ponder in the chapel, which the daylight has deserted. The country-people are still on their knees, still careless of the frescoed forms around them, still praying to the Madonna of the Miracles. The service is well-nigh done. The benediction has been given, the organist strikes up his air of Verdi, and the congregation shuffles off, leaving the dimly-lighted chapel for the vast sonorous dusky nave. How strange it is to hear that faint strain of a feeble opera sounding where a short while since, the trumpet-blast of Signorelli's angels seemed to thrill our ears!

The Pearl Mosque, India

THE BUILDINGS OF SHAH JEHAN
G. W. Steevens

The north-eastern approach to Agra is through a waste of land at the same time flat and broken. Formless hillocks and ditches, colourless sand and dead turf, the whole scene was mean and depressing. I raised my eyes, and there, on the edge of the ugly prairie, sat a fair white palace with domes and minarets. So exquisite in symmetry, so softly lustrous in tint, it could hardly be substantial, and I all but cried, "Mirage!" It was the Taj Mahal.

And now we were clanking over an iron bridge above a dark-green river that filled barely a quarter of its sandy bed; deep, broad staircases stepped down to its further bank with pillared pleasure-houses overlooking them. Now on the right rose a great mosque, its bellying domes zig-zagged with red and white; dawn from the left frowned the weather-worn battlements of a great red fortress. This was the city of Shah Jehan, emperor and devotee, artist and lover.

And this, in a few words, is the passionate story of

Shah Jehan. He was the grandson of Akbar the Great, the first Mogul Emperor of Hindustan. While yet Prince Royal, conquering India for the Moguls, he married the beautiful Persian, Arjmand Banu, called Mumtaz-i-Mahal, the chosen of the palace, and loved her tenderly beyond all his wives for fourteen years. But only a year after he became Sultan she died in travail of her eighth child. Shah Jehan in his grief swore that she should have the loveliest tomb the world ever beheld, and for seventeen years he built the Taj Mahal. Also he built the palace of Agra, the fort and palace of Delhi, and the great mosque of Agra; he took to wife many fair ladies, and lived in all luxuriousness, ministering abundantly to every sense, till he had reigned thirty years. Then his son Aurungzebe rose up and dethroned him, and kept him a close prisoner in his own private mosque, which he had built within the palace of Agra. There he lived seven years more, attended by his daughter Jehanara, who would not leave him, till at last, in 1645, being grown very feeble, he begged to be laid in a chamber of the palace wherefrom he could see the Taj Mahal. This was granted him, so that he died with his eyes upon the tomb of the love of his youth. There they buried him beside her. And his daughter, when her time came, wrote a Persian stanza begging that no monument should be set up to "the humble transitory Jehanara," and praying only for her father's soul.

Agra is the mirror of Shah Jehan. In the fort and palace you can read all the story of the warrior and the lover—in the fort so nakedly grim without and the palace so richly voluptuous within. Under the brow of the sheer sandstone walls you are dwarfed to a pigmy. Before and beneath the great gateway stands a double curtain of loophole and machicolation and tower: you go in through cavernous guard-houses, up a ramp between sky-closing walls. Only thus do you reach the real entrance—the great Elephant Gate—two jutting octagon towers supporting spacious chambers thrown across the passage. On the lower storey all is closed, and only white plaster designs relieve the savage masses of the sandstone; in the upper balconies are windows and recesses, all decked with white, and above all runs a gallery crowned with cupolas.

Under this arch you go, a dome above, deep and lofty recesses on either hand; now you are past the sternness. Shah Jehan is soldier no longer but artist and amorist at large. You come to the Pearl Mosque. There is a Pearl Mosque at Delhi, sandstone slabs without, marble within, as this is; but the Delhi mosque is a bauble to this. This is a broad court, paved with slabs of marble, veined with white and blue, gray and yellow. This is all marble—marble walls with moulded panels, marble cloisters of multifoliate arches, marble gateways breaking three walls of the square, marble columns supporting bell-cupolas above them and at each corner, a marble basin in the centre of the court, a marble sundial beside it. Along the west side of the court shines the glorious face of the mosque itself—only a roofed quarter of the whole space, a mere portico, but colonnaded with three rows of seven pillars apiece, each branching to right and left, to front and back, with eight-pointed, nine-leaved arches. Along the entablature above runs a Persian inscription in mosaic of black marble; on the roof, over each pillar of the front row is a cupola with four columns, and at each corner a cupola with eight columns. Three domes fold their broad white wings behind and above all.

Three steps for the mullah to preach from, and that is all the catalogue. No altar or shrine or image: there is no god but God. No carving or lattice-work: but the simple pillars and arches, the few cupolas and domes, are yet the richest of ornamentation. No paint or gems—only the clear harmonious veining of the marble. Only space and proportion, form and whispers of colour—and it is so beautiful that you can hardly breathe for rapture. The radiant marble ripples from shade to shade—snow-white, pearl-white, ivory-white—till it seems half alive. The bells and pinnacles are so light that they seem to float in the air. It cannot be a building, you whisper: it is enchantment.

But now go on to the palace. It has been battered and sacked—the Jats of Bhurtpur carried away the precious stones from the walls; but through the restorations you can dream of some of its delights when it held the houris of Shah Jehan. Dream this and it is all enchantment; you have arrived at last—at last, after so many years, after so many leagues—in the dear country of your earliest dreams, and the Arabian nights are come to life. Under this pillared hall the ambassadors of Shiraz and Samarkand are making their obeisance and displaying rich gifts. Above, in the marble alcove festooned with flowers and tendrils in pietra dura, reclines the Sultan of the Indies on a couch of white marble. Up the stairs—and here, enclosed by a colonnade of two storeys, is the fish-pond; on the upper terrace under that canopy, which is one block of creamy marble embossed with flowers, sits the lovely favourite Schemselnihar, and makes believe to angle. She rises and follows the other lights of the harem into the little square court and portico that miniature the great Pearl Mosque without. But some of the beauties turn aside to the gallery, where, below, is an enclosed bazaar; handsome young merchants of Baghdad tempt them with silks and brocades—and with looks that sigh and languish. They had best be prudent: eyes as fathomless as theirs have grown dim in the dungeons under the terraces, below the water. From lust to cruelty is only a step; and when the Sultan raised the marble and the gems he sank the dungeon, remote in a labyrinth of tunnels. Across it is a beam with a noose for soft necks and a shoot for frail bodies that tumbles them into the Jumna.

The Sultan has risen from his audience: he walks round the terrace, through the delicious Hall of Private Audience, whose walls are marble, whose pillars are festooned with creepers in agate and jasper, jade and cornelian, whose ends are profound and graceful recesses, half-arch, half-dome. He passes to the heavy slab of the black marble throne on the riverside brink of the quadrangle; in the pit below they let out buffaloes and tigers to fight before him; on the white seat behind him sits the court jester to make him merry.

And now—it is the full moon that rises from an arch of the pavilion to the right—the full moon, though it is still broad day? It is the Sultaness-in-Chief looking out at the fight from her abode in the Jasmine Tower. She has grown tired of throwing the dice, while her handmaidens stand for pieces on the pachisi-board that is let into her marble pavement—there, behind those duenna screens, the gauze of lattice-work that encloses her courtyard. She has grown tired of dabbling in the fountain that tinkles on the shallow basin of figured marble, weary of her bower of marble inlaid with gems. The Sultan rises, and it is the signal for the bath—the bath in the dark Mirror Palace, lighted with a score of flambeaux and walled with a million tiny mirrors, that reflect.... No; we must not think of it—nor of the feast in the Private Palace, under the ceiling emblazoned with blue and crimson and gold—nor yet of the disrobing in the Golden Pavilion, where the ladies thrust their jewels into holes in the wall too narrow for a man's arm to follow them.... No; you should not listen to what the Jester is saying now.

But if you envy Shah Jehan, look again later into the tiny Gem Mosque and the cupboard at the side, too small to turn in, where he is the uncrowned prisoner of his son. No Mirror Palace now; the ceiling is black where they heat the water for his bath, in a hole of a cistern where he cannot stretch out his limbs. Look again into the little gilt-domed cupola, where he lies dying, and Jehanara's voice sounds suddenly far away; and the very Taj, though he knows every angle and curve of it, swims in a grey-white blur; and nothing is left clear save the voice and face of the beautiful Persian, Arjmand Banu, whose palankeen followed all his campaigns in the days when empire was still a-winning, whose children called him father—Arjmand Banu, silent and unseen now for four-and-thirty years, the wife of his youth.

Now follow him to the Taj. Under the great gateway of strong sandstone ribbed with delicate marble, its vaulted red arch cobwebbed with white threads, and then before you—then the miracle of miracles, the final wonder of the world. In chaste majesty it stands suddenly before you, as if the magical word had called it this moment out of the earth. On a white marble platform it stands exactly four-square, but that the angles are cut off; nothing so rude as a corner could find place in its soft harmonies. Seen through the avenue, it looks high rather than broad; seen from the pavement below it, it looks broad rather than high; you doubt, then conclude that its proportions are perfect. Above its centre rises a full white dome, at each corner of whose base nestles a smaller dome, upheld on eight arches. The centre of each face is a lofty-headed gateway rising above the line of the roof; within it is again a pointed caving recess, half arch, half dome; within this, again, a screen of latticed marble. On each flank of these, and on the facets of the cut-off angles, are pairs of smaller, blind recesses of the same design, one above the other. From each junction of facets rises a slim pinnacle. Everywhere it is embellished with elaborate profusion. Moulding, sculpture, inlaid frets and scrolls of coloured marbles, twining branches and garlands of jade and agate and cornelian—here is every point of lavish splendour you saw in the palace combined in one supreme embodiment—superb dignity matched with graceful richness.

But it is vain to flounder amid epithets; the man who should describe the Taj must own genius equal to his who built it. Description halts between its mass and its fineness. It makes you giddy to look up at it, yet it is so delicate you feel that a brick would lay it in shivers at your feet. It is a rock temple and a Chinese casket together—a giant gem.

Nothing jars; for if the jewel were away the setting would still be among the noblest monuments on earth. The minarets at the four corners of the platform are a moment's stumbling-block: they look irreverently like the military masts of a battleship, and the hard lines where the stones join remind you of a London subway. But look at the Taj itself, and the minarets fall instantly into place; they set off its glories, and, standing like acolytes, seem to be challenging you not to worship it. At each side, below the Taj, is a triple-domed building of sandstone and marble; the hot red throws up the pearl-and-ivory softness of the Taj. The cloisters round the garden, the lordly caravanserai outside the gate, the clustering domes and mosaic texts from the Koran on the great gate itself—all this you hardly notice; but when you do, you find that every point is perfection. As for the garden, with shady trees of every hue, from sprightly yellow to funereal cypress, with purple blossoms cascading from the topmost boughs, with roses and lilies, phloxes and carnations—and the channel of clear water with twenty fountains that runs through the garden, and the basin with the goldfish.... It is pure Arabian Nights! You listen for the speaking bird and the singing tree. And was it not hither that Prince Ahmed, leaving his brother Ali to cuddle Nuronnihar in the palace, followed his arrow? And is not that the fairy Peri-Banu coming out of the pleasure-house to welcome him? Surely man never made such a Paradise: it must be the fabric of a dream wafted through gates of silver and opal.

O Shah Jehan, Shah Jehan, you are bewitching a respectable newspaper-correspondent. The thought of you is strong wine. Shah Jehan, with your queens and concubines without number, their amber feet mirrored in marble, their ivory limbs mirrored in quicksilver; Shah Jehan, who starved them in the black oubliettes, and hung them from the mouldy beam, and sluiced their beautiful bodies into the cold river; Shah Jehan, with elephants and peacocks; Shah Jehan, returning from the conquered Dekhan, dismounting in the Armoury Square, hastening through the Grape Garden, hastening past the fair ones in the Golden Pavilion to the fairest within the Jasmine Tower!

Shah Jehan—Grape Garden—Golden Pavilion—Jasmine Tower—there is dizzy magic in the very names. And when I turn aside in your garden, shunning your fierce black-and-scarlet petals to bring back my senses with English stocks and pansies, the sight of your Taj through the trees sends my brain areel again. I go in and stand by your tomb. The jewel-creepers blossom more luxuriantly than ever in the trellised screen that encloses it, and the two oblong cenotaphs are embowered in gems. But here it is dark and cool: light comes in only through double lattices of feathery marble. You look up into a dome, obscure and mysterious, but mightily expansive, as it were the vault of the heaven of the dead. It is very well; it is the fit close. In this breathless twilight, after his battles and buildings, his ecstasies and torments, his love and his loss, Shah Jehan has come to his own again for ever.

THE PRIORY AND CHURCH OF ST. BARTHOLOMEW, ENGLAND
Charles Knight

Of all the persons whom the mighty business of providing sustenance for the population of London leads among the pens, and crowds, and filth of the great Metropolitan beast-market—of all those whom pleasure attracts to the gingerbread and shows, and gong-resounding din of the great Fair—or, lastly, of all those whom chance, or a dim remembrance of the popular memories of the place, its burnings, tournaments, etc., or any other motive, brings into Smithfield—we wonder how many, as they pass the south-western corner of the area, look through the ancient gateway which leads up to the still more ancient church of St. Bartholomew, with a kindly remembrance of the man (whose ashes there repose) from whom these, and most of the other interesting features and recollections of Smithfield, are directly or indirectly derived? We fear very few. Time has wrought strange changes in the scene around; and it is not at all surprising that we should forget what has ceased to be readily visible. Who could suppose, from a mere hasty glance at the comparatively mean-looking brick tower, and the narrow restricted site of St. Bartholomew, that that very edifice was once the centre only, of the splendid church of a splendid monastery—a church which extended its spacious transepts on either side, and sent up a noble tower high up into the air, to overlook, and, as it were, to guard, the stately halls, far-extending cloisters, and delightful gardens that surrounded the sacred edifice? Or, again, who would suspect that the site of this extensive establishment (now in a great measure covered with houses), and most probably the entire space of Smithfield, was, prior to the foundation of the former, nothing but a marsh "dunge and fenny," with the exception of a solitary spot of dry land, occupied by the travelers' token of civilization, a gallows? Yet such are the changes that have taken place, and for all that is valuable in them our gratitude is due to the one man to whom we have referred—Rahere.

The history of the Priory is indeed the history of this singular individual; and, by a fortunate coincidence, the historical materials we possess are as ample as they are important. Among the manuscripts of the British Museum is one entirely devoted to the life, character, and doings of Rahere, written evidently shortly after his death by a monk of the establishment, and which, for the details it also gives of the circumstances attending the establishment of a great religious house in the Twelfth Century, its glimpses into the manners and customs, the modes of thought and feeling of the time—and, above all, for its marked superiority of style to the writings that then generally issued from the cloister—forms one of the most extraordinary, as it certainly is one of the most interesting, of monastical documents.

Rahere, it appears, was a "man sprung and born from low *kynage*: when he attained the flower of youth, he began to haunt the households of noblemen and the palaces of princes; where under every elbow of them, he spread their cushions with japes and flatterings, delectably anointing their eyes, by this manner to draw to him their friendships. And he still was not content with this, but often haunted the King's palace, and among the noiseful press of that tumultuous court informed himself with polity and cardinal suavity, by the which he might draw to him the hearts of many a one. There in spectacles, in meetings, in plays, and other courtly mockeries and trifles intruding, he led forth the business of all the day. This wise to the King and great men, gentle and courteous known, familiar and fellowly he was." The King here referred to is Henry I. Stow says Rahere was "a pleasant-witted gentleman; and therefore in his time called the *king's minstrel*." To continue: "This manner of living he chose in his beginning, and in this excused his youth. But the *inward Seer* and merciful God of all, the which out of Mary Magdalen cast out seven fiends, the which to the Fisher gave the Keys of Heaven, mercifully converted this man from the error of his way, and added to him so many gifts of virtue." Foremost in repentance as he had been in sin, Rahere now "decreed himself to go to the court of Rome, coveting in so great a labour to do the works of penance. And while he tarried there, in that meanwhile, he began to be vexed with grievous sickness; and his dolours little and little taking their increase, he drew to the extreme of life. He avowed that if health God would him grant, that he might return to his country, he would make an hospital in recreation of poor men, and to them there so gathered, necessaries minister after his power." And not long after the benign and merciful Lord beheld this weeping man, gave him his health, approved his vow.

When he would perfect his way that he had begun, in a certain night he saw a vision full of dread and sweetness. It seemed to him to be borne up on high of a certain beast, having four feet and two wings, and set him in a high place. To whom appeared a certain man, pretending in cheer the majesty of a king, of great beauty and imperial authority, and his eye on him fastened. "O man," he said, "what and how much service shouldest thou give to him that in so great a peril hath brought help to thee?" Anon he answered to this saint, "Whatsoever might be of heart and of might diligently should I give in recompence to my deliverer." And then, said he, "I am Bartholomew, the apostle of Jesus Christ, that come to succour thee in thine anguish and to open to thee the secret mysteries of Heaven. Know me truly, by the will and commandment of the Holy Trinity *and the common favour of the celestial court and council*, to have chosen a place in the suburbs of London, at Smithfield, where in my name thou shalt found a church."

A man like this could not but succeed in whatever he essayed; and accordingly the work "prosperously succeeded, and after the Apostle's word all necessaries flowed unto the hand. The church he made of comely stonework, tablewise. And an hospital-house, a little longer off from the church by himself he began to edify. The church was founded (as we have taken of our elders) in the month of March, 1113. President in the Church of England, William, Archbishop of Canterbury, and Richard, Bishop of London;" who "of due law and right," hallowed a part of the adjoining field as a cemetery. "Clerks to live under regular institution were brought together, and Rahere, of course, was appointed Prior, who ministered unto his fellows necessaries, not of certain rents, but plenteously of oblations of faithful people." The completion of the work, under such circumstances, evidently excited a large amount of wonder and admiration, not unmixed with a kind of superstitious awe. In 1410, during the prelacy perhaps of brother John the Priory was rebuilt. At this time, and perhaps before, it possessed within itself every possible convenience for the solace and comfort of its inmates. We read of Le Fermery, Le Dorter, Le Frater, Les Cloysters, Les Galleries, Le Hall, Le Kitchen, Le Buttry, Le Pantry, Le olde Kitchen, Le Woodehouse, Le Garnier, and Le Prior's Stable, so late as the period of the dissolution in the Sixteenth Century. There was also the Prior's house, the Mulberry-garden, the Chapel now the Church of St. Bartholomew the Less, etc., etc. It was entirely enclosed within walls, the boundaries of which have been carefully traced in the *Londini Illustrata*, and for which we abbreviate the following description:—The north wall ran from Smithfield, along the south side of Long Lane, to its junction with the east wall, about thirty yards west from Aldersgate Street. It is mentioned by Stow, and shown in Aggas' plan, who represents a small gate or postern in it. This gate stood immediately opposite Charter House Lane, where is now the entrance into King Street or Cloth Fair. The west wall commenced at the south-west corner of Long Lane, and continued along Smithfield, and the middle of Duc Lane (or Duke Street) to the south gate, or Great Gate House, now the principal entrance into Bartholomew Close. The south wall, commencing from this gate, ran eastward in a direct line towards Aldersgate Street, where it formed an angle and passed southward about forty yards, enclosing the site of the present Alboin Buildings, then resumed its eastern direction and joined the corner of the eastern wall, which ran parallel with Aldersgate Street, at the distance of about twenty-six yards. This wall was fronted for the most part by houses in the street just mentioned, some of them large and magnificent, particularly London House, between which and the wall was a ditch. At first there were no houses in the immediate neighbourhood; but the establishment of the monastery, and the fair granted to it, speedily caused a considerable population to spring up all around, and ultimately within. This grant was obtained from Henry II. The fair was to be kept at Bartholomew tide for three days, namely, the eve, the next day, and the morrow; and unto it "the clothiers of England and the drapers of London repaired, and had their booths and standings within the churchyard of this priory, closed in with walls and gates, locked every night and watched, for safety of men's goods and wares." A Court of Pie-powders sat daily during the fair holden for debts and contracts.

Although the present church, which was the choir of the more ancient structure belonging to the Priory, stands some distance backwards from Smithfield, there is little doubt that its front was originally on a line with the small gateway yet remaining, and that the latter indeed was the entrance from Smithfield into the southern aisle of the nave, the part of the church now entirely lost. It is useless to inquire what kind of front was here presented to the open area before it; but if we may judge of it by this gateway, and by the general style of the interior parts of the choir, it must have been a grand work. The gateway is of a very beautiful character, with a finely pointed arch, consisting of four ribs, each with numerous mouldings, receding one within the other, and decorated with roses and zigzag ornaments. Straight before us as we pass through this gateway are the churchyard and church, the former having around it a range of large and very dingy-looking lath-and-plaster houses, which, however, derive somewhat of a picturesque appearance from their gable ends, and their windows scattered about in "most admired disorder." The exterior of the church, as it here appears to us, consists of a brick tower, erected in 1628, and by its side the end of the church, from which the nave has been cut away, and the wall and large window erected to terminate the structure at this point. The foundations of the nave still lie below the soil of the churchyard some three or four feet. The wall of the latter, on the right or southern side, now faced with brick, is very ancient and of immense thickness, and forming most probably the original wall of the south aisle. On stepping into the apartments of the adjoining public-house, to which the wall now belongs, we find traces of a past very different from what we see at present. Rooms with arched ceilings, a cornice with a shield extending through two or three of them, and thus showing that they have formed but one room, and a chalk cellar below the house—all betoken that we are wandering among the ruins of the old Priory. By the side of this house is a yard, filled with costermongers and their donkeys, and surrounded by black and decayed sheds and habitations, with balconied galleries.

Entering the church by the gateway below the tower, we get the first glimpse of the new world as it were that opens upon us, or rather we should say the old world of seven hundred years ago that has passed away. Everything is solemn, grand, and apparently eternal. Those immense pillars that we look upon have lost nothing as yet of their original strength; there is no token that they will ever lose it. Within the porch are the remains of a very elegant pointed arch in the right wall, leading we presume into the cloisters, but of an older date than those glorious Norman pillars to which some, of as peculiarly slender make, belonging to another and opposite arch, appear to have been attached, somewhat we think to the injury of their simple character. One of the most interesting features of the choir is the long-continued aisle, or series of aisles, which entirely encircle it, opening into the former by the spaces between the flat and circular arch-piers of the body of the structure. It is about twelve feet wide, with a pure arched and vaulted ceiling in the simplest and truest Norman style, with windows of different sizes slightly pointed. The pillars against the wall opposite the entrance into the choir are flat. One of the most beautiful little architectural effects of a simple kind that we can conceive is to be found at the north-eastern corner of the aisle. Between two of the grand Norman pillars projecting from the wall is a low postern doorway; and above, rising on each side from the capitals, a peculiarly elegant arch, something like an elongated horse-shoe. The connexion between two styles so strikingly different in most respects as the Moorish, with its fantastic delicacy and variety and richness, and the Norman with its simple (occasionally uncouth) grandeur, was never more apparent. That little picture is alone worth a visit to St. Bartholomew's.

Let us now enter the Choir, and, ascending the gallery to the side of the organ, gaze on the impressive and characteristic work before us, which seems scarcely less fresh and solid than when Rahere beheld in its vast piers and beautiful arches the realization of the vision for which he had so long yearned. We are standing in the centre of four arches of the most magnificent span, fit bearers of the great tower that they lifted so airily, as it were a thing of nought, into the air. Two of these are round and two slightly pointed. The last (which were originally open and formed the commencement of the transepts) have been referred to as among the various instances of the occasional use of pointed arches by the Normans before their systematic introduction as a style. In each of the spandrels formed by these arches is a small lozenge-shaped panel containing ornaments which bear a striking resemblance to the Grecian honeysuckle, and deserve notice from their singularity. Behind us are arches showing the original continuation of the church into the nave. The roof is very ancient, and not particularly handsome looking. It consists of massy timbers, some of them braced up in the middle, apparently to prevent their falling. Prior Bolton's elegant oriel window in the second story appears to have been built as a kind of pew or seat, from which the Prior could overlook the canons when he pleased, without their being aware of his presence, as it communicated with his house at the eastern extremity of the church. The piers which support the range of pointed arches forming the uppermost story are pierced longitudinally, so as to leave open a passage all round the upper part of the building. The dimensions of the church are stated somewhat differently by different writers, and we have no means of reconciling the discrepancy. According to Malcolm, the height is about forty feet, the breadth sixty feet, and the length one hundred and thirty-eight feet; to which if we add eighty-seven feet for the length of the nave, we have two hundred and twenty-five feet as the entire length of the Priory church within the walls. Osborne, in his *English Architecture*, gives the height as forty-seven feet, the breadth fifty-seven feet, and the length of the present church one hundred and thirty-two feet. We may here observe that when the fire broke out in 1830, the interior of the church was much injured, and the entire pile had a narrow escape from destruction.

Lastly, and as we began, so should we end, with Rahere, who is the presiding spirit of the place, we find the monument of the founder in the north-eastern corner, almost immediately opposite the beautiful oriel window which Prior Bolton there erected, in order, perhaps that when he sat in it the home of the ashes of his illustrious predecessor might be forever before him. This is a work in every way worthy of the man whom it enshrines. It is one of the most elegant specimens of the pointed style of architecture, consisting mainly of a very highly wrought stonework screen, enclosing a tomb on which Rahere's effigy extends at full length. The roof of the little chamber, as we may call it, is most exquisitely groined. At what period the monument was erected is uncertain; but the style marks it as of a later date than that of the founder's decease. But it was most carefully restored by Bolton; and the fact is significant of its antiquity. As the latter found, no doubt, a labour of love in making these reparations, so Time itself seems to have seconded his efforts, and to have shared in the hopes of its builders that a long period of prosperity should be granted to it, by touching it very gently. Here and there the pinnacles have been somewhat diminished of their fair proportions, and that is pretty well the entire extent of the injury the work has experienced. The monument, it must be added, is richly painted as well as sculptured, and shows us the black robes of Rahere and of the monks who are kneeling at his side—the ruddy features of the former, and the splendid coats-of-arms on the front of the tomb below. Each of the monks has a Bible before him, open at the fifty-first chapter of Isaiah. And often and often, no doubt, has Rahere, as he read such verses as that (the third) we are about to transcribe, received fresh accession of strength to complete his arduous task, until what he had first looked upon as holy words of encouragement only became to his rapt fancy a prophecy which he was chosen to fulfil. When others spoke of the all but impossible task (for such it was generally esteemed) he had undertaken, of cleaning and building upon the extensive marsh allotted, he smiled in his heart to think what One had said greater than they:—"The Lord shall comfort Zion: he will comfort all her waste places; and he will make her wilderness like Eden, and her desert like the garden of the Lord; joy and gladness shall be found therein, thanksgiving and the voice of melody."

KUTB MINAR, INDIA
G. W. Steevens

Delhi is still seamed with the scars of her spoilers, and still jewelled with remnants of the gems they fought for. If you take them in order, you will go first, not into the city, but eleven miles south, to the tower Kutb Minar. Through the dust of the road, rising out of the springing wheat, among the mud-and-mat huts before which squat the brown-limbed peasants, you see the country a litter of broken walls, tumbling towers, rent domes. There are fragments of seven cities built by seven kings before the present Delhi was. Eleven miles of them bring you to the tower and mosque of Kutb.

Kutb-ed-Din was a slave who raised himself to Viceroy of Delhi when the Mussulmans took it, then to Emperor of Hindustan and founder of a dynasty. Whether he or his son or the last of the Hindu kings built the tower, antiquaries are undecided and others careless. It is enough that here is one landmark in Delhi's history, one splendid monument reared for a symbol of triumph by a victor whom now nobody can certainly identify. It is a colossal, five-storied tower, two hundred and forty feet high, of nearly fifty feet diameter at the base, and tapering to nine feet at the top. Tiny balconies with balustrades mark the junctions of the stories: the three lower are red stone, the two upper—dwarfed just under the sky—faced with white marble. All the red part is fluted into alternate semicircles and right angles, netted all over with tracery, and belted with inscriptions under the balconies. But the details strike you little: the vertical lines of the fluting only give the impression that this is one huge pillar with a red shaft and a white capital—a pillar that might form part of the most tremendous temple in the world, yet stands quite seemly alone by reason of its surpassing bigness.

Pant to the top. It will do you good, though the view is nothing. The country is an infinite green-and-brown chess-board of young corn and fallow, dead-flat on every side, ugly with the complacent plainness of all very rich country. Beyond the sheeny ribbon of the Jumna, north, south, east, west, into the blurred horizon, you can see only land and land and land—a million acres with nothing on them to see—except the wealth of India and the secret of the greatness of Delhi.

Then look down past your toes and you will see the evidence of some of Delhi's falls. From the ground you will have noticed ruins about you; but there the Kutb Minar dwarfs everything. Now you see that you stand above a field of broken arches, solitary pillars, stumps of towers, and in the middle of what must once have been a town of mosques and tombs. Before it was that, it was a town of Hindu temples and palaces. In the court of the ruined mosque stands a solid wrought-iron pillar—little enough to look at, but curious, because it is at least fifteen hundred years old, and there is nothing else quite like it in the world. It bears a Sanskrit inscription to the effect that this is "the Arm of Fame of Raja Dhava, who conquered his neighbours and won the undivided sovereignty of the earth."

Poor Raja Dhava! The temples of generations that had already forgotten him are swept utterly away; the mosque of their conquerors stands now only as a few shattered red arches and pillars with defaced flowers wilting on them. Beyond that is the base of what was once to be a tower more than twice as high as the Kutb Minar, but was never even finished. The very tower you stand on has been buffeted by earthquake, and great part of it is mere restoration. And Delhi, which in the year One stood here, has drifted away almost out of sight from the summit and left these forlorn fragments to decay without even the consolation of neighbourhood.

Kutb Minar
André Chévrillon

I take a carriage to visit the Kutb Minar, the great tower that rears itself up about ten miles from Delhi.

This is Asia's Appian Way. Ruins from every century, left by three races and three religions, are scattered over a large and dismal plain. The remains of ancient Hindu Delhi, of Afghan Delhi, and of Mogul Delhi, cover a dead expanse of seventy square miles. Slowly, during the flow of centuries, the city has changed its site, as a river changes its bed. As far as the eye can reach, dilapidated domes and broken columns reveal themselves in the midst of the dry brushwood. These yellowish hillocks are the ruins of Indra-Partha, the city of Indra, for which the five brothers of Mahabarata fought three thousand years ago. Farther away a granite pillar, covered with Pali characters, proclaims the edicts of the Buddhist King Asoka. Everywhere, like tombs in a cemetery, the *débris* of Mongolian art, monumental mausoleums and domes surrounded by kiosks are heaped together, all corroded by time and merged into the uniform tint of the sad and dry vegetation that Nature provides. Several tombs are as large as those of Akbar at Secundra and rise up solitary upon the arid steppe. The blue peacocks that are roaming about are the only living things that haunt the place. Generations have swarmed here and of their living past this almost imperceptible residue is all that is left, just as ancient forests have had to exist in order to make a little piece of coal. The Vedic age, the Brahmanical age, the Buddhist age, the first Mussulman dynasties, the Mogul Empire,—each historical period has left here a small deposit.

You can gather this history around the Kutb: four old

Hindu forts, still quite recognizable, once surrounded a large city and some Buddhist temples where the monks in yellow robes with shaven heads walked about peacefully; there remains a large iron post charged with some Sanskrit inscriptions. About the year 1000, over the wall of the Himalayas overflowed the first hordes of the Mussulmans. The city was razed and from the stones of the great temple a mosque was built, the ruins of which now lie around us. Here is a triple colonnade where you recognize the old Buddhist pillars, and the patient, complicated, confused work of the poor Hindu workman, with all of its childish indecency. They are deeply worked, overcharged with chisellings that time has made almost illegible; here and there, figures of a symbolical obscenity appear, a few mutilated by the moral superiority of the conqueror. Little by little, you accustom yourself to read what the eaten away stone has to say, the lines form themselves afresh. You recognize processions of gods surrounded by guards and faithful followers, animals, tigers, lewd monkeys and elephants, which, from a very early period, occupy the Hindu mind. These thousands of stones, which ought to be arranged in irregular chapels and leafy roofs, the Mussulmans have erected into columns, rectangular galleries, or in geometrical and simple rows. Upon the great bare walls, cabalistic numbers and letters that look like the tracks of birds are directed against the unbelievers. Above all, dominating the immense cemetery-like plain, inviolate through time, the Kutb throws its straight rocket of red stone and white marble, two hundred and fifty feet into the sky. Six centuries ago, from its top the sharp chant of the Muezzin broke the silence of the great plain when the sun dropped behind the horizon.

KENILWORTH CASTLE, ENGLAND
Sir James D. Mackenzie

Apart from the great historical interest attaching to these magnificent ruins, they deserve, architecturally, the closest examination and study, containing, as they do, elaborate specimens of the best constructions, in both military and domestic branches, during the different periods of the art in this country. We find first the massive square Norman keep, which had its protecting moat. This was the work of the original grantee, Geoffrey de Clinton, the treasurer and chamberlain of Henry I. Next comes an era, from 1180 to 1187, when we find entries for building and repairs to walls and fortifications; and again, from 1212 to 1216, the castle being then in the hands of King John, vast sums were expended upon the outer line of walls, with their flanking defences of Lunn's Tower and the Water Tower, and upon a chamber and other accommodation for the King, most of which still remains, though the timber constructions inside and against the walls have, of course, not survived. The next development is in the Late Decorated or Perpendicular style including the ruins of the great Hall and some other buildings at the west end of the inner court still called Lancaster's

Buildings, of the Fourteenth Century, rather late in the reign of Edward III., being some of the additions made by John of Gaunt, after he obtained Kenilworth by his first wife.

After this portion come the various alterations and insertions of the Elizabethan period, the beautiful gatehouse on the north side, and the towers and works added by Robert Dudley, Earl of Leicester and called the Leicester Buildings. Here are, therefore, examples of four different periods in each of which the particular work is capable of proof by existing documents, showing the gradations and changes which these buildings underwent, according to the requirements of the different ages, in passing from the barbarism of a military despotism to the comforts and splendour of later civilization. It is a magnificent specimen, and one easy of access. As we have said, the Manor of Kenilworth was bestowed by Henry I. upon Geoffrey de Clinton, who founded here a castle and a monastery; deriving, doubtless, from a Norman follower of Duke William, he must have been of worth and eminence among the barons, since besides the Royal posts which he occupied, the King appointed him to the Chief Justiceship of England. He was succeeded by his son Geoffrey, married to Agnes, daughter of Roger, Earl of Warwick, whose son, Henry, parted with Kenilworth, most probably on compulsion, to King John, who made it a Royal residence. One of the rebellious sons of Henry II. had taken possession of it, and held it for a time. Henry III., on his sister, the Princess Eleanor, marrying Simon de Montfort, Earl of Leicester, settled Kenilworth on her for life but in 1254 it was granted for the joint lives of the Earl and Countess of Leicester, and they made their home here. During the Baron's War which followed, this castle was made the base of operations by de Montfort, who provided it with warlike engines of defense not then known in England, and stores of all sorts, and after the battle of Lewis, Richard, King of the Romans, Henry's brother, with his youngest son, Edmund, was sent prisoner to Kenilworth, under the care of Leicester's second son Simon. In 1265, after effecting his escape from the custody of the barons at Hereford, Prince Edward, by a daring night attack, beat up the quarters of young de Montfort at Kenilworth, and took temporary possession of the place, making prisoners thirteen knights bannerets, with their followers, who were unguardedly sleeping in houses around the castle perhaps for the sake of an early bath. Young de Montfort and his pages narrowly escaped capture and only did so by a headlong race "some stark naked, some in breeches or drawers, some in shirts and many with their clothes under their arms." Departing thence Prince Edward rapidly effected a junction with his friends in the West, and overwhelmed and slaughtered the Earl of Leicester at the battle of Evesham. After this the Royal forces returned to Kenilworth which still held out manfully under the Earl's second son Simon and underwent a close siege that lasted for six months.

Trenches were cut on the land side of the castle and huge wooden towers, holding slingers and archers, were advanced against the wall, while barges, transported overland from Chester maintained the attack across the castle lake; but the garrison which numbered 1,200 men, met these assaults with the mangonels and other engines of de Montfort, and only gave in when reduced by famine, when, with the surrender of Kenilworth, the Civil War came to an end in December, 1265.

Having thus recovered possession of the fortress, King Henry bestowed it and the manor upon his youngest son Edmund, whom he created, two years later, Earl of Lancaster. In 1279, under the encouragement of that martial prince, Edward I., a very magnificent tournament was held at Kenilworth, under Mortimer, Earl of March, for the space of three days, at which, besides the sports of tilting and the barriers, the new military game of the Round Table was introduced. King Edward II., after his flight and capture, was brought a prisoner here to meet the commission appointed by Parliament, from whose lips he received the announcement of his deposition in favour of his son, at hearing which he fell senseless to the ground. Of the presence chamber, where this mournful scene was enacted, little remains but fragments of walls and two large bay windows festooned with ivy. The unfortunate King was shortly after, on December 5, removed hence to his hideous doom at Berkeley Castle on January 25. On the accession of Edward III., the castle again became the seat of baronial splendour under the Earls of Lancaster, the third of whom, Henry, was created Duke of Lancaster, but dying s. p. male (35 Edward III.), his two daughters became heirs to his great estates: Blanche, the younger, inheriting Kenilworth and bringing it, and afterwards, on her sister's death the whole property of her father, in marriage to John of Gaunt, fourth son of Edward III., who shortly after revived in him the title of Duke of Lancaster. The wealth thus obtained from his father enabled in great measure the duke's son and heir, Henry of Bolingbroke, in later days to oust his cousin, Richard II., from the throne, and to take his place thereon as King Henry IV., being greatly driven thereto by the King's treatment of him in regard to Kenilworth.

The range called Lancaster Buildings was caused to be erected by John of Gaunt between his accession to the property and his death in 1399. They lie on the south side of the inner quadrangle and there is a tower with three stories of arches adjoining the hall on the north, also of this date; the same origin is given to the Strong, or Mervin's Tower, as it is called by Sir Walter Scott. The ancient garden of the castle was situated near the north-east angle of the outer wall, where the Swan Tower meets the lake and wet ditch on the north.

Of course on Henry IV. succeeding, the crown resumed the ownership of the fortress, and thus it continued, often enlivened by the visits of royalty, until the days of Elizabeth, who bestowed it on her favourite, Robert Dudley, fifth son of the Duke of Northumberland, with all the royalties thereto belonging. Without enlarging on the history of this courtier, it is enough to say that he seems to have expended the enormous emoluments derived from the many dignities with which Elizabeth overwhelmed him in his lavish outlay upon Kenilworth. The additions and alterations made there by this Dudley involved an expenditure of £60,000—an incredible sum in those days. He erected the great gatehouse on the north, also the mass of square rooms from the north-east angle of the upper court, the buildings, called after him, and the gallery and lower gatehouse towers, together with a great range of stabling. He removed the Norman windows from the keep, replacing them by more modern ones; and it is evident that the great object of his outlay was to provide magnificent accommodation for the entertainment of his Queen and her Court.

This reception took place in July, 1575, and the festivities were continued for seventeen days during which every sort of prodigal extravagance possible at that age was indulged in. It cost Leicester £1,000 a day. At his death he bequeathed the castle to his brother Ambrose, Earl of Warwick, for life, and afterwards to his own son Sir Robert Dudley, upon whose birth and legitimacy the father (who is certainly one of the dark characters in English history) chose to throw doubts.

This seems to have incited that greedy monarch, James I., to refuse the succession to Sir Robert, whom he forced to consent to a nominal sale of the property to Henry, Prince of Wales, at one-third of its value, and even that was never paid. Dudley, in disgust, withdrew from England, and lived in much honour at Florence, when he died about the year 1650.

When the place fell into the hands of Oliver Cromwell, a sort of commission of army officers was sent to Kenilworth to divide and share the property between them, and they, caring nothing for historical associations, the splendour of the structure, or the richness of the furniture and plenishing (it was but seventy-five years after the entertainment of Elizabeth there) proceeded to strip the place, to cut the timber, kill the deer, and even to sell the walls and roofing, for the value of the bare materials.

At the restoration, Charles II. granted the reversion of the manor to Lawrence, Lord Hyde, second son of Chancellor Clarendon, whom he created Baron Kenilworth and Earl of Rochester. His grandson leaving only a daughter, the lands and ruins came by marriage to the Essex family and, afterwards, by marriage to Thomas Villiers, the second son of the Earl of Jersey, created, in 1756, Baron

Hyde, in whose family they still continue.

At Kenilworth was immured Eleanor Cobham, the wife of Humphrey, Earl of Gloucester, after the performance of her penance on a charge of practicing witchcraft against Henry VI. and here she ended her days.

As in most other cases the Norman baron founded his castle on the site of a Saxon home with a fortified burh; a square keep was built on the most commanding position, perhaps on the mound, and a large walled enclosure was made, defended on the west, south and east sides by a lake and by a deep ditch across the north front. Somewhat on the west side of this was formed the inner ward a rectangular enclosure, nearly one and one-half acres in area, the north-east corner of which was occupied by Clinton's keep. This is a plain late Norman edifice with a forebuilding on the west side, and containing a vaulted basement and one upper floor only, the former being entirely filled with earth. The main floor formed one immense room thirty-four feet by sixty-four and about forty feet high. The forebuilding contained the staircase of approach to the entrance doorway, and above was a room, possibly an oratory. Large corner turrets, three containing mural chambers and one large spiral stair, cap the angles of the keep, the walls of which are of immense thickness. There is no evidence as to what was the nature of the Norman buildings in this ward, since they have been replaced by the work of the Earls of Lancaster, and of John of Gaunt, and are called by their name. West from the keep are the ruined kitchens, showing a huge fireplace and baking ovens. At the north-west angle is the Strong Tower, of three stages, which was, perhaps, used as a prison for persons of consequence. Adjoining this is the Hall, a pure Perpendicular building, due to John of Gaunt, beyond which was the white hall, and next the State rooms, which are connected with a large garderobe tower. Then at the south-east corner comes the range to which the name of Leicester's Buildings has been given, and the east face to the keep is made up by the site of Dudley's Lobby and Henry VIII.'s lodgings, but all this has perished.

The outer ward is a large oblong enclosure, 270 yards

long from east to west by 174; at its east end were domestic offices, the entrances and the chapel. Originally this ward was divided by a ditch seventy feet wide running north and south with a bridge for access to the inner ward, part of it remaining in front of Leicester's buildings, and the rest having probably been filled in by Dudley after the visit of Elizabeth. This outer ward contains about nine acres, having a circumference of 750 yards; it is formed by a strong curtain wall embracing six important buildings; namely, the octagon Swan Tower on the north-west, Mortimer's Tower, or the gatehouse, at the head of the dam across the lake, called either after Lord Mortimer of Wigmore (temp. Edward III.), or from Sir John Mortimer, imprisoned here in the reign of Henry V. Then towards the east came the Warden's Tower, and next the Water Tower at the south-east corner, a complete mural bastion of Early Decorated style; whence the curtain runs to Lunn's Tower at the north-east angle, a round building thirty-six feet in diameter and forty high. At the back of this part of the wall is a long range of stabling and farm buildings, with an upper half-timbered storey, said to have been built by the great Earl Thomas of Lancaster, in the reign of Edward II., but some part is Late Perpendicular. Next to this is the chapel. West of Lunn's Tower is the building called Leicester's Gatehouse, built in 1570, a rectangular tower with octangular corner turrets. On the north side of the great ditch, which is cut through the rock and forms the north defense, is Clinton's green, where are still banks of earth, probably survivals of the great siege by Henry III.

In front of Mortimer's Tower is the dam, eighty yards long, across the valley, having at its further end the remains of a flood-gate and outer gatehouse, or the gallery tower, with a drawbridge here over the outer ditch. This was the point at which Queen Elizabeth made her entry. Beyond it was called the Brayz, where tournaments were held, as they also were on the dam itself. On both sides of the dam extended a lake, half a mile long on the west, and some twelve feet deep, upon which the attack by ships was made by Henry III. Finally, beyond the Brayz was a great curved outwork forming a tête-du-pont in front of the entrance.

The keep, or Clinton's Tower was perhaps built between 1170 and 1180. Lunn's Tower may be the work of King John. Henry III. expended large sums at Kenilworth, and to him is ascribed the great dam, the Water and Warden's Towers, and much of the curtain on the south and east. Robert Dudley, Earl of Leicester, altered the keep into Tudor Style, and besides the buildings called by his name, added the Gallery Tower and the gatehouse at the northeast, "a very fine example of a declining period in English architecture." John of Gaunt certainly built the great Hall (circ. 1390), "one of the most beautiful examples of Early Perpendicular work in the kingdom," and he is said to have built the portion called Lancaster's Buildings, between Cæsar's Tower and the hill. It was at Kenilworth, during one of her visits in August, 1572, while out hunting, that Queen Elizabeth read, as she rode, the terrible news of the massacre of Saint Bartholomew.

SANTA MARIA DELLA SALUTE, ITALY
John Ruskin

"SANTA MARIA DELLA SALUTE," Our Lady of Health, or of Safety, would be a more literal translation, yet not perhaps fully expressing the force of the Italian word in this case. The church was built between 1630 and 1680, in acknowledgment of the cessation of the plague:—of course to the Virgin, to whom the modern Italian has recourse in all his principal distresses, and who receives his gratitude for all principal deliverances.

The hasty traveler is usually enthusiastic in his admiration of this building; but there is a notable lesson to be derived from it, which is not often read. On the opposite side of the broad canal of the Guidecca is a small church, celebrated among Renaissance architects as of Palladian design, but which would hardly attract the notice of the general observer, unless on account of the pictures by John Bellini which it contains, in order to see which the traveller may perhaps remember having been taken across the Guidecca to the Church of the "Redentore." But he ought carefully to compare these two buildings with each other, the one built "to the Virgin," the other "to the Redeemer" (also a votive offering after the cessation of the plague of 1576): the one, the most conspicuous church in Venice, its dome, the principal one by which she is first discerned, rising out of the distant sea; the other, small and contemptible, on a suburban island, and only becoming an object of interest, because it contains three small pictures! For in relative magnitude and conspicuousness of these two buildings, we have an accurate index of the relative importance of the ideas of the Madonna and of Christ in the modern Italian mind.

The Church of Santa Maria della Salute on the Grand Canal, one of the earliest buildings of the Grotesque Renaissance, is rendered impressive by its position, size, and general proportions. These latter are exceedingly good; the grace of the whole building being chiefly dependent on the inequality of size in its cupolas, and pretty grouping of the two campaniles behind them. It is to be generally observed that the proportions of buildings have nothing whatever to do with the style or general merits of their architecture. An architect trained in the worst schools, and utterly devoid of all meaning or purpose in his work, may yet have such a natural gift of massing and grouping as will render all his structures effective when seen from a distance: such a gift is very general with the late Italian builders, so that many of the most contemptible edifices in the country have good stage effect so long as we do not approach them. The Church of the Salute is farther assisted by the beautiful flight of steps in front of it down to the

Canal; and its façade is rich and beautiful of its kind, and was chosen by Turner for the principal object in his well-known view of the Grand Canal. The principal faults of the building are the meagre windows in the sides of the cupola, and the ridiculous disguise of the buttresses under the form of colossal scrolls; the buttresses themselves being originally a hypocrisy, for the cupola is stated by Lazari to be of timber, and therefore needs none. The sacristy contains several precious pictures: the three on its roof by Titian, much vaunted, are indeed as feeble as they are monstrous; but the small Titian, "St. Mark, with Sts. Cosmo and Damian," was, when I first saw it, to my judgment, by far the first work of Titian's in Venice. It has since been restored by the Academy, and it seemed to me entirely destroyed, but I had not time to examine it carefully.

At the end of the larger sacristy is the lunette which once decorated the tomb of the Doge Francesco Dandolo; and at the side of it, one of the most highly finished Tintorets in Venice, namely *The Marriage in Cana*, an immense picture, some twenty-five feet long by fifteen feet high, and said by Lazari to be one of the few which Tintoret signed with his name.

THE RAMPARTS OF CARCASSONNE, FRANCE
A. Molinier

To what race shall we attribute the foundation of the city of Carcassonne? We cannot say exactly, so many races having occupied this part of the valley of the Aude in turn; the first in point of time was that of the Iberians, that mysterious people, who had colonized Southern Europe long before the coming of the Aryan race. Without taking any more account than is necessary regarding the hypothesis of the etymologists, we may recall the fact that the celebrated William von Humboldt attaches the vocable

Carcaso, as well as many others from the south of Gaul and the north of Spain, to the Iberic language.

Erected into a Latin colony by Cæsar himself, or by his adopted son, Augustus, Carcassonne vegetated obscurely for three centuries until the day when the invasion by the Barbarians and the civil wars brought about the ruin of the Empire. At this moment she was shorn of her ancient glory; and from a Latin colony, she became a simple *castrum*, which many manuscripts of the *Notitia dignitatum*, written about the year 400, do not even mention. But if the old city lost her importance with regard to civil life, she gained it in military life. At the moment the Germans, those hereditary enemies of Rome, spread over the whole of Gaul, the cities repaired their too long neglected fortifications in great haste; open spaces they surrounded with high walls; the ancient citadels were reinforced; and in their haste, just as happened later during the Hundred Years' War, many sumptuous buildings erected by Latin architects, were sacrificed to make the defences. Carcassonne is now furnished with a strong enclosure, the honour of which many archæologists, among them Viollet-le-Duc, wish to give to the Visigoths; but it seems more prudent to attribute them to the last engineers of the expiring Empire. This enclosure, of which some parts still exist to-day, is composed of curtains of medium height, surmounted by a parapet without projections and flanked at intervals with semicircular towers opened at the gorge, or closed by a flat wall.

The towers were bare up to the level of the circling road, higher they comprised two or three stories. Viollet-le-Duc supposes that they were covered with a roof, and restored one according to this hypothesis. Much more elevated than the curtain, these Gallo-Roman towers commanded it from above, and on each of their flanks the curtain is interrupted by a gap connected by a narrow bridge, which was easy to destroy in case of an attack.

One must imagine the city of Carcassonne, with this enclosure composed of high curtains with parapets and turrets, and, at intervals, high towers, dominating the country and commanding the neighbouring defences. Such she was at the end of the Empire and such she remained for several centuries. Occupied by the Visigoths, vainly besieged several times by Clovis and by the successors of that prince, she was not forced before the Eighth Century. At this date, she fell into the hands of the Arabs, with all of the surrounding country. The domination of the Mussulmans, however, was very ephemeral; occupied by them about 720, Carcassonne again became Christian thirty years later, in 759.

Carcassonne became an important town. The city remains a fortress of the first order, almost impregnable, with its towers, its curtains and its vast *château*; but around it, on the slopes and at the base of the hill between the Aude and the city, extensive and flourishing boroughs are forming. These *bourgs* are mentioned in 1067; more recent discoveries tell us that the two principal ones were Saint-Vincent and Saint-Michel. The latter was a commercial town inhabited by common people and workmen whose turbulent character caused great embarrassment to the viscounts during the Twelfth Century. From the beginning of that century, the notables of Carcassonne took the side of the enemy of their legitimate master, the Count of Barcelona, gave him their oath, and on two different occasions the Viscount, Bernard Aton, was chased by them from his capital. When he returned, in 1125, he took rigorous measures to assure his rule in the future. Each tower on the wall was confided to the care of a faithful noble who had to live in it with his family and his men, to do what was called *le service d'estage*. The feudal acts have preserved for us the name of several towers, the *turris monetaria vetus*, for example, but it would be difficult to state precisely to which of the existing towers the old names were given.

To the same viscount, Bernard Aton, is attributed the construction of a great part of the present wall of the city, and almost the entire *château*; from the reign of the same prince dates also the old part of the church Saint-Nazaire. Let us begin with the *château*. An act of the year 1034 already mentions the residence of the Counts of Carcassonne, and the *sala*, in which the Bishop of Gerona,

Pierre Roger, lived; it speaks of the kitchens, the chambers, the stables and the chapel Saint-Marcel. Later, the *castellum Carcassonne* is always carefully distinguished from the citadel; the acts, in mentioning a *camera rotunda*, speak of the elm that ornamented the court and under which the feudal lords rendered justice, as Saint Louis did later at Vincennes. But these give very meagre information which the study of this building will happily permit us to complete.

The ordinary residence of the suzerain, the *Château de Carcassonne*, like the donjons of the North, was designed to protect him against all attacks that came from outside as well as from within the town. A last refuge for faithful defenders, it had to be a shelter during a regular siege, or a personal attack, and to protect the suzerain against enemies without and traitors within. Therefore, a special wall was erected against the town and against the country. The *Château de Carcassonne* was no exception to the general rule. Supported by the exterior wall on the side of the town, it is defended by a wide moat and by a circular barbican over the end of a bridge that was thrown over the moat; it forms a parallelogram, flanked by towers and high curtains. The masonry is the same and is composed of yellowish stones placed in regular layers of from fifteen to twenty centimetres in height. The domes have the form of hemispherical caps, with regular arches and are unornamented. The bays are semicircular without mouldings, or projections; nowhere is there any sacrifice to decoration, with the exception of certain upper openings that are inaccessible to attack, and these have received a few ornaments,—mouldings and little columns of marble that garnish the corners of the windows. The principal entrance towards the city was defended by two portcullises and two successive gates; after having passed these obstacles, you find yourself in a large court of honour which was flanked on one side by the walls of the city, and on the other by dwellings, shops, and light wooden buildings, that have disappeared to-day, or have been restored in the style of the Thirteenth Century. A few halls of the Twelfth Century have, however, survived; they are not very attractive, with their surbased vaults and their narrow openings.

Let us now turn our back on the *château* and enter the *lices*, for this is what they called the space circumscribed by the two walls of the City. We have seen above that from 1240 the town had a double wall, but the first, probably much damaged by the lords of Trencavel, was doubtless reconstructed in, and appears to date almost entirely from, the reign of St. Louis. It is composed of curtains elevated upon the rock and which never could have been of a great height: since the ground of the *lices* was made, it has gained in height. Sometimes the two curtains were quite far apart, sometimes, on the contrary, they are close together, and the straight passage between them was formerly closed by walls with battlements and solid gates. Most of the towers which flank the exterior wall are very simple and are quite low; as a rule, they are composed of two storeys and their platform is covered with a pointed roof covered with slate.

The interior enclosure, which is much stronger and better preserved than the exterior, dates only in part from the Thirteenth Century, but if the royal architects have respected the work of their predecessors as scrupulously as possible, they have never hesitated to transform the defective or insufficient portions, whenever they felt it practical. This second enclosure is at once higher and stronger than its neighbour, the towers are closer together and better arranged for defense. The elevated and spacious curtains still carry traces of the *hourds* which surmounted them in times of war; in many of those near the *château*, the base dates from the time of a remote epoch,—perhaps the time of the Romans, but the tops were remodelled in the Thirteenth Century by Saint-Louis, or Philip the Bold. Moreover, these princes made no other changes in the whole wall that extends from the *château* to the Tower of the Inquisition; you particularly notice the Tower of Justice, a beautiful building with four stories of the feudal period, and the Visigoth Tower, cleverly restored, too cleverly perhaps, by Viollet-le-Duc, but an interesting example of the military system of the Gallo-Romans of the

Decadence.

The Tower of the Inquisition appears to date from the reign of Philip the Bold. It is a beautiful building of four storeys which in the Thirteenth and Fourteenth Centuries, sheltered the ecclesiastical tribunal the name of which it bears.

Before the Revolution, the city was deserted; in 1744, the bishop followed the general example and left his old palace of the Thirteenth Century. The new *régime* was not equally just. For a long time, the city remained a military post, mutilated by military genius, on the pretext of maintaining and improving it; a great number of towers were razed and transformed into low curtains, absurd defenses which could not have held out two hours against a strong attack. This admirable collection of mediæval military art was exposed to the greatest danger; let us thank the archæologists who interested the State in the preservation of these venerable remains. Restored to-day with a reverent care, the old citadel is assured a long life. As for the City herself, she can never become what she was in the Thirteenth Century, a rich and populous town, but she will certainly remain forever an admirable museum, where everyone who is interested in national history will come to study the military art of old France.

THE CATHEDRAL OF MODENA, ITALY
Edward Augustus Freeman

The student of the Romanesque who transports himself suddenly from the Arno and the Apenines to the river-basin of the Po will find himself spirited away into a new architectural world. Let him flit from Pisa to Modena. Pistoia, a city of high interest on other grounds, will not long detain him. A single noble campanile is attached to a basilican *duomo* which would hold a third or fourth-rate place at Lucca, and which at Pisa no one would think of mentioning at all. But at Modena his halt must be longer.

The church of Pisa and the church of Modena are contemporary buildings, and the Great Countess is honoured as a benefactress by both; but they are as unlike one another as any two buildings of the same date and general style well can be. At Modena we get our first glimpse of the genuine Lombard form of the Italian Romanesque, a form wholly unlike either the domical or basilican type, and which makes a far nearer approach to the Romanesque of the lands beyond the Alps. The approach is indeed only an approach; the *duomo* of Modena is Italian, and not English, French, or German; still it is a form of Italian far less widely removed from English, French, or German work than the style of Pisa or St. Vital. As at Pisa, the architect seems to have halted between two opinions. The church is cruciform, but the transepts have no projection on the ground-plan; there are real lantern-arches, not obscured as they are at Pisa, but they do not bear up any central dome or tower. The lantern-arches are pointed; but here, as at Pisa, the pointed form is more likely to be Saracenic than Gothic. Without, three eastern apses, rising from between pinnacles of quite Northern character, group boldly with one of the noblest campaniles of Italy, which is certainly not improved by the later addition of a spire. The great doorways rest on lions; the west front has a noble wheel window; the greater part of the outside is lavishly arcaded, but the arcading is of a different type from the long rows of single arcades at Lucca and Pisa; the favourite form at Modena is that of several small arches grouped under a containing arch.

With such an outside, we are not surprised to find, on entering the church, an elevation more nearly after the Northern type than anything which we have yet seen in Italy. At Pisa we saw an arcade, triforium, and clerestory; but the triforium was not so much the Northern type itself as the Northern type translated into Italian language. But at Modena we find as genuine a triforium as in any minster of England or Normandy. Its form indeed seems somewhat rude and awkward, as if the containing arch had been crushed by the lofty clerestory above. And eyes familiar with Norman detail may possibly be amazed at the sight of mid-wall shafts, and those of a somewhat rough type, showing themselves in such a position. But the mid-wall shaft is constructively as much in its place in a triforium as it is in a belfry window, and in the whole elevation there is nothing lacking. There is pier-arch, triforium, and clerestory, and the deep splay of the highest range hinders the presence of any continuous blank spaces such as we have seen in the Basilican churches. The capitals are a strange mixture of classical and barbaric forms, and in the alternate piers, supporting the arches which span the nave, we find huge half-columns, which form a marked contrast to the tall slender shafts commonly used in like positions in Northern churches. Altogether the Cathedral of Modena is strictly an Italian church, yet the approaches to Northern forms are very marked, and they are of a kind which suggests the direct imitation of Northern forms or the employment of Northern architects.

THE CATHEDRAL OF RHEIMS, FRANCE
Louis Gonse

The basilica of Rheims is the ideal type of a great Gothic cathedral. Everything has been gathered together here to enchant the eye and touch the mind.

From the outside, with its eight spires, and the lace-work of its bell-towers, and its galleries boldly mounting to the sky, with the breadth of its arrangement, the splendid development of its cruciform plan, with its two cloisters and its magnificent dependencies, it appears as the sublime expression of western genius and the culminating point of the Christian idea.

Within, it is dazzling. All the resources of decoration have been prodigally employed. Indeed, the eye does not know which of the marvels to select, and if this stupendous whole has been preserved to us by a miracle, nothing in the world can be compared to it. The brilliant series of windows, one of the most complete and beautiful in existence; the pavement, with its labyrinth and countless mortuary tombs; the rich altars and chapel paintings; the tomb of St. Nicaise; the pulpit of St. Remi; the rood-screen, a master work by Colard de Givry, made in 1417; the railings of the choir, with precious hangings and stalls; the high altar charged with relics, and presents from the Kings of France; its golden retable and its splendid ciborium of the Thirteenth Century, in silver gilt; the sacrarium, the fonts, and the sepulchres;—form a great mass of treasure.

And how greatly is the feeling increased by memories when you reconstruct the public life of Notre-Dame of Rheims, and the events of which she was the theatre during the long course of centuries; when you dream of all the coronations, councils, and meetings that have taken place beneath its vaults! No edifice, in truth, is, in this respect, more worthy of our honour and admiration.

Notre-Dame of Rheims measures in round numbers one hundred and thirty-nine metres long and thirty-eight metres high beneath the vault; it is not surpassed in length by the Cathedral of Mans, thanks to the unusual dimensions of its absidal chapel, nor in height by Beauvais, Cologne, Metz, Amiens, or Saint-Quentin. The great divisions of the whole, founded upon a triple scale, in height and breadth, are clearly accentuated. From the lower part of the nave the view is one of striking grandeur and harmony; the dazzled glance loses itself in these vast depths, under the luminous sheets of light which spread out from the lateral bays, while the large vault, clouded in the mysterious penumbra of the high windows, ornamented with their glass, invites you to meditation. No cathedral offers so powerful an opposition to light. The arrangement of the great piers cantoned by four half-columns bound together also increases the fleeting perspective.

Of the whole building, I have only to criticize the composition of the triforium, which is truly not of the first order; it demands more elegance and firmness; the arches of that gallery, the decorative function of which is so important in a Gothic church, seem heavy and as if crushed between the robust piers of the ground-floor and the large bays of the upper story.

In all that belongs to the Thirteenth Century, the execution bears witness to an extreme care and luxury. The Cathedral of Rheims, principally in its interior work, is a model that has never been surpassed from the point of view of technique, of show and of the judicious use of material. The carving is of the first order. The capitals of Rheims are celebrated, and very justly. The independence of the *Style champenois* has introduced some elements of life and fantasy which give them a character of their own. Some of the most beautiful, notably the capital of the *Vendanges* (The Vintages), have been made popular by the mouldings in the Musée of the Trocadéro; but all of them are remarkable on account of the variety of the motives that decorate them. Viollet-le-Duc has justly observed that the capitals of Rheims present a decisive progress in the union of the capital of the principal column with the capitals of the connected columns: a very great difficulty which Gothic architects did not solve until after numerous groupings. Here the monotony has been avoided by a division of the bound columns into two segments, separated by an astragal. The effect of this division is most happy and constitutes one of the most striking peculiarities of the Cathedral of Rheims.

The choir is unanimously admired. However, it has not the breadth nor the spring of the great choirs of Bourges, Amiens and Mans; but it derives its originality from its depth and its radiating chapels; and to the preservation of its most exquisite windows it owes a poetic charm that very few interiors can equal. The windows of Rheims are, in reality, the most perfect we have seen after those of Chartres, Bourges, Mans and Auxerre. In purity of expression they surpass the windows of Soissons, Troyes, and Châlons. The windows in the apsis are masterpieces; their sweet intensity, in the scale of blue, is truly enchanting. They were executed from 1227 to 1240 under the episcopate of Henri de Braisne, whose figure appears in the principal window, in the centre of nine large, high windows, between the twelve suffragans of Rheims, arranged in order, according to their rank in the province: Soissons, Laon, Beauvais, Noyon, Senlis, Tournai, Cambrai, Châlons, Thérouanne, Amiens, etc., each having at his side a Gothic cathedral.

These figures of bishops of gigantic proportions have a majesty that cannot be described. But in the midst of these splendours, it is the rose of the western window which is perhaps the most worthy of everything to hold your attention. Composition, brilliancy, harmony and elegance of position,—it possesses all these qualities. It would be difficult to find a more admirable witness of the decorative sense of the old glass-workers. When across the network of the immense surface, the light from the setting sun is thrown, the whole interior of the church is illuminated as if by a conflagration. The preservation of this masterpiece is unfortunately greatly compromised by the crack like a sabre cut which crosses the façade near the rose. The high windows in the nave represent the Kings, just as in the Cathedral of Sacres; they are still more beautiful, however, of deep rich colours, but of a less careful execution than the great rose and the windows in the choir.

All these marvels, however, pale before the carved decoration that surrounds on the inside the lower part of the three doors of the façade, a kind of drapery in relief, as unique by the character of its invention as by the perfection of its workmanship.

This extraordinary decoration envelops up to their summits the three ogival windows that open upon the porch. It goes up as high as the triforium, by a succession of seven rows of niches closed by trefoil arches, and separated from them by panels and corner-pieces of leaves borrowed from the flora of the country and divinely carved. You see in turn: the laurel, the vine, the pear, the apple, the holly, the oak, the ivy, the water-lily, the bulrush, the peony, the clover, the chestnut, the liverwort, and the olive. A hundred and twenty-two statues of incomparable beauty, rivalling the most beautiful productions of sculpture of former times, occupy the niches, and, deliciously set off by the floral decoration of the plain surfaces, stand out like living personages from the dark background of the niches.

Each one of these figures is a most precious work, studied from nature with a sovereign knowledge of drapery and movement. Here is a priest officiating in his chasuble and holding the Eucharist; there, is a warrior in coat-of-mail, who seems to have just returned from the Crusades; moreover, there are some prophets of heroic mien, noble virgins with trailing robes, and martyrs, illuminated with ecstasy. All this mural decoration was made in the spirit of the architecture, intended to complete the iconography of the great door and to amplify still further the cyclic character,—the general theme being the history of Christ and the glorification of the Virgin, with the accessory scenes that belong to it.

Let us cross the threshold: we are outside, before the façade. We must walk farther away in order to embrace all the lines and take in the masterly idea of the whole. It is most celebrated, that is well-known; for a long time, its richness has been a synonym of beauty in mediæval art. I have already said that the general conception is of the highest order, the upward movement is magnificent, the statues blossom with a bewildering luxuriance, and the infinite multiplication of the details, which—miraculous fact—do not obliterate the majestic section of the lower stages, so happily cut by the tall bays scattered in the bell-towers. Nevertheless, when you come nearer, you are surprised at finding so much uncertainty in the conduct of this terrible enterprise! How much weakness and lassitude in the highest parts! You perceive both haste and economy there. All that dates from the end of the Fourteenth and the beginning of the Fifteenth Century is mediocre; the sculpture, cut in bad materials that are injured by the frost, is coarse and flabby: the nobility of the contours is lost beneath the excessive ornamentation, and the absence of the spires deprives this aërial building of its necessary finish.

To be satisfied, the eye must rest below the row of Kings made during the reign of Charles V.

While the upper stories have been made of soft stone of a bad quality, the lower parts, built of hard stone, have acquired in the course of time the hues of Florentine bronze. It is here that the Champagne sculptor has lavishly exhibited the treasures of his spirit, his audacity and his genius. When the great statues of the portals of Rheims are mentioned, everybody is of one accord.

The Queen of the basilica, the Virgin, is the soul of this cosmos, the centre from which everything radiates.

She is crowned by Christ beneath the daïs of the great gable, and this composition, which is still brightened by the remains of the gold background from which it stands out, is one of the most exquisite creations of Christian Art; the Virgin is also on the pier; she is directly or indirectly in every scene of the life of Jesus. Her memory, her legend, her poetry are everywhere: she is at once the culminating point and the humble pretext of all this magnificence. At Paris, at Bourges and at Amiens, it is Christ; here, it is the Virgin; and around this admirable theme a powerful thought has quickened into being a race of statues, a people in whom life, movement and fantasy circulate, beneath the compassionate gaze of the Mother of God and under the influence of her adorable grace. Charm is really the special characteristic of the sculpture at Rheims,—a special charm that is always evident, a charm carried to the point of *morbidezza* which in certain figures has been compared, and not without reason, to the mysterious charm of Leonardo da Vinci.

All these personages of high stature, blackened and polished by time, possess an indescribable grace, smiling and familiar, an indescribable and eloquent gravity that puts them into communion with the spectator; they are indeed of our country and of our race; their idealism, always youthful despite the centuries, is not too far removed from earth to respond even now to the secret aspirations of our souls; they are the glory of the portals of Rheims, the glory of French sculpture.

Beautiful as these figures are, they must not let us forget the population of two thousand five hundred statues that make the Cathedral of Rheims a unique monument of decorative and monumental sculpture. All the images of this old basilica deserve attentive study. An entire volume would scarcely suffice to enumerate them. It is necessary to take a trip to the roof to measure fully this incredible wealth: giants of stone, angels with spread wings, apostles, saints and royal figures, fantastic animals, more than forty metres high, which occupy the pinnacles of the buttresses, are lined along the galleries of the transepts or fortify the balustrade of the roof; figures full of vitality that project from the corners, the springs of the arches, the junction of curves, as crowns, supports, caryatides, mascarons, and gargoyles; capricious, expressive and energetic figures, to execute which the Champagne chisel, the freest and most supple of Gothic chisels, has given itself full scope, with an exuberant joy.

Despite the devastations of the rococo period, to which was added that of the Revolutionary period, the Cathedral of Rheims has not been entirely stripped of her incomparable artistic treasures. She has preserved a great portion of her tapestry hangings, and her Treasury is still one of the richest in France.

The tapestries of Rheims have been very learnedly described by M. Ch. Loriquet. Before the Revolution the collection was unique. Hincmar, Hérivée, Regnault de Chartres, Juvénal des Ursins, Robert de Lenoncourt, the great Cardinal of Lorraine, the Cardinal of Guise, Henri de Lorraine, the Kings of France and the Chapter were the principal donators.

These tapestries were used to decorate the cathedral on days of special solemnity. Of the magnificent collection there only remain the fifteen pieces by Lenoncourt, two of the six tapestries of the *Grand Roi Clovis*, given by the Cardinal of Lorraine, fifteen tapestries executed by Pepersack, at the order of Henri de Lorraine, the four pieces ordered from Lombart d' Aubusson by the Chapter, four tapestries called the *Cantiques* and two Gobelins after Raphael's Cartoons.

The most remarkable are certainly those by Lenoncourt and those of the Clovis set. The first were offered to the cathedral by the Archbishop Robert de Lenoncourt; one of them bears the dedication of 1530. They represent the *Life of the Virgin*. They are of Flemish origin and of a very fine execution. The composition is rich, spirited and of an extremely graceful style. Some of them have not lost the freshness of their colours and can still be counted among the best specimens of the art of tapestry at the beginning of the Sixteenth Century. These precious hangings occupy the wall surfaces of the side-aisles of the nave, where they produce a sumptuous effect.

THE CASTLE OF S. ANGELO, ITALY
Augustus J. C. Hare

The Ponte S. Angelo is the Pons Elius of Hadrian, built as an approach to his mausoleum, and only intended for this, as another public bridge existed close by, at the time of its construction. It is almost entirely ancient, except the parapets. The statues of St. Peter and St. Paul, at the extremity, were erected by Clement VII., in the place of two chapels, in 1530, and the angels, by Clement IX., in 1688. The pedestal of the third angel on the right is a relic of the siege of Rome in 1849, and bears the impress of a cannon-ball.

These angels, which have been called the "breezy maniacs" of Bernini, are only from his designs. The two angels which he executed himself, and intended for this bridge, are now at S. Andrea della Fratte. The idea of Clement IX. was a fine one, that "an avenue of the heavenly host should be assembled to welcome the pilgrim to the shrine of the great apostle."

From the Ponte S. Angelo, when the Tiber is low, are visible the remains of the bridge by which the ancient Via Triumphalis crossed the river. Close by, where Santo Spirito now stands, was the Porta Triumphalis, by which victors entered the city in triumph.

Facing the bridge, is the famous Castle of S. Angelo, built by the Emperor Hadrian as his family tomb, because the last niche in the imperial mausoleum of Augustus was filled when the ashes of Nerva were laid there. The first funeral here was that of Elius Verus, the first adopted son of Hadrian, who died before him. The Emperor himself died at Baiæ, but his remains were transported hither from a temporary tomb at Pozzuoli by his successor Antoninus Pius, by whom the mausoleum was completed in A.D., 140. Here also were buried, Antoninus Pius, A.D., 161; Marcus Aurelius, 180; Commodus, 192; and Septimius Severus, in an urn of gold, enclosed in one of alabaster, A.D., 211; Caracalla, in 217, was the last Emperor interred here. The well-known lines of Byron:

"Turn to the mole which Hadrian rear'd on high,
Imperial mimic of old Egypt's piles,
Colossal copyist of deformity,
Whose travell'd phantasy from the far Nile's
Enormous model, doom'd the artist's toils
To build for giants, and for his vain earth,
His shrunken ashes, raise this dome! How smiles
The gazer's eye with philosophic mirth,

To view the huge design which sprung from such a birth, seem rather applicable to the Pyramid of Caius Cestius than to this mausoleum.

The Castle, as it now appears, is but the skeleton of the magnificent tomb of the Emperors. Procopius, writing in the Sixth Century, describes its appearance in his time. "It was built," he says, "of Parian marble; the square blocks fit closely to each other without any cement. It has four equal sides, each a stone's throw in length. In height it rises above the walls of the city. On the summit are statues of men and horses, of admirable workmanship in Parian marble." Canina, in his *Architectura Romana*, gives a restoration of the mausoleum, which shows how it consisted of three stories: 1, A quadrangular basement, the upper part intersected with Doric pillars, between which were spaces for epitaphs of the dead within, and surmounted at the corners by marble equestrian statues; 2, a circular story, with fluted Ionic colonnades; 3, circular story, surrounded by Corinthian columns, between which were statues. The whole was surmounted by a pyramidal roof, ending in a bronze fir-cone.

The history of the Mausoleum, in the Middle Ages is almost the history of Rome. It was probably first turned into a fortress by Honorius, A.D., 423. From Theodoric it derives the name of "Carcer Theodorici." In 537, it was besieged by Vitiges, when the defending garrison, reduced to the last extremity, hurled down all the magnificent statues which decorated the cornice, upon the besiegers. In A.D., 498, Pope Symmachus removed the bronze fir-cone at the apex of the roof to the court of St. Peter's, whence it was afterwards transferred to the Vatican garden, where it is still to be seen between two bronze peacocks, which probably stood on either side of the entrance.

Belisarius defended the castle against Totila, whose Gothic troops captured and held it for three years, after which it was taken by Narses.

It was in 530 that the event occurred which gave the building its present name. Pope Gregory the Great was leading a penitential procession to St. Peter's, in order to offer up prayers for the staying of the great pestilence which followed the inundation of 589; when, as he was crossing the bridge, even while the people were falling dead around him, he looked up at the Mausoleum and saw an angel on its summit, sheathing a bloody sword, while a choir of angels around chaunted with celestial voices, the anthem, since adopted by the church in her vesper service—"*Regina cœli, lœtare—quia quem meruisti portare—resurrexit, sicut dixit, Alleluja.*"—To which the earthly voice of the Pope solemnly responded: "*Ora pro nobis Deum, Alleluja.*"[10]

In the Tenth Century the fortress was occupied by the infamous Marozia, who, in turn, brought her three husbands (Alberic, Count of Tusculum; Guido, Marquis of Tuscany; and Hugo, King of Italy), thither, to tyrannize

---

[10] The pictures at Ara Cœli and Sta. Maria Maggiore both claim to be that carried by St. Gregory in this procession. The song of the angels is annually commemorated on St. Mark's Day, when the clergy pass by in procession to St. Peter's, and the Franciscans of Ara Cœli and the canons of Sta. Maria Maggiore, halting here, chaunt the antiphon, *Regina cœli, lœtare.*

with her over Rome. It was within the walls of this building that Alberic, her son by her first husband, waiting upon his royal stepfather at table, threw a bowl of water over him, when Hugo retorted by a blow, which was the signal for an insurrection, the people taking part with Alberic, putting the King to flight, and imprisoning Marozia. Shut up within these walls, Pope John XI. (931–936), son of Marozia by her first husband, ruled under the guidance of his stronger-minded brother Alberic; here, also, Octavian, son of Alberic and grandson of Marozia, succeeded in forcing his election as John XII. (being the first Pope who took a new name), and scandalized Christendom by a life of murder, robbery, adultery and incest.

In 974, the Castle was seized by Cencio (Crescenzio Nomentano), the consul, who raised up an anti-pope (Boniface VII.) here, with the determination of destroying the temporal power of the popes and imprisoned and murdered two popes, Benedict VI. (972), and John XIV. (984), within these walls. In 996, another lawful pope, Gregory V., calling in the Emperor Otho to his assistance, took the Castle and beheaded Cencio, though he had promised him life if he would surrender. From this governor the fortress long held the name of Castello de Crescenzio, or Turris Crescentii, by which it is described in mediæval writings. A second Cencio supported another anti-pope, Cadolaus, here in 1063, against Pope Alexander II. A third Cencio imprisoned Gregory VII. here in 1084. From this time the possession of the Castle was a constant point of contest between popes and anti-popes. In 1313, Arlotto degli Stefaneschi, having demolished most of the other towers in the city, arranged the same fate for S. Angelo, but it was saved by cession to the Orsini. It was from hence, on December 15, 1347, that Rienzi fled to Bohemia, at the end of his first period of power, his wife having previously made her escape disguised as a friar.

"The cause of final ruin to this monument," is described by Nibby to have been the resentment of the citizens against a French governor who espoused the cause of the anti-pope (Clement VII.) against Urban VI. in 1378. It was then that the marble casings were all torn from the walls and used as street pavements.

A drawing of Sangallo of 1465 shows the upper part of the fortress crowned with high square towers and turreted buildings; a cincture of bastions and massive square towers girding the whole; two square-built bulwarks flanking the extremity of the bridge, which was then so connected with these outworks that passengers would have immediately found themselves inside the fortress after crossing the river. Marlianus, 1588, describes its double cincture of fortifications,—"a large round tower at the inner extremity of the bridge; two towers with high pinnacles, and the cross on their summits, the river flowing all around."

The Castle began to assume its present aspect under Boniface IX. in 1395. John XXIII., 1411, commenced the covered way to the Vatican, which was finished by Alexander VI.; and roofed by Urban VIII., in 1630. By the last named pope the great outworks of the fortress were built under Bernini, and furnished with cannon made from the bronze roof of the Pantheon. Under Paul III. the interior was decorated with frescoes, and a colossal marble angel erected on the summit, in place of a chapel (S. Angelo inter Nubes), built by Boniface XIV. for the existing angel of bronze, by a Dutch artist, Verschaffelt.

Of the Castle, as we now see it externally, only the quadrangular basement is of the time of Hadrian; the round tower is of that of Urban VIII., its top added by Paul III. The four round towers of the outworks, called after the four Evangelists, are of Nicholas V., 1447.

The interior of the fortress can be visited by an order. Excavations made in 1825 have laid open the sepulchral chamber in the midst of the basement. Here, stood in the centre, the porphyry sarcophagus of Hadrian, which was stolen by Pope Innocent II. to be used as his own tomb in the Lateran, where it was destroyed by the fire of 1360, the cover alone escaping, which was used for the tomb of Otho II., in the atrium of St. Peter's, and which, after filling this office for seven centuries, is now the baptismal font of that basilica. A spiral passage, thirty feet high and eleven wide, up which a chariot could be driven, gradually ascends through the solid mass of masonry. There is wonderfully little to be seen. A saloon of the time of Paul III. is adorned with frescoes of the life of Alexander the Great, by Pierino del Vaga. This room would be used by the pope in case of his having to take refuge in S. Angelo. An adjoining room, adorned with a stucco frieze of Tritons and Nereids, is that in which Cardinal Caraffa was strangled (1561) under Pius IV., for alleged abuses of authority under his uncle, Paul IV.—his brother, the Marquis Caraffa, being beheaded in the castle the same night. The reputed prison of Beatrice Cenci is shown, but it is very uncertain that she was ever confined here,—also the prison of Cagliostro, and that of Benvenuto Cellini, who escaped, and broke his leg in trying to let himself down by a rope from the ramparts. The statue of the angel by Montelupo is to be seen stowed away in a dark corner. Several horrible trabocchette (oubliettes) are shown.

On the roof, from which there is a beautiful view, are many modern prisons, where prisoners suffer terribly from the summer sun beating upon their flat roofs.

Among the sculptures found here were the Barberini Faun, now at Munich, the Dancing Faun, at Florence, and the Bust of Hadrian at the Vatican. The sepulchral inscriptions of the Antonines existed till 1572, when they were cut up by Gregory XIII. (Buoncompagni), and the marble used to decorate a chapel in St. Peter's! The magnificent easter display of fireworks (from an idea of Michael Angelo, carried out by Bernini), called the girandola, used to be exhibited here, but now takes place at S. Pietro in Montorio, or from the Pincio. From 1849 to 1870, the Castle was occupied by French troops, and their banner floated here, except on great festivals, when it was exchanged for that of the pope.

Running behind and crossing the back streets of the Borgo, is the covered passage intended for the escape of the popes to the Castle. It was used by Alexander VI. when invaded by Charles VIII. in 1494, and twice by Clement VII. (Giulio de' Medici), who fled, in 1527, from Moncada, viceroy of Naples, and in May, 1527, during the terrible sack of Rome by the troops of the Constable de Bourbon.

"The Escape" consists of two passages; the upper open like a loggia, the lower covered, and only lighted by loopholes. The keys of both are kept by the pope himself.

S. Angelo is at the entrance of the Borgo, promised at the Italian invasion of September, 1870, as the sanctuary of the papacy, the tiny sovereignty where the temporal sway of the popes should remain undisturbed,—the sole relic left to them of all their ancient dominions.

SALISBURY CATHEDRAL
W. J. Loftie

Salisbury Cathedral, from the point of view of the architectural artist, is the most beautiful and the most perfect in England. The visitor who sees it first on a bright day, can never forget the impression it has made on his mind. Unlike the architects of the so-called "Great Gothic Revival," the builders of Salisbury put their trust in proportion. Incidentally they made their details as elaborate and perfect as possible; but they were subordinated to the general effect, and when during the frightful ravages of the "restorers," let loose upon the church in the past and present centuries, many of the best and most precious of these details and ornaments perished or were renewed, the main building survives, raising its exquisitely graceful spire into the blue sky, its thousand pinnacles all pointing upward and gleaming white against the deep green of the old trees and the emerald turf of the surrounding close. "How long," asked an American visitor, "does it take to grow such turf?" "Oh! not long," was the reply; "only a couple of centuries." One feels at Salisbury that whether the answer was given there or at Oxford, of no place could it be more true. Though when we look near enough, we can see that fresh and white as is the general effect, the masonry of Salisbury is of great antiquity, except, of course, where it has been restored; and antiquity adds another charm, for Salisbury was the first complete cathedral built after the Romanesque tradition had died out, as St. Paul's is the first built after it had been revived. In other cathedrals there are portions and fragments of the same style, and they are always the most beautiful features of the whole building. We can recall the western porch at Ely, and the angel choir at Lincoln, and the Chapter-house at Southwell; but here at Salisbury, we have the whole vast cathedral, all in the same supreme style, every part fitting into its place, and adding its contribution to the general effect, never in contrast, but always in harmony until the effect is attained. What that is may be read in countless books of travel or criticism. Salisbury cathedral, like the Parthenon and all the other— there are not many—buildings which tempt one to call them poems in stone—produces a different feeling in the minds of all who see it. I am not going to add another to the descriptions of the view. On the contrary, I am going about the prosaic task of trying to find out to what circumstances its beauty is due, and why the name of Richard Poore is honoured among lovers of good architecture with that of Christopher Wren, no other Englishman being worthy to make a third. The chief points to be noted about Salisbury are these. The effect does not in any way depend upon ornamental details. This may be proved by two examples taken from the building. The west front was greatly injured at different times, its carving broken, and its figures defaced. The carving has been copied and "restored," and new figures have replaced the old. The front is now neat and spick and span, but the general effect is in no wise improved, but rather deteriorated, by having its antiquity destroyed. It is the same with the chromatic decoration of the interior, and with the "improvement" of the Chapter-house. The painting on the roof tends to lower it; the gaudy, shiny aspect of the Chapter-house goes far to spoil, if it could spoil, the exquisite design and subtle proportions.

Another point to be noticed is this: Salisbury does not owe its beauty to size, nor yet altogether to the style in which it is built. This is easily proved. The great French cathedral of Amiens exceeds Salisbury in all its dimensions, and was built, allowing for the difference between France and England, in the self-same style. Both are examples of First Pointed, and Amiens is, according to Fergusson, at least twice as large in its cubic contents. "The French church covers 71,000 square feet, the English only 55,000. The vault of the first is one hundred and fifty-two feet in height, the latter only eighty-five." There is still a more remarkable difference between the central spires of the two churches. That of Amiens rises to a height of 422 feet; that of Salisbury, the tallest in England, only to 404. Yet the great height of the roof at Amiens robs its spire of any preponderance it might otherwise boast, and leaves the comparatively small steeple of Salisbury a feature of grandeur and beauty only approached by the still lower dome of St. Paul's, which rises at its highest part, the cross, to 365 feet above the ground level.

It will be seen, therefore, that Salisbury owes its effect to something beyond ornament or size. The extraordinary order and regularity of the masonry may have something to say to it, although the stones, as compared with what may be seen in Egypt, and elsewhere, are not very large. But you can trace the same course all round the church and the same stone, oolite from the quarry at Chilmark, has been used throughout. This communicates a certain look of stability to the structure, which is, in itself, more pleasing to the eye than any amount of ornament out of place, or intended, as in modern Gothic, to divert the eye from the poverty of the materials or the absence of proportion. The proportions of Salisbury, like those of St. Paul's, or the Parthenon, are calculated to give the building its full measure of beauty, without anything extraneous.

That Salisbury should have this unity of age and design is owing to a curious fact in the history of the place. The "bishop's stool" had been upon the bleak, chalk down which borders Salisbury Plain. The place was really a castle whose fortifications are still visible; the cathedral within the walls must have been Norman in design, to judge in dry seasons from the marks still visible among the grassy mounds, and from fragments of carved stone built into the wall or cross. Mr. Walcott gives its dimensions as follows: "A nave one hundred and fifty feet by seventy-two feet, a transept one hundred and fifty feet by sixty feet, and a choir sixty feet in length, in all two hundred and seventy feet." The situation was in every way inconvenient, having been chosen for security not comfort. After the King took the fort and filled it with his own soldiers, a governor superseding the bishop, the position of the ecclesiastics became unendurable. The inhabitants in times of comparative peace and security migrated to the rich pastures by the Avon and the Bourne below, while cold winds in winter, and a scarcity of water in summer, finally determined Bishop Poore and his canons, for Sarum was a church of the old foundation, to seek a better country. The old legend says that the site of the new cathedral was determined by the fall of an arrow in Merrifield (or more likely Mirifield), shot by a stalwart archer from the ramparts. The church was raised in a green vale, surrounded by the downs. Pepys, in describing his journey from Hungerford says, "So, all over the Plain by the sight of the steeple, the Plain high and low; to Salisbury by night."

"Of the cathedral," Pepys remarks that it is "most admirable; as big, I think, and handsomer than Westminster, and a most large close about it." Pepys' comparison of Westminster and Salisbury is a very just one; both were built in the then new First Pointed style, but there is no doubt about the superiority of Salisbury in either design or completeness.

In the close, which occupies an extent of half a square mile, there are three gates, the South or Harnham, the East or St. Anne's, and the North or Close Gate, built about 1327. The ground-plan of the church embraces a nave of ten bays, with aisles; a northern porch; a main and a choir transept of four and three bays each; to the east a choir and presbytery, each of three bays, and the so-called Lady Chapel, all having aisles. The cloister is on the south side, and to eastwards of the cloister is the Chapter-house. An octangular canon's vestry and muniment room is to the south of the south-east transept. The pyramidal disposition of the leading lines is very observable from certain points of view. It is the only ancient cathedral in England begun and finished on a uniform plan and in one style. The foundations were laid under Bishop Poore, on the Feast of St. Vitalis (April 28), 1220, and it was built by Elias of Dereham, clerk of the works, and by Nicholas of Portland, and Richard of Farleigh, his successors, the last named completing the spire in 1375. The Beauchamp and Hungerford Chapels, both subsequently removed, were built in the Lady Chapel in the Fifteenth Century. Bishop Audley's Chantry in the choir was built in 1502. In the close, near the north aisle of the nave, as at Chichester, was the Clochard or Campanile. There are several points of resemblance, of which this is one, between Chichester and Salisbury. This bell-tower was taken down in "cold blood" as we may say, or by way of "restoration" in 1799. About the same time Wyatt made many structural and other alterations, which are detailed with undisguised approbation by contemporary writers. Dodsworth gives particulars received from Wyatt himself. They are in form and language, and, I may add, conceit, so like what the "restorer" of to-day uses of a building which he has done his best to ruin, and are besides so interesting, historically, that I am tempted to quote some sentences. Wyatt was first let loose on Salisbury about 1789. He went to work without a doubt or a scruple. The Hungerford and Beauchamp Chapels were "defects." He "expressed his astonishment at the temerity of their builders. They were destroyed, though the consent of their owners had to be obtained first. Their fragments were used in the alterations, some in the organ screen, some in the choir. The walls and buttresses of the Lady Chapel were restored, the windows brought to their proper level, the seats which disfigured it removed, and the pavement was raised a few inches to give an ascent from the choir." The phrase "proper level" is good. Then came almost the worst of Wyatt's "restorations." It was found "necessary" to remove several monuments. New sites were prepared—the result being what we now see in the nave, where the mixture of the fragments of one monument with the ruins of another of a different period has not even the merit of being picturesque. The tomb ascribed traditionally to Bishop Poore and nine others were destroyed, portions being neatly arranged as in a kind of museum "along the plinth between the series of pillars on each side of the nave." Two small porches, one at the north end of the great transept, and the other on the south side, near the Lady Chapel, "were considered as neither adding to the beauty, nor to the convenience of the building. They were accordingly taken down." The "accordingly" is another happy expression. We might be reading a report of Sir G. Scott, or Mr. Pearson, or Mr. Butterfield. Yet this was written close on a hundred years ago. A very interesting series of paintings, representing the months or the Zodiac, were on some of the eastern bays of vaulting. They were highly admired, we are told, by those "regard the mere antiquity of an object as a sufficient title to admiration." These are precisely the words used lately by an architect about the north transept of Westminster Abbey. Wyatt promptly wiped off the traces of these decorations, and "judiciously coloured the arches and ribs of the choir like the original stone. As the Campanile intercepted the most striking view of the structure it was taken down."

When we enter by the west door the first view is hardly so striking as the first view of the exterior. A closer examination and a comparison with other cathedrals shows how far Salisbury is in advance of everything else of its kind. The exquisite lightness and delicate proportions of the steeple are equally apparent in the nave and its aisles, the slender columns, the pointed arches, the light triforium, the lancets of the clerestory, and the soaring vault. The same "order," as the classical architect would say, is practically carried round the church. As we advance eastward, and reach the crossing of the transepts, we observe the curious four centred buttressing arches erected by Bishop Wayte, 1415, to increase the supports of the tower. Similar precautions are seen in Canterbury, Hereford and Wells Cathedrals. Under the tower is a brass plate in the pavement which was placed here in 1737, and marks the fact that the spire inclines twenty-two and a half inches to the south-west. This inclination, which is perfectly visible on the outside, was first calculated by Sir Christopher Wren, who put iron "bandages" round the masonry, and made other repairs. No increase of the deflection has been observed since his time, although the spire was struck by lightning in 1741. The choir screen is by Skidmore. The organ is divided. Some ancient glass may be seen in the triplet windows at the ends of the transepts. The altar stood to the eastward of the second or choir transept, and some parts of the old stalls are still to be seen, but almost everything in this part of the church is new. The Audley chantry (1524), in the latest style of Gothic, is on the north side. There are some remains of the very curious and interesting if not unique iron chantry of Lord Hungerford, formerly in the Lady Chapel, made into a kind of pew or cage, about a hundred years ago, by the heirs of the family when Wyatt destroyed it. A somewhat similar example, or part of one, the Chantry of Edward IV. in St. George's Chapel at Windsor, has already been "restored" away.

The Lady Chapel is probably not correctly described by that name. The whole church is dedicated to the Blessed Virgin. It is perhaps more correctly called Trinity Chapel. Here the colouring, modern, of the roof, and other amendments and improvements made and suggested by Scott, for the most part, though Clutton also showed himself a worthy successor of Wyatt, are exceedingly offensive.

The cloisters are entered from the south-western transept. They are slightly later, in the same style as the church, but were evidently not built till it was finished. In churches of the old foundation cloisters were an ornament, a luxury, and not a necessity, as at Canterbury or Gloucester, where they were needed for the use of the monks. The cloisters of Salisbury are the largest in England, each walk being, within, 181 feet long, or from wall to wall, without, 195 feet. Over the east walk is a fine Library, containing many illuminated and other manuscripts, including some early liturgies.

THE CASTLE OF ANGERS, FRANCE
Henri Jouin

On the 7th of September, 1661, as night was falling, a company of musketeers crossed the drawbridge of the Castle of Angers. Scarcely had they entered the fortress when these musketeers expelled the garrison. This was the King's order. A sub-lieutenant commanded these men: it was d'Artagnan. A prisoner had been confided to him: this was Nicholas Fouquet. The superintendent's servant, La Vallée, and his physician, Pecquet, taking pity upon Fouquet, who was the prey of a quartan fever, obtained leave to share his captivity. The Castle then had shut within it three prisoners, who were subjected to the most rigorous treatment. We know by the official account of Fouquet's detention that the bed in which he had to sleep on the 7th of September "was not of the cleanest." Now for the rest, d'Artagnan, and his two officers, Saint Mars and Saint Leger, maintained an extreme reserve towards their guests. There is no news from outside. Pecquet, before leaving Nantes, had, it is true, fortuitously met Gourville. It was from him that Pecquet got the news of the arrest of Pellisson and the exile of Madame Fouquet. Sorrowful presage! The accused one began first of all to prepare his defense. He wrote several memoirs, but at the end of a few days, writing was prohibited. The president of Chalain, suspected of having wished to bribe a musketeer was also apprehended to be conducted to the Bastille. Louis XIV., Colbert, Le Tellier, and Séguier kept their eyes fixed on Angers. Fouquet lived there until the first of December, having no other pastime between his two attacks of fever than to contemplate with a melancholy look "*la fillette du Roi.*" This was the name by which they designated an iron cage, in which, according to legend, a queen of Sicily had been shut up by her husband "for having built the church of Saint-Maurice at Angers too magnificently." This legend was not calculated to reassure the Superintendent. He knew that he was accused precisely of having used the money of the Treasury to build Vaux-le-Vicomte, the magnificence of which had offended the King. If, through misfortune, the thought of keeping him under such good guard, between these bars, had entered the heads of his enemies, of what advantage was the little bit of liberty that he still enjoyed? Moreover, he was not unaware of the refinements of cruelty that had been practiced for the past two centuries upon the prisoners of State. The "*fillette du Roi,*" made at the order of Louis XI., had not been empty at any period. Had not Cardinal Balue, bishop of Angers, known this instrument of torture at the *Château d'Onzain,* near Blois? Fouquet might well be afraid, for there entered perhaps far more passion than justice in his disgrace. They did not go so far, however, as to put him in a cage. The vigilance and the loyalty of d'Artagnan, and the thickness of the walls of the Castle seemed to Fouquet's enemies, a sufficient safeguard against all danger of his escape. What is then the Castle of Angers?

Péan de la Tuilerie—the *d'Argenville angevin*—comes to tell us. "The Castle is at one of the extremities of the city, on a rock, and surrounded with deep moats, cut in the rock, which is an escarpment on the bank of a river that flows at its base, and from which they lift, by means of a very convenient machine, all the munitions which are necessary. It is of a triangular form, all built of slate and flanked by eighteen round towers and a crescent, which is the gate of the faubourg."

Péan de la Tuilerie wrote in 1778. His description is still very nearly exact. To speak the truth, this military post forms less of a triangle than a pentagon, but the appearance of the Castle remains what it was in the last century. The girdle of moats has been, however, a little changed. The Maine rolls no longer beneath its towers. It is not, as you will readily believe, that the course of the river has been turned. To change the position of the fortress would have been difficult. They considered it simpler to fill up the canal. Some factories, some counting-houses, and some private dwellings occupy the place of the moat, and the traveler seeks vainly at the present moment for that "very convenient machine," of which Péan speaks. Moreover, it would be useless. The Castle has no more need of munitions. English, Bretons and Normans have left it. Their attacks are ended. Angers ignores to-day those savage incursions and perpetual threats, which for several centuries, troubling its repose, kept its independence in check. Then the Castle had to sustain repeated sieges. The silence that envelops it has grown out of the clank of arms and the cries of the combatants, who many times made this stone colossus tremble to its very foundations. Ah! the noble rampart of the city! Its great days and its glorious past, haunt my memory.

Who chose its site? Count Eudes, under the royal approbation of Charles the Bald. The Plantagenets seem to have embellished and fortified the north turret of the building, but it is to Louis IX. that the primitive castle is indebted to its transformation into a military post. Its imposing towers, firmly planted on their bases of schist, are the work of Louis IX. Its large canals hollowed out of the slate date from the last years of the Fifteenth Century. They give character to the citadel. You judge it most impregnable in measuring the depth of its moats with your eye; but how many times had the enemy been repulsed by the rain of projectiles thrown from the Castle?

In 1444, the English approached the city. They ravaged the country mercilessly, and pillaged and ruined according to their good pleasure. The army encamped near the fortress, intending to open the siege on the following day. On the following day the English troops took their departure. What could have been the cause of their retreat? One of the English chiefs was hit in the forehead by a shot and instantly killed. This occasioned such confusion that the assailants fled. An artilleryman thus saved the city.

The Fifteenth Century was, moreover, the great epoch for the Castle of Angers. Louis XI., profound politician and crafty of action, meditated upon uniting the Duchy of Anjou to the crown of France. This was shown on two occasions. The second time, the Prince being at war with Bretagne had levied previously upon the city of Angers for subsidies for his troops. He came again. Behnard Guillaume Cerizay, his secretary, and three chamberlains entered Angers. They convoked and consulted with the notables. At this time *plébiscites* were unknown. People did not have the character to defend their rights and their interests. They were minors. But if the Angevin populace could have spoken, it would not have spoken better than its representatives. The notables chose for France. "The assembly," wrote M. Port, "through the voice of the Chancellor of Anjou, pledged its faith to the King. On the following day, Louis XI. had come to the Castle offering a favourable reply to all requests, granting to the most zealous petitions leave to have a house in the city." The Castle in which this act of submission to the King of France took place, was formerly the property of the Duc d'Anjou, who was at the same time Count of Provence and King of Sicily, René, son of Yolande, poet, amateur, bibliophile, collector, and patron of poets, sculptors, goldsmiths, tapestry-workers and illuminators who filled his court,

> *"René le prince populaire,*
> *Doux artiste aux yeux éblouis*
> *Des peintres que, pour lui plaire*
> *Lui fait offrir le roi Louis."*

It was at the Castle of Angers, in a kind of little manor-house flanked by four turrets, that René first saw the light on the 16th of January, 1409. The Maugine was his nurse in the citadel, the Maugine, Tiphaine, to whom in after years he erected a tomb, the touching inscription upon which is from his hand. Married at the age of twelve to Isabelle de Lorraine, René d'Anjou, fighting everywhere for twenty-five years, made only rare appearances at the Castle of Angers; but soon comes the death of Isabelle and upon it quickly follows the second marriage of the prince with Jeanne de Laval, upon which he establishes his residence at Angers. Farewell war, diplomacy, treaties and conquests! René yields himself up to the charm of his young wife. To her the poet consecrates his loving stanzas of *Regnault and Jeanneton*, a kind of autobiography of the husband and wife. *The Shepherd and the Shepherdess*, a delicate pastorale composed in honour of Jeanne de Laval, will be put into its final form under the skies of Provence, at Tarascon; but it is in the Angevin country that the poet finds all his ideas as he strolls at the side of the beautiful Jeanne. The writers of the time show us René going out of the Castle without escort, accompanied solely by his royal spouse, and taking the *chemin de la Baumette*. After passing through the field-gate, the illustrious personages got into a fisherman's boat below the *Basse-Chaîne*, and descended the Maine to that solitary hermitage, where Rabelais will presently come to study at the Cordeliers.

It is also from this Castle that René d'Anjou issues to cross his "beautiful city" on foot to his dear hermitage, where he loved to consort "with the citizens of Angers, the artists and the men of learning of his Court."

René disappeared; Louis XI. reigned. A century elapsed. Henri III. yielded to the request of the common people of the city who wished for the destruction of the Castle. The citadel suffered. Letters patent from the King authorized the governor of Anjou to "raze to the ground the stones of all the walls, towers, lodgings, buildings and fortifications of the Castle." Already the workmen are called. Who will direct this barbarous piece of work? Donadieu, Sieur de Puycharic, claims this honour. Puycharic is the governor of the Castle. They grant his wish. But a man of heart, a soldier, can he conscientiously annihilate the ramparts of a city? This military post of which he is the keeper has its past of glorious traditions. It is worthy of respect. Its services, it seems to him, ought to be taken into consideration. This is what Puycharic thought aside, and for ten years—you have read of this—for ten years—with clever ingenuity, Puycharic kept his army of destroyers busy without destroying anything. He yielded to the necessities of the hour by demolishing the outside buildings of the Castle which he had inherited from his predecessors; a garden pavilion, built by Louisa of Savoy, disappeared; the field-gate, whose defence was difficult, was altered; two useless towers lost their turrets, and in proportion as the waggons full of stones left the Castle, the common people exulted, proud of their success. From time to time, it is true, public opinion complained of the slowness of the workmen at the town's expense. "Isolated during the troubles," M. Port has said of him, "in the heart of the Angevin league, the valiant captain was not merely satisfied to guard the place but bravely attacked the foe in the field, one day the Lion d'Angers, another Brissac, Rochefort, Beaupreau, and Chemillé, fighting for about ten years in every kind of warlike adventure, fought against and fighting, holding the country in hand and preparing the place for the King." His headquarters were at the Castle. It was here that he rallied his men and came to heal his wounds between encounters. Peace being restored, Puycharic, being appointed senechal of Anjou, dismissed his workmen, who were greatly astonished and perhaps greatly pleased at having repaired, embellished and fortified the Castle that they thought they were pulling down.

Puycharic died in 1605. His funeral was magnificent. He rests in the chapel of the Jacobins; and his brothers, the bishops of Saint-Papoul and d'Auxerre erected to his memory a monument surmounted by his statue.

THE PAGODA OF TANJORE, INDIA
G. W. Steevens

Southward out of Madras you still run through the new India, the old India of the nursery. Now it is vivid with long grass, now tufted with cotton, then dark-green with stooping palm-heads or black with firs; anon brown with fallow, blue with lakes and lagoons, black with cloud-shadowing pools starred with white water-lilies. Presently red hills break out of the woods, then sink again to sweeping pastures dotted only with water-hoists and naked herdsmen.

Then in the placid landscape you are almost startled by the sight of monuments of religion. A tall quadrangular pyramid, its courses lined with rude statues, a couple of half-shaped human figures, ten times human size, a ring of colossal hobby-horses sitting on their haunches like a tea-party in Wonderland—they burst grotesquely out of meadow and thicket, standing all alone with the soil and the trees. No worshippers, no sign of human life near them, no hint of their origin or purpose—till you almost wonder whether they are artificial at all, and not petrified monsters from the beginning of the world.

These are the outposts of the great pagodas of Southern India—those sublime monstrosities which scarce any European ever sees, which most have never heard of, but which afford perhaps the strongest testimony in all India at once to the vitality and the incomprehensibility of Hinduism. The religion that inspired such toilsome devotion must be one of the greatest forces in history; yet the Western mind can detect neither any touch of art in the monuments themselves nor any strain of beauty in the creed. Both command your respect by their size: that which is so vast, so enduring, can hardly, you tell yourself, be contemptible. And still you can see nothing in the temples but misshapen piles of uncouthness, nothing in the religion but unearthly superstitions, half meaningless and half foul.

The nearest approach to a symmetrical building is the great pagoda of Tanjore. Long before you near the gate you see its tall pyramidal tower, shooting free above crooked streets and slanting roofs. Presently you see the lower similar towers, so far from the first that you would never call them part of the same building. In reality they are the outer and inner gateways—*gopura* is their proper name—built in diminishing courses, garnished with carving and statuary. From a distance the massive solemnity of their outlines, the stone lace of their decorations, strike you with an overwhelming assertion of rich majesty. But you are in India, and you wait for the inevitable incongruity.

It comes at the very gate. The entrance is not under the stately gopura, but under a screen and scaffolding of lath and plaster daubed with yellow and green grotesqueness—

men with lotus-eyes looking out of their temples, horses with heads like snakes, and kings as tall as elephants. There is to be a great festival in a day or two, explains the suave Brahman; therefore the gopuras are boarded up with pictures beside which the tapestries of our pavement-artists are truth and beauty. You walk through scaffold-poles into a great square round the great tower, and with reverence they show you that colossal monolith, the great bull of Tanjore. I wish I could show you a picture of him, for words are unequal to him. In size he stands, or rather sits, thirty-eight hands two. His material is black granite, but it is kept so piously anointed with grease that he looks as if he were made of toffee. In attitude he suggests a roast hare, and he wears a half-smug, half-coquettish expression, as if he hoped that nobody would kiss him.

From this wonder you pass to the shrines of the chief gods. The unbeliever may not enter, but you stand at the door while a man goes along the darkness with a flambeau. The light falls on silk and tinsel, and by faith you can divine a seated image at the end. Next you are at the foot of the great tower, and the ridiculous has become the sublime again. Every story is lined with serene-faced gods and goddesses, dwindling rank above rank, a ladder of deities that seems to climb half-way up to heaven. Then the Brahman shows you a stone bull seated on the ground, like a younger brother of the great one. "It is in existence," he says, throwing out his words in groups, dispassionately, as though somebody else were speaking and it were nothing at all to do with him—"it is in existence—to show the dimensions—of four other bulls—which are in existence—up there." You lay your head back between your shoulder-blades, and up there, at the very top, among gods so small that you wonder whether they are gods or only panels or pillars, are four more little brothers of the hare-shaped toffee-textured monster below.

Reduplication is the keynote of Hindu art. The same bulls everywhere, the same gods everywhere, and all round the cloistered outer wall scores on scores of granite, fat-dripping, flower-crowned emblems, so crudely shapeless that you forget their gross significance—but all absolutely alike. Next the Brahman leads you aside to piles and piles of what look like overgrown, gaudily painted children's toys. This is an exact facsimile of the Tower, reduced and imitated in wood. It is all in pieces, but at the festival the parts are fitted together and carried on a car. Every god sculptured on the pyramid is represented in a section of this model, waiting to be fitted into his place. Only what is richly mellow in tinted stone is garishly tawdry in king's yellow and red lead—and again you tumble from the sublime to the infantile.

Next, a little shrine that is a net of the most delicate carving—stone as light and fantastic as wood; pillar and panel, moulding and cornice, lattice and imagery, all tapering gracefully till they become miniatures at the summit. It is a gem of exquisite taste and patient labour. And the very next minute you are again among flaming red and yellow dragon-tigers and duck-peacocks, and the one is just as holy and just as beautiful to its worshippers as the other. From which objects of veneration the Brahman passes lightly to the domestic life of the frescoed rajahs of Tanjore. "This gentleman—marry seventeen wives—all one day—doubtless in anxiety of getting son." It is quite true. The Rajah, having but three wives and no child, resolved to marry six more young ladies, and collected seventeen to choose them from. But the fathers and brothers of the rejected eleven were affronted; and rather than have any unpleasantness on his wedding-day, his Majesty tactfully married the whole seventeen, nine in the morning and eight in the afternoon. "And here," pursued the Brahman automatically, showing a tank, "he will let in water—and here he will play—with all his females—and all that."

That is all, except to write your name in the visitor's book. As I went in to sign, I noticed a band of musicians standing at the door and thought no more of it. But as my pen touched the paper, suddenly reedy pipes and discordant fiddles and heady tom-toms began to play "God Save the Queen." A huge chaplet of muslin and tinsel, like a magnified Christmas-tree stocking, was cast about my neck; betel and attar-of-rose were brought up in silver vessels, and flowers and fruits on silver trays. The pagoda keeps its character to the end: the compliment was sublime—and I ridiculous.

Yet the temple of Tanjore is the most simple and orderly of all its kind. Visit the great pagoda of Madura and you will come out mazed with Hinduism. All its mysteries and incongruities, its lofty metaphysics and its unabashed lewdness, seem to brood over the dark chambers and crannying passages. The place is enormous. Over the four chief gateways rise huge pyramid-towers, coloured like harlequins, red tigers jostling the multiplied arms and legs of blue and yellow gods and goddesses so thick that the gopuras seem built of them. In the pure sunlight you almost blush for their crudity, just as you would blush if the theatre roof were lifted off during a matinée. But inside the place is nearly all half-lighted, dim, and cryptic. You go through a labyrinth, that seems endless, of dark chambers and aisles. Now you are in thick blackness, now in twilight, now the sun falls on fretwork over pillared galleries and damp-smelling walls. But as the light falls on the pillar you start, for it is carved into the shape of an elephant-headed Ganesh, or a conventionally high-stepping Shiva. On you go, from maze to maze, till there is no more recollection of direction or guess at size: you are lost in an underground world of gods that are half devils; you hardly distinguish the silent-footed, gleaming-eyed attendants from the stone figures. Some of the fantastic images are smeared with red-lead to simulate blood: all drip with fat. A heavy smell of grease and stagnant tank-water loads your lungs.

You feel that you are bewitched—lost and helpless among unclean things. When you come out into the sun and the cleaner dirt of the town, you draw long breaths. If you could understand the Hindu religion, you tell yourself, you would understand the Hindu mind. But that, being of the West, you never, never will.

THE VENDRAMIN-CALERGI, ITALY
Théophile Gautier

Following a vagabond method, let us regain the Grand Canal and give some details upon the Vendramin Palace, now occupied by the Duchesse de Berry. It is of a rich and noble architecture, probably by Pietro Lombardo; in the entablature and above the windows, little cherubs uphold storied shields adorned with exquisite taste, and contribute much elegance to this façade. A garden of somewhat restricted space contributes some green trees alongside this palace, which would not be distinguished from the others if the large white and blue posts with ropes did not indicate, by means of the fleur-de-lis painted upon them, a princely and semi-royal dwelling.

After having obtained permission to visit this palace, *valets* in green livery welcome you very politely at the base of the staircase, the steps of which are laved by the waters, fasten your boat to the posts, and take you into a vestibule, where you wait until all the formalities of admission are complied with.

This vestibule is just as long as the palace; it opens

upon a kind of court similar to the courts of our hotels.

Two hitched gondolas and a few earthen pots containing small firs and other poor plants that are dying of thirst are all that adorn the bareness of this vast waiting-room that is found in every Venetian palace,—an antechamber that is also a landing-place.

In the centre of this vestibule, a little to the left, a wide stairway between two walls is seen where the same decoration of miserable plants appear. A narrow carpet covers the steps leading to an immense hall resembling a vestibule, without furniture and without adornment. From this, you enter the dining-room, the walls of which are hung with family portraits.

This is a long square room. It is very well lighted by two enormous French windows.

An oval table stands in the centre and a screen shields the entrance. Upon the wall to the right you notice the portrait of the Duchesse de Bourgogne in a blue velvet dress; also of the Comte d'Artois and Madame la Princesse de Lamballe and several others. Upon the left wall opposite, is the full length portrait of Louis XV., and on either side of him, his daughters.

In this dining-room, a masked door opens into a dark chapel, so small that it will barely hold six persons. You can count four *Prie-Dieu* there. On the right, a large door opens into a very modern drawing-room filled with pictures and a great number of small pieces of furniture: English tables, Parisian coffers,—nothing is lacking to produce that charming home-like feeling that is derived from luxurious trifles. Two portraits of Her Royal Highness are placed opposite one another; that by Lawrence in a dress of white satin, with a rose on her breast, exhibits the most charming little foot that can possibly be admired in a white satin slipper.

On walking through the dining-room, you enter, by a door on the left, a little salon, which seems relatively small after the preceding rooms, and perhaps overwhelmed by the sumptuous furniture that adorns it. It contains thirty splendid pictures; this is a kind of Uffizi or *Salon carré*, where scarcely one of the greatest names in painting is missing. Among these great masterpieces shines a Virgin by Andrea del Sarto, so beautiful that it would make cold chills run through the most elementary connoisseur and the most hide-bound and prosaic Philistine.

This Salon illumincd by a soft and well distributed light, seems to me the select spot, the very heart of the building, and I left it with deep regret to go and visit the famous salon which contains those two porphyry columns whose value is so great that they are worth more than the entire palace. They are placed in front of a door, and thus produce as little effect as the lapis lazuli in the "Salon Serra" in Genoa, which you might well believe were painted and varnished, and which strongly resemble a metallic blue watered silk.

There is still another salon, but it is not remarkable in any way. In the four corners, four bracket pedestals support four busts: those of the Duc de Berry, of Charles X., and other members of the royal family.

The Vendramin-Calergi has gained an additional interest in recent years on account of the fact that Richard Wagner died in it on Feb. 13, 1883.—E. S.

Fountain Of The Old Seraglio, Turkey

A VISIT TO THE OLD SERAGLIO, CONSTANTINOPLE
Pierre Loti

The rising sun gilds the mosque, gilds it under the fresh plane-trees; in the air there is a white mist which is like the original veil of day. The little Turkish *cafés* begin to open, and two or three *minims* are already being shaved in the open air under the trees.

It is evidently very early, and I have time to stop here before returning to Pera. I sit down under the trellis ordering coffee with those warm little *bonbons* that they sell here in the morning, and I think this better than the most delicate breakfast.

About two hours afterwards, about eight o'clock, a carriage takes me back to Stamboul in the company of an aide-de-camp of His Majesty; and in a solemn and desert-like quarter, where the grass pushes up between the stones of the pavement, our coachman stops before a forbidding enclosure like that of a Mediæval fortress.

These walls shut in a little corner of earth which is

absolutely special and unique, and which is the extreme point of Oriental Europe,—a promontory that juts out towards neighbouring Asia, and which was, moreover, for many centuries, the residence of the Caliphs and a place of incomparable splendour. This, and the sacred suburb of Eyoub contain all that is most exquisite in Constantinople: this is the "Old Seraglio,"—a name that alone evokes a world of dreams.

They open for us a door in this wall, and, then, as soon as the barrier is passed, the delicious melancholy of interior things is revealed to us, and the dead Past takes us to itself and envelops us with its winding-sheet.

At first, there is silence and shadow. Empty, desolate courts, where the neglected grass pushes through the flag-stones and where still live ancient trees that were contemporaries of the magnificent sultans of former times: black cypresses as tall as towers, plane-trees which have acquired unwonted forms, all hollowed out by time, being supported only by immense shreds of bark and bent like old men.

Then come the galleries with colonnades in the ancient Turkish style, painted with strange frescoes, under which the great Solomon forced the ambassadors of the European kings to enter. And this place, happily never open to profane visitors, has not yet become a common promenade for tourists; behind the high walls, it preserves a little mysterious peace, it is all imprinted with the sadness of dead splendour.

Crossing these first courts, we have upon the right impenetrable gardens, where you see rising above the clumps of cypress old kiosks with closed windows,—the residences of imperial widows and aged princesses who wish to end their days here in this austere retreat in one of the most wonderful sites in the world.

It is all bathed in sunlight, all dazzling in tranquil light, the last portion of this walled-in spot to which we have now come,—the very last point of the Old Seraglio, and of Europe. It is a solitary esplanade, very elevated and very white, dominating the distant blue of the sea and of Asia. The clear morning sunlight inundates those depths of space out yonder, where the towns, the islets and the mountains are sketched out in light tints above the motionless sheet of Marmora.

Around us are old buildings also white, which contain all that is rarest and most precious in Turkey.

First the kiosk, forbidden to infidels, where the cloak of the Prophet is kept in a cover embroidered with jewels. Then the kiosk of Bagdad, the interior of which is entirely clothed in those old Persian faïences; which are priceless to-day: the branches of red flowers were made upon them with coral that they liquified by a process now lost and spread upon them like pigment.

Then the Imperial Treasury, very white also under its layers of whitewash and barred like a prison; and whose iron gates will be opened for me presently.

And finally, a palace, uninhabited, but well maintained, which we entered and sat down. Steps of white marble led us to the salons of the first floor, which were furnished about the middle of the last century in the European taste. They are of the Louis XV. style, to which an imperceptible mixture of Oriental singularity gives a special charm. The white and gold wainscots with old cherry or old lilac damask with white flowers show nothing but light tints mellowed by time. There are some large Sèvres and Chinese vases, and few other objects, but all of them are old and rare. Much space, air, and light, and a tranquil symmetry in the arrangement of everything—give a feeling of changelessness and neglect.

And there in a sort of sumptuous solitude, seated on these *fauteuils* of a deliciously pale rose, before large open windows, we have from this last promontory of Europe, the splendid view that charmed the Sultans of the past. To our left, and very far below us, the Bosphorus spreads, furrowed with ships and caïques; the whiteness of the marble quays are reflected in it; the whiteness of the new imperial residences, Dolma Bagtche and Tcheragan, are mirrored inverted in long, pale lines; the row of palace and mosques is pictured magnificently upon its banks. Opposite is Asia, still bluish in the remaining drifts of the morning mist; it is Scutari, with its domes and minarets, with its immense cemetery and its forest of dark cypresses. To the right, the infinite expanse of Marmora;—distant steamboats are moving upon it, lost in all that diaphanous blue,—little grey silhouettes trailing delicate clouds of smoke.

How well it was chosen, this site, to dominate and watch from above that Turkey, seated superbly on two divisions of the world! And to-day, what peace and what melancholy splendour in this complete isolation from all the agitations of modern life, in this great silence of abandonment, under this clear and mournful sun!

When the guardian of the Treasury—an old man with a white beard—is ready to open the iron door with his enormous keys, twenty individuals come to form a hedge, ten to the right, ten to the left, on each side of the entrance.

We pass between this double row and enter the rather dark halls, into which they all follow us.

The cavern of Ali Baba could never have been filled with such wealth! For eight centuries they have been heaping up here the rarest jewels and the most astonishing marvels of art. As our eyes become rested from the outside sunlight, and get accustomed to the shadowy interior, the diamonds begin to sparkle everywhere. Things in profusion, without age or price, classified by species upon shelves. Arms of all periods, from Genghis Khan to Mahomet; weapons of silver and gold set with jewels. Then there are collections of golden coffers of all sizes and of all styles; some are covered with rubies, others with diamonds and others with sapphires; some of them are even cut out of a single emerald as big as an ostrich's egg. Then there are services for coffee, for drinking, and ewers of antique and exquisite forms. And the stuffs fit for fays; the saddles; the harness, the housings of parade in brocades of gold and silver, embroidered and encrusted with flowers in precious stones; the large thrones made to sit upon cross-legged: all these in ruby and fine pearl together produce a rosy brilliancy; elsewhere, others covered with emeralds and brilliant in their green reflections, look as if bathed in sea-water.

In the last hall, there is waiting for us behind the

windows a motionless and terrible company: twenty-eight *macabre* dolls, of human size, standing up straight in a military row with their elbows touching each other. They all wear that high pear-shaped turban that has not been in use for a century, and which is only to be seen upon the catafalques of distinguished personages, in the twilight of mortuary kiosks, or carved upon the tombs—so that this kind of a turban is for me absolutely associated with the idea of death. Until the beginning of this century, whenever a sultan died, they brought here a doll clothed in the ceremonial robes of the dead sovereign, they placed marvellous arms in his belt, put on his turban, and his magnificent jewelled aigrette,—and it remained here forever covered with this eternally wasted wealth. The twenty-eight Sultans who succeeded each other from the capture of Constantinople until the end of the Seventeenth Century are standing here in their imperial robes in facsimile; slowly has the sombre and sumptuous assembly increased, new funeral dolls came one by one to range themselves in line with the old ones, who had awaited them for hundreds of years, sure of seeing them at last—and they are now touching each other's elbows.

Their long robes are of the strangest brocades, with great mysterious designs whose tints are dimmed by time; priceless poignards with large handles made of a single precious stone, rust, notwithstanding the care, in the silken belts; it even seems that the enormous diamonds of the aigrettes have lost some of their fire, and shine with a yellowish and dulled light.

And this unheard of luxury, all powdered with dust, is sad to look upon. Fabulously magnificent, the dolls with the high coiffure, objects of so much human covetousness guarded there behind the double doors of iron, useless and dangerous, see the seasons, years, reigns, revolutions and centuries pass by with the same immobility and the same silence, with scarcely any daylight through the gratings of the old windows and in total darkness after the sun sets. Each one bears his name, written like a common name upon a faded ticket—illustrious names that were formerly terrible: Mourad the Conqueror, Soliman the Magnificent,

Mohammed and Mahmoud. I believe that these dolls give me the most terrifying lesson of fragility and nothingness.

THE DUOMO, THE LEANING TOWER. THE BAPTISTERY AND THE CAMPO-SANTO OF PISA
H. A. TAINE

There are two Pisas: one in which people are bored and where they have lived in a provincial manner since the decadence; this is the greater part of the city, with the exception of a secluded corner: the other is this corner, a marble sepulchre, where the Duomo, the Baptistery, the Leaning Tower and the Campo-Santo repose silently like beautiful things that are dead. The true Pisa is here, and in these relics of an extinguished life, you find a world.

A renaissance before the renaissance, a second and almost antique budding of an antique civilization, a spring-time after six centuries of snow,—such are the ideas and words that crowd into the mind. Everything is of marble, white marble, whose immaculate whiteness shines in the azure. On all sides are large solid forms, the cupola, the full wall, the balanced stories, the firmly-planted round or square mass; but over these forms, revived from the antique, like delicate foliage that clothes an old tree-trunk, there is spread an individual invention and a new decoration of the small columns surmounted by arcades, and the originality and grace of this architecture thus renewed cannot be described.

Duomo, Leaning Tower, Baptistery and Campo Santo, Italy

In 1083, to honour the Virgin who had given them the victory over the Saracens of Sardinia, the Pisans began to build their Duomo.

This is almost a Roman basilica, I should say a temple surmounted by another temple, or if you like better, a house having its gable for a façade, and this gable is cut off at the peak to support a still smaller house. Five stories of columns cover the entire façade with their superimposed porticoes. Two by two they are coupled together to support the little arcades; all these lovely columns of white marble under their black arcades make an aërial population that is most graceful and unexpected. In no place here do you perceive that sorrowful reverie of the Mediæval north; it is the holiday of a young nation that is awakening, and, in the joy of its newly acquired wealth, honours its gods. She has gathered from the distant shores to which her wars and trade led her, capitals, ornaments and entire columns and these fragments of antiquity fit into the work without any incongruity; for the work is instinctively cast into the ancient mould and is only developed with a grain of fantasy on the side of delicacy and charm. All the antique forms re-appear, but remodelled in the same spirit, by a new and original vivacity. The exterior columns of the Greek temple are reduced, multiplied and elevated into the air and are not only a support but have become an ornament. The Roman or Byzantine dome is elongated and its natural heaviness diminished beneath a crown of slender little columns with a mitre ornament which girds it in the centre with its delicate gallery. On the two sides of the great door two Corinthian columns are enveloped with the luxuriant leaves, buds and twining stems of the acanthus, and from the threshold we see the church with its rows of black, and white columns of nave and transept, with their multitude of slender and beautiful forms rising up like an altar of candelabra. A new spirit appears here, a more delicate sense of feeling; it is not excessive and confused as in the north, but, at the same time, it is not contented with merely the grave simplicity and the robust nudity of antique architecture. This spirit is the daughter of a pagan mother, healthy and gay, but more feminine than her mother.

She is not yet an adult, sure of her steps; she makes awkward mistakes. The lateral façades outside are monotonous. The cupola within is a reversed funnel, of a strange and disagreeable form. The union of the two arms of the cross is unpleasing, and a number of modernized chapels dispel the charm of the purity found in Sienna. At the second glance, however, all this is forgotten, and the effect of the whole is felt again. Four rows of Corinthian columns, surmounted by arcades, divide the church into five naves and form a forest. A second passage also as richly peopled with columns crosses the first one, and above the beautiful grove, rows of still smaller columns are carried along and intersect each other in order to uphold in the air the quadruple gallery, also prolonged and intersected. The ceiling is flat; the windows are little, and most of them without panes; they allow the walls to exhibit the grandeur and solidity of their mass, and down these long lines of straight and simple windows the untempered daylight makes these innumerable columns glow with the serenity of an ancient temple.

It is not, however, wholly an ancient temple, and there lies its peculiar charm: at the back of the choir the entire hollowed out apsis is occupied with a large Christ[11] in a golden robe, with the Virgin and another smaller saint. His face is gentle and sad: on this golden background in the dimness of the pale daylight he seems like a vision. Certainly, a number of pictures and constructions of the Middle Ages supply all the needs of ecstasy. Other fragments show the decadence and the deep barbarism from which they sprang. There remains one of those ancient bronze doors covered with formless and horrible bronze bas-reliefs.

Such is what the descendants of the sculptors preserved out of antiquity, such is what the human mind became in the chaos of the Tenth Century at the time of the Hungarian invasions, of Marozzia and Theodora: sad, mournful, anæmic, dislocated and mechanical figures, God the Father and six angels, three on one side and three on the other, all leaning at the same angle like a row of cards leaning against one another; the twelve apostles all in a row, six in front and six in the intervening spaces, like those round rings with holes for eyes and long lines for arms that children scribble in their exercise-books. On the other hand, the entrance doors, carved by John of Bologna,[12] are full of life: leaves of the rose, the grapevine, the medlar, the orange and the laurel with their berries, their fruits and their

---

[11] By Jacopo Turrita, the restorer of the mosaic.
[12] 1602.

flowers, amongst which are birds and animals, twine about and make frames for animated figures and groups that are energetic and imposing. This wealth of truthful and vital forms is peculiar to the Sixteenth Century: it discovered nature and man at the same time. Five centuries lie between the work of these two doors.

There is nothing more to say about the Baptistery or the Leaning Tower; the same idea, the same taste and even the same style are seen in them. The one is a simple isolated dome; the other is a cylinder; each has its exterior decoration of columns. However, each has its own distinct and speaking physiognomy; but too much time would be occupied in either talking or writing about them and too many technical terms would be needed to distinguish the subtle differences. I will only mention the inclination of the Tower. It is supposed that when the Tower was half-finished, it leaned and that the architects kept on, and since they went on with it this inclination did not seem to have troubled them. At all events, there are other leaning towers in Italy,—at Bologna, for instance; voluntarily, or involuntarily, this fondness for oddity, this search for paradox and this yielding to fantasy, is one of the characteristics of the Middle Ages.

In the centre of the Baptistery is a superb eight-sided basin; each one of three sides is incrusted with a rich and complicated flower in full bloom, and each flower is different. There is a circle of large Corinthian columns around it, supporting round-arched arcades; most of them are ancient and are ornamented with antique bas-reliefs: Meleager with his barking dogs and the nude bodies of his companions is assisting at Christian mysteries. On the left, there is a pulpit similar to the one in Sienna, the first work of Nicholas of Pisa,[13] a simple marble coffer supported on marble columns and covered with carvings. The feeling of the strength and nudity of antiquity is exhibited here in a striking manner. The sculptor understood the postures and movements of the body. His figures, a little massive, are grand and simple; sometimes he reproduces the tunics and

---

[13] 1260.

---

the folds of the Roman costume; one of his nude personages, a kind of Hercules carrying a lion on his shoulders, has that large chest and the strained muscles that the sculptors of the Sixteenth Century loved so much. What a difference to human civilization and what a hastening of it there would have been if these restorers of ancient beauty, these young Republics of the Twelfth and Thirteenth Centuries, these precocious creators of modern thought had been left to themselves like the ancient Greeks, if they had followed their natural bent, if mystical tradition had not intervened to limit and divert their effort, if secular genius had developed among them, as it formerly did in Greece, amongst free, rude and healthy institutions, and not, as it did, two centuries later, in the midst of the servitude and the corruptions of the decadence.

The last of these edifices, the Campo-Santo, is a cemetery, the earth of which, brought from Palestine, is holy. Four high walls of polished marble surround it with their white and highly ornamented panels. Within, a square gallery forms a promenade and opens upon a court through arcades trellised with ogival windows. It is filled with mortuary monuments, busts, inscriptions, and statues of every form and of every age. Nothing could be nobler or simpler. A framework of dark wood supports the vault, and the naked crest of the roof cuts the crystal of the sky. At the corners four cypresses rustle their leaves in the light breeze. The grass grows in the court with freshness and wild luxuriance. Here and there a climbing flower twines itself around a column, a little rosebush, or tiny shrub, glowing in a ray of sunlight. Not a sound,—this quarter is deserted; now and then you hear only the voice of a stroller which echoes as if beneath the vault of a church. It is the veritable cemetery of a free and Christian city; here before the tombs of the great, you can well reflect upon death and public affairs.

ROCHESTER CASTLE, ENGLAND
Arthur Shadwell Martin

The Romans, who always had a keen eye for favourable defensive sites, were scarcely likely to miss the high ground in the great bend of the Medway not far from where it falls into the Thames. The Watling Street from Dover to London passed the river, moreover, at this point and received protection from the Roman camp. The Saxons and Danes also maintained the Castle of Hrofa here. The usual timber fortifications were constructed in an oblong enclosure of about seven acres, including a large conical mound of the Eastern chalk range called Bully Hill. It must even at that date have been a place of some strength, because when it was besieged by the Danes in 885, it was able to hold out long enough for Alfred to come to its relief. At the Conquest, the Normans recognized the strength of the position and added their own improved methods of fortification, enclosing a quadrangular space close to the river with a strong curtain wall and afterwards building a massive square keep in the enclosure. The Saxon works were left outside and used merely as an outpost, as was the case at Warwick and Canterbury. The original quadrangular enclosure had a wall-circuit of 580 yards, the North and

South walls measuring 160, and the East and West 130 each. The East front faced the cathedral which even at that day was venerable. The West wall ran along the river front. The other three walls were defended by a broad and deep moat, traces of which still remain. Much of the outer wall, with square open towers recurring at intervals also exists. The main entrance or gatehouse with drawbridge, which no longer exists, was at the North-east angle, from which there was a steep descent to what is now the High Street. At the North-west angle, was a bastion tower with a postern gate. Although this tower no longer exists, it was still standing as late as 1735, immediately on the shore, commanding the bridge. A large round tower still stands at the South-east angle. It measures thirty feet in diameter; it has two floors and is loop-holed for archery. Two rectangular towers that defended the East front are still in existence. Throughout the constructions, we cannot fail to notice and admire the strength and massiveness of the masonry. To this the ruin owes its preservation, for besides the destroying hand of time, the neglect of unappreciative generations, and the destruction wrought by greed and fanaticism, it has also suffered from several sieges.

On the highest ground of the enclosure, near the South-east angle, stands the keep. In grandeur and impressiveness, this tower does not suffer in comparison with any English keep of the Norman period. Neither the smaller keep of Newcastle, nor the larger ones of Colchester, Canterbury, Norwich and Hedingham show the original arrangement better than Rochester. Its base is more than seventy feet square, and it is 113 feet high. It is buttressed at the angles with four small towers each twelve feet square. These, rising twelve feet above the principal mass, add greatly to the picturesque effect of the whole. Clinging like a limpet to the East angle of the keep is a smaller tower twenty-eight feet square and about seventy-five feet high. This contained the chief entrance to the keep. It had a flight of steps and an arched gateway enriched. This and the other arches are constructed of Caen stone brought from Normandy; the walls, from ten to twelve feet thick, are built with Kentish rag. Even when this smaller tower was taken in an assault, the besiegers still had trouble to get into the keep proper, for the vestibule was divided from the rooms of the great keep by a portcullis in the main wall. The groove in which it worked and traces of the ironwork still remain.

The keep contains three storeys of lofty apartments, with a vault beneath. As in the tower of London, it is divided into two nearly equal parts by a wall running East and West that rises to the roof. Its thickness allows it to contain a well two feet nine inches in diameter with openings by which each apartment might be supplied with water. By this arrangement, it was impossible for besiegers to cut off the drinking supply of the garrison. The thickness of the walls also admits of mural galleries, as in the White Tower, and a well staircase leading from the vault to the roof, communicating with each apartment. The basement and first floor received their light through loop-holes; the rooms of the higher storeys have their walls pierced with windows.

On the second storey were the rooms of state, thirty-two feet high. It has two tiers of windows, the upper tier having a passage in the wall in front of the windows. On this floor, the apartments open into one another through the central dividing wall by four arches; and in the north-east corner is a large doorway leading into an oratory or chapel built over the great entrance. A flight of steps ascends to the wall gallery which goes all round the tower: as in the White Tower, it is vaulted. It is three feet high. In these apartments, there are fireplaces with enriched arches from which the smoke escaped through openings in the wall near the hearth. This primitive contrivance must have rendered the council-chamber and banqueting-hall uncomfortable with draughts.

Twenty-three steps lead from the wall gallery to the top floor which contains two handsome rooms twenty-five feet high. From this storey, the visitor may enjoy a lovely view, including the town and banks of the winding river, the Cathedral and its close, extending in the distance to the junction of the Thames and Medway.

Above the third floor, are the battlements which had a

rampart walk. The floorings were all carried by timber joists, and in the basement was a prison.

The striking resemblance between this keep and the White Tower at London of the same date would lead us to conclude that both were designed by the same architect. They were in fact both planned originally by Gundulf, who was consecrated Bishop of Rochester in the year after the Conquest. Besides his other great attainments, this bishop was a very able architect, and when the Conqueror wanted to erect a strong castle at Rochester, Gundulf was naturally entrusted with the task.

The first important historical event connected with the castle was the rebellion of Odo, Bishop of Bayeux and Earl of Kent, half (and perhaps full) brother to William the Conqueror. Kent had already suffered greatly from his rapacity, and his conduct finally led to his dramatic arrest by William's own hands. After William's death, he plotted in Robert's interest against his nephew Rufus. He attributed his imprisonment to Archbishop Lanfranc, and when war broke out between the brothers Robert and William in 1088, he plundered Kent, paying especial attention to the Archbishop's estates. Finally, being captured at Pevensey, he was forced to give up all his possessions in England, including Rochester, and leave the country. He was sent under guard to Rochester to complete the surrender and take ship for Normandy; but on his arrival, Eustace of Boulogne and Robert de Belême and other supporters rescued Odo and refused to surrender the city. The castle was garrisoned and William Rufus besieged it in person. It surrendered after a blockade of six weeks. William was very reluctant to grant any terms, and indignantly refused Odo's request for the honours of war. The English portion of William's army, who were principally Kentishmen, were very bitter against the Bishop who had harried and oppressed them, and cried: "Halters! halters for the traitor bishop! Let not the doer of evil go unharmed!" Counsels of clemency, however, prevailed; and Odo was allowed to go; and on this occasion Rochester saw the last of him.

The castle had been considerably injured in the siege, and William commissioned Gundulf to spend £60, a large sum in those days, in building a new tower.

In the twenty-seventh year of William's successor, Henry, the king, with the consent of his barons, granted to the church of Canterbury, William (of Corbeil), archbishop of that see, the custody of the castle of Rochester for ever, with liberty to build a fort and a tower. This archbishop, who had the support of the king in the rivalry of Canterbury and York, was a great builder. He rebuilt Rochester Cathedral and attended its dedication in 1130. Shortly before, he had with great pomp completed and dedicated the great cathedral at Canterbury begun by Lanfranc. It was therefore about 1130 that the new castle was also completed.

The castle with its splendid and strong keep was far too important a military post to remain in possession of the see of Canterbury for any length of time in that turbulent age. When the see became vacant, and on other occasions, the Crown resumed possession of it. In 1141, William of Ypres, a Fleming, was its governor for Stephen, as the archbishop had sworn allegiance to the Empress Maud. When the Earl of Gloucester, a natural son of Henry I. was captured at Winchester, he was imprisoned in this castle until exchanged for Stephen, who was taken at Lincoln later in the year. William of Ypres being banished, Henry II. gave his earldom of Kent and the castle of Rochester to Philip, Earl of Flanders, but the Earl never took possession.

In 1202, the castle was again restored to the archbishop, then Stephen Langton, who later, during John's wars with his barons, turned it over to William de Albini, a valiant and able commander, to be held in the interests of the barons. John invested the stronghold in 1215, and succeeded in gaining possession after an obstinate defence lasting three months. The military engines could produce little impression, but the walls were undermined, and then the keep was attacked in the same way. The following year, Louis the Dauphin, being invited over by the barons to assist them against John, landed at Sandwich and led his army to Rochester. The damage had not yet been repaired and so the castle easily fell. With other Crown possessions, it then came into the hands of Henry III. Much money was spent in repairs, especially in 1225–6–7. This was while Hubert de Burgh was constable of Rochester castle. In 1240, the tower was ordered to be whitewashed where it had not yet been done; and in 1247 both chapels were ordered to be wainscoted. One of these was in the outer ward, and used by the garrison.

In 1264, the king gave the charge of the castle to the celebrated Roger de Leybourne who had just joined his cause. He furnished it with sufficient arms, garrison, and provisions to stand a siege. Early in April, the attack being imminent, the king's brother-in-law, the Earl of Surrey, arrived at the castle with reinforcements. Just before Easter, Simon de Montfort came to besiege the castle. On reaching the western bank of the Medway, he found the passage of the bridge disputed, and a palisade and breastwork thrown up on the opposite side, well defended. Having sent Gilbert de Clare to attack the south side of the town, the Earl of Leicester in person assaulted the bridge, but was twice driven back by the citizens. At length, with the aid of boats loaded with combustibles, he set fire to the bridge and the tower upon it which were both built of wood. During the confusion caused by the fire, he crossed the river and destroyed the church and what was left of the priory. Richard de Leybourne for purposes of defence had already burned down all the suburbs and part of the priory. Simon de Montfort next made a furious assault upon the castle and captured the outworks and all the towers except the great keep. The latter made such an obstinate resistance that after a seven days' close siege, Simon suddenly relinquished the attempt and retreated to London. Shortly afterwards, in 1264, most of the garrison, under Leybourne, who had been badly wounded, left Rochester and joined the Royal army at Lewes. The king's disastrous defeat there resulted in the surrender of Rochester castle to the Baron's forces. When however the tide of success turned two years later, on the death of de Montfort at Evesham, and the fall of Kenilworth, Leybourne resumed his governorship.

In 1274, Robert de Hougham died constable of this castle, and was followed by Robert de Septvans. Two other constables of Rochester during this reign were Sir John de

Cobham and Stephen de Dene. During the next two centuries the following names occur among the holders of this office: William Skarlett, Lord Grey of Codnor, John de Newtrun, William Criol and Sir Thomas Cobham.

In 1367–8, extensive repairs were undertaken by Edward III., under Prior John of Rochester as chief of the works. Stone was imported from Beer, Caen, and Reigate, with copings and crests for battlements, probably for buildings in the court. Edward IV. also repaired the castle, but afterwards it lost its military importance and fell into decay. A drawing, of the year 1518, shows the turrets domed over and capped with vanes, like those of the White Tower.

Rochester much resembles Hedingham, which is a very perfect Norman keep with three floors, the remains of a forebuilding and upper gallery in the main floor. In each ornamentation, the chevron moulding is profusely employed.

Santa Croce, Florence, Italy
John Ruskin

Your Murray's Guide tells you that this chapel of the Bardi della Libertà, in which you stand, is covered with frescoes by Giotto; that they were whitewashed, and only laid bare in 1853; that they were painted between 1296 and 1304; that they represent scenes in the life of St. Francis; and that on each side of the window are paintings of St. Louis of Toulouse, St. Louis King of France, St. Elizabeth of Hungary, and St. Claire,—"all much restored and repainted." Under such recommendation the frescoes are not likely to be much sought after; and accordingly, as I was at work in the chapel this morning, Sunday 6th September, 1874, two nice-looking Englishmen, under guard of their valet de place, passed the chapel without so much as looking in.

You will perhaps stay a little longer in it with me, good reader, and find out gradually where you are. Namely, in the most interesting and perfect little Gothic chapel in all Italy—so far as I know or can hear. There is no other of the great time which has all its frescoes in their place. The Arena, though far larger, is of earlier date—not pure

Gothic, nor showing Giotto's full force. The lower chapel at Assisi is not Gothic at all, and is still only of Giotto's middle time. You have her developed Gothic, with Giotto in his consummate strength, and nothing lost, in form, of the complete design.

By restoration—judicious restoration, as Mr. Murray usually calls it—there is no saying how much you have lost. Putting the question of restoration out of your mind, however, for a while, think where you are, and what you have got to look at.

You are in the chapel next the high altar of the great Franciscan Church of Florence. A few hundred yards west of you, within ten minutes' walk, is the Baptistery of Florence. And five minutes' walk, west of that is the great Dominican Church of Florence, Santa Maria Novella.

Get this little bit of geography, and architectural fact, well into your mind. There is the little octagon Baptistery in the middle; here, ten minutes' walk east of it, the Franciscan Church of the Holy Cross; there, five minutes' walk west of it, the Dominican Church of St. Mary.

Now, that little octagon Baptistery stood where it now stands (and was finished, though the roof has been altered since) in the Eighth Century. It is the central building of Etrurian Christianity,—of European Christianity.

From the day it was finished, Christianity went on doing her best, in Etruria and elsewhere, for four hundred years,—and her best seemed to have come to very little,— when there rose up two men who vowed to God it should come to more. And they made it come to more, forthwith; of which the immediate sign in Florence was that she resolved to have a fine new cross-shaped cathedral instead of her quaint old little octagon one; and a tower beside it that should beat Babel:—which two buildings you have also within sight.

But your business is not at present with them; but with these two earlier churches of Holy Cross and St. Mary. The two men who were the effectual builders of these were the two great religious Powers and Reformers of the Thirteenth Century;—St. Francis who taught Christian men how they should behave, and St. Dominic, who taught Christian men what they should think. In brief, one the Apostle of Works; the other of Faith. Each sent his little company of disciples to teach and to preach in Florence: St. Francis in 1212; St. Dominic in 1220.

The little companies were settled—one, ten minutes' walk east of the old Baptistery; the other five minutes' walk west of it. And after they had stayed quietly in such lodgings as were given them, preaching and teaching through most of the century; and had got Florence, as it were heated through, she burst out into Christian poetry and architecture, of which you have heard so much talk:—burst into bloom of Arnolfo, Giotto, Dante, Orcagna, and the like persons, whose works you profess to have come to Florence that you may see and understand.

Florence then, thus heated through, first helped her teachers to build finer churches. The Dominicans, or White Friars, the Teachers of Faith, began their church of St. Mary's in 1279. The Franciscans, or Black Friars, the Teachers of Works, laid the first stone of this church of the Holy Cross in 1294. And the whole city laid the foundations of its new cathedral in 1298. The Dominicans designed their own building; but for the Franciscans and the town worked the first great master of Gothic art, Arnolfo; with Giotto at his side, and Dante looking on, and whispering sometimes a word to both.

And here you stand beside the high altar of the Franciscan's Church, under a vault of Arnolfo's building, with at least some of Giotto's colour on it still fresh; and in front of you, over the little altar, is the only reportedly authentic portrait of St. Francis, taken from life by Giotto's master. Yet I can hardly blame my two English friends for never looking in. Except in the early morning light, not one touch of all this art can be seen. And in any light, unless you understand the relations of Giotto to St. Francis, and of St. Francis to humanity, it will be of little interest.

Observe, then, the special character of Giotto among the great painters of Italy is his being a practical person. Whatever other men dreamed of, he did. He could work in mosaic: he could work in marble; he could paint; and he could build; and all thoroughly: a man of supreme faculty, supreme common sense. Accordingly, he ranges himself at once among the disciples of the Apostle of Works, and spends most of his time in the same apostleship.

Now the gospel of Works, according to St. Francis, lay in three things. You must work without money, and be poor. You must work without pleasure, and be chaste. You must work according to orders, and be obedient.

Those are St. Francis's three articles of Italian opera. By which grew the many pretty things you have come to see here.

And now if you will take your opera-glass and look up to the roof above Arnolfo's building, you will see it is a pretty Gothic cross vault, in four quarters, each with a circular medallion, painted by Giotto. That over the altar has the picture of St. Francis himself. The three others, of his Commanding Angels. In front of him, over the entrance arch, Poverty. On his right hand, Obedience. On his left, Chastity.

Poverty, in a red patched dress, with grey wings and a square nimbus of glory above her head, is flying from a black hound, whose head is seen at the corner of the medallion.

Chastity veiled, is imprisoned in a tower, while angels watch her.

Obedience bears a yoke on her shoulders, and lays her hand on a book.

Now, this same quatrefoil, of St. Francis and his three Commanding Angels, was also painted, but much more elaborately, by Giotto, on the cross vault of the lower church of Assisi, and it is a question of interest which of the two roofs was painted first.

Your Murray's Guide tells you the frescoes in this chapel were painted between 1296 and 1304. But as they represent, among other personages, St. Louis of Toulouse, who was not canonized till 1317, that statement is not altogether tenable. Also, as the first stone of the church was only laid in 1294, when Giotto was a youth of eighteen, it is little likely that either it would have been ready to be painted, or be ready with his scheme of practical divinity, two years later.

Farther, Arnolfo, the builder of the main body of the church, died in 1310. And as St. Louis of Toulouse was not a saint till seven years afterwards, and the frescoes therefore beside the window not painted in Arnolfo's day, it becomes another question whether Arnolfo left the chapels or the church at all, in their present form.

On which point—now that I have shown you where Giotto's St. Louis is—I will ask you to think awhile, until you are interested; and then I will try to satisfy your curiosity. Therefore, please leave the little chapel for the moment, and walk down the nave, till you come to two sepulchral slabs near the west end, and then look about you and see what sort of a church Santa Croce is.

Without looking about you at all, you may find, in your Murray, the useful information that it is a church which "consists of a very wide nave and lateral aisles, separated by seven fine pointed arches." And as you will be—under ordinary conditions of tourist hurry—glad to learn so much, *without* looking, it is little likely to occur to you that this nave and two rich aisles required also, for your complete present comfort, walls at both ends, and a roof on the top. It is just possible, indeed, you may have been struck on entering, by the curious disposition of painted glass at the east end;—more remotely possible that, in returning down the nave, you may this moment have noticed the extremely small circular window at the west end; but the chances are a thousand to one that, after being pulled from tomb to tomb round the aisles and chapels, you should take so extraordinary an additional amount of pains as to look up at the roof,—unless you do it now, quietly. It will have had its effect upon you, even if you don't, without your knowledge. You will return home with a general impression that Santa Croce is, somehow, the ugliest Gothic church you ever were in. Well, that is really so; and now, will you take the pains to see why?

There are two features, on which, more than on any others, the grace and delight of a fine Gothic building depends; one is the springing of its vaultings, the other the proportion and fantasy of its traceries. *This* church of Santa Croce has no vaultings at all, but the roof of a farmhouse barn. And its windows are all of the same pattern,—the exceedingly prosaic one of two pointed arches, with a round hole above, between them.

And to make the simplicity of the roof more conspicuous, the aisles are successive sheds, built at every arch. In the aisles of the Campo Santo at Pisa, the unbroken flat roof leaves the eye free to look to the traceries; but here, a succession of up-and-down sloping beam and lath gives the impression of a line of stabling rather than a church aisle. And lastly, while, in fine Gothic buildings, the entire perspective concludes itself gloriously in the high and distant apse, here the nave is cut across sharply by a line of ten chapels, the apse being only a tall recess in the midst of them, so that, strictly speaking, the church is not of the form of a cross, but of a letter T.

Can this clumsy and ungraceful arrangement be indeed the design of the renowned Arnolfo?

Yes, this is the purest Arnolfo-Gothic; not beautiful by any means; but deserving, nevertheless, our thoughtfullest examination. We will trace its complete character another day: just now we are only concerned with this pre-Christian form of the letter T, insisted upon in the lines of chapels.

Respecting which you are to observe, that the first Christian churches in the catacombs took the form of a blunt cross naturally; a square chamber having a vaulted recess on each side; then the Byzantine churches were structurally built in the form of an equal cross; while the heraldic and other ornamental equal-armed crosses are partly signs of glory and victory, partly of light, and divine spiritual presence.

But the Franciscans and Dominicans saw in the cross no sign of triumph, but of trial. The wounds of their Master were to be their inheritance. So their first aim was to make what image to the cross their church might present, distinctly that of the actual instrument of death. And they did this most effectually by using the form of the letter T, that of the Furca or Gibbet,—not the sign of peace.

Also their churches were meant for use; not show, nor self-glorification, nor town-glorification. They wanted places for preaching, prayer, sacrifice, burial; and had no intention of showing how high they could build towers, or how widely they could arch vaults. Strong walls and the roof of a barn,—these your Franciscan asks of his Arnolfo. These Arnolfo gives,—thoroughly and wisely built; the successions of gable roof being a new device for strength much practised in his day.

This stern humour did not last long. Arnolfo himself had other notions; most of all, Nature and Heaven. Something else had to be taught about Christ than that He was wounded to death. Nevertheless, look how grand this stern form would be, restored to its simplicity. It is not the old church which is in itself unimpressive. It is the old church defaced by Vasari, by Michael Angelo, and by modern Florence. See those huge tombs on your right hand and left, at the sides of the aisles, with their alternate gable and round tops, and their paltriest of all sculpture, trying to be grand by bigness, and pathetic by expense. Tear them all down in your imagination; fancy the vast hall with its massive pillars,—not painted calomel-pill colour, as now, but of their native stone, with the rough true wood for roof,—and a people praying beneath them, strong in abiding, and pure in life, as their rocks and olive forests. That was Arnolfo's Santa Croce. Nor did his work remain long without grace.

That very line of chapels in which we found our St. Louis shows signs of change in temper. They have no penthouse roofs, but true Gothic vaults: we found our four square type of Franciscan Law on one of them.

It is probable, then, that these chapels may be later than the rest—even in their stonework. In their decoration, they are so, assuredly; belonging already to the time when the story of St. Francis was becoming a passionate tradition, told and painted everywhere with delight.

And that high recess, taking the place of apse, in the centre,—see how noble it is in the coloured shade surrounding and joining the glow of its windows, though their form be so simple. You are not to be amused here by patterns in balanced stone, as a French or English architect would amuse you, says Arnolfo. "You are to read and think, under these severe walls of mine; immortal hands will write upon them."

THE CERTOSA OF PAVIA, ITALY

The Certosa of Pavia leaves upon the mind an impression of bewildering sumptuousness: nowhere else are costly materials so combined with a lavish expenditure of the rarest art. Those who have only once been driven round together with the crew of sightseers can carry little away but the memory of lapis-lazuli and bronze work, inlaid agates and labyrinthine sculpture, cloisters tenantless in silence, fair painted faces smiling from dark corners on the senseless crowd, trim gardens with rows of pink primroses in Spring and bigonia in Autumn, blooming beneath colonnades of glowing terra-cotta. The striking contrast between the Gothic of the interior and the Renaissance façade, each in its own kind perfect, will also be remembered; and thoughts of the two great houses, Visconti and Sforza, to whose pride of power it is a monument, may be blended with the recollection of art treasures alien to their spirit.

Two great artists, Ambrognio Borgognone and Antonio Amadeo are the presiding genii of the Certosa. To minute criticism, based upon the accurate investigation of records and comparison of styles, must be left the task of separating their work from that of numerous collaborators. But it is none the less certain that the keynote of the whole music is struck by them. Amadeo, the master of the Colleoni chapel at Bergamo, was both sculptor and architect. If the façade of the Certosa be not absolutely his creation, he had a hand in the distribution of its masses and the detail of its ornaments. The only fault in this otherwise faultless product of the purest quattrocento inspiration is that the façade is a frontispiece, with hardly any structural relation to the church it mocks: and this, though serious from the point of view of architecture, is no abatement of its sculpturesque and picturesque refinement. At first sight it seems a wilderness of loveliest reliefs and statues—of angel faces, fluttering raiment, flowing hair, love-laden youths, and stationary figures of grave saints, mid wayward tangles of acanthus and wild vine and cupid-laden foliage; but the subordination of these decorative details to the main design, clear, rhythmical and lucid, like the chant of Pergolese, or Stradella, will enrapture one who has the sense for unity evoked from divers elements, for thought subduing all caprices to the harmony of beauty. It is not possible elsewhere in Italy to find the instinct of the earlier Renaissance, so amorous in its expenditure of rare material, so lavish in its bestowal of the costliest workmanship on ornamental episodes, brought into truer keeping with a pure and simple structural effect.

All the great sculptor-architects of Lombardy worked in succession on this miracle of beauty; and this may account for the sustained perfection of style, which nowhere suffers from the languor of exhaustion in the artist or from repetition of motives. It remains the triumph of North Italian genius, exhibiting qualities of tenderness and self abandonment to inspiration which we lack in the severer masterpieces of the Tuscan school.

To Borgognone is assigned the painting of the roof in nave and choir—exceeding rich, varied, and withal in sympathy with stately Gothic style. Borgognone, again, is said to have designed the saints and martyrs worked in *tarsia* for the choir-stalls. His frescoes are in some parts well preserved, as in the lovely little Madonna at the end of the south chapel, while the great fresco above the window in the south transept has an historical value that renders it interesting in spite of partial decay.

The Certosa is a wilderness of lovely workmanship. From Borgognone's majesty we pass into the quiet region of Luini's Christian grace, or mark the influence of Leonardo on that rare Assumption of Madonna by his pupil Andrea Solari. Like everything touched by the Leonardesque spirit, this great picture was left unfinished; yet Northern Italy has nothing finer to show than the landscape outspread in its immeasurable purity of calm, behind the grouped Apostles, and the ascendant Mother of Heaven. The feeling of that happy region between the Alps and Lombardy, where there are many waters—*et tacitos sine labe lacus sine murmure rivos*—and where the last spurs of the mountains sink in undulations to the plain, has passed into this azure vista, just as all Umbria is suggested in a twilight background of young Raphael or Perugino.

The portraits of the dukes of Milan and their families carry us into a very different realm of feeling. Medallions above the doors of sacristy and chancel, stately figures reared aloft beneath gigantic canopies, men and women slumbering with folded hands upon their marble biers—we read in all these sculptured forms a strange record of human restlessness resolved into the quiet of the tomb. The iniquities of Gian Galeazzo Visconti, *il gran Biscione*; the blood-thirst of Gian Maria; the dark designs of Fillipo and his secret vices; Francesco Sforza's treason; Galeazzo Maria's vanities and lusts; their tyrant's dread of thunder and the knife; their awful deaths by pestilence and the assassin's poniard; their selfishness, oppression, cruelty and fraud; the murders of their kinsmen; their labyrinthine plots and acts of broken faith;—all is tranquil now, and we can say to each what Bosola found for the Duchess of Malfi ere her execution:

> Much you had of land and rent;
> Your length in clay's now competent:
> A long war disturbed your mind;
> Here your perfect peace is signed!

From the church it is delightful to escape into the

cloisters flooded with sunlight, where the swallows skim and the brown hawks circle and the mason bees are at work among the carvings. The arcades of the two cloisters are the final triumph of Lombard terra-cotta. The memory fails before such infinite invention, such facility and felicity of execution. Wreaths of cupids gliding round the arches among grape-bunches and bird-haunted foliage of vine; rows of angels, like rising and setting planets, some smiling and some grave, ascending and descending by the Gothic curves; saints stationary on their pedestals and faces leaning from the rounds above; crowds of cherubs and courses of stars and acanthus-leaves in woven lines and ribands incessantly inscribed with Ave Maria! Then, over all, the rich red light and purple shadows of the brick, than which no substance sympathizes more completely with the sky of solid blue above, the broad plain space of waving summer grass beneath our feet.

It is now late afternoon, and when evening comes the train will take us back to Milan. There is yet a little while to rest tired eyes and strained spirits among the willows and poplars by the monastery wall. Through that grey-green leafage, young with early spring, the pinnacles of the Certosa leap like flames into the sky. The rice-fields are under water, far and wide, shining like burnished gold beneath the level light now near to sundown. Frogs are croaking; those persistent frogs whom the muses have ordained to sing for aye in spite of Bion and all tuneful poets dead. We sit and watch the water snakes, the busy rats, the hundred creatures swarming in the fat, well watered soil. Nightingales here and there, newcomers, tune their timid April song. But, strangest of all sounds in such a place, my comrade from the Grisons jodels forth an Alpine cowherd's melody—*Auf den Alpen droben ist ein herrliches Leben!*

Did the echoes of Gian Galeazzo's convent ever wake to such a tune as this before?

THE END